The Masters of Truth in Archaic Greece

Translated by Janet Lloyd

The Masters of Truth
in Archaic Greece

Marcel Detienne

Foreword by Pierre Vidal-Naquet

ZONE BOOKS · NEW YORK

1996

© 1996 Urzone, Inc.
611 Broadway, Suite 608
New York, NY 10012

Originally published in France as *Les Maîtres de vérité
dans la grèce archaïque* © 1967 Librarie François Maspero,
© 1990 Editions la Découverte.

Printed in the United States of America.

Distributed by The MIT Press,
Cambridge, Massachusetts, and London, England

Library of Congress Cataloging-in-Publication Data

Detienne, Marcel.
  [Maîtres de vérité dans la grèce archaïque. English]
  The masters of truth in Archaic Greece / by Marcel
Detienne; foreword by Pierre Vidal-Naquet; translated
by Janet Lloyd.
    p.   cm.
  Includes bibliographical references and index.
  ISBN 0-942299-85-X
    1. Truth. 2. Philosophy, Ancient. 3. Greece –
Religion. 4. Alētheia (The Greek word) I. Title.
B187.T7D413   1995
180–dc20   95-33454
                                               CIP

Contents

Foreword

Pierre Vidal-Naquet

The title of Marcel Detienne's book announces both a paradox and a program. Are there such creatures as "masters of truth"? Already in Antiquity, one view of education held that a master must be independent of the truth he teaches, which is both beyond him and beyond us. In the nineteenth century this view seemed triumphant in the strict sciences and even the social sciences. It was because Marx believed social reality could be an object of science and hence independent of the observer that he once declared that he was not a Marxist. Today that kind of universalism is widely questioned, although it is not my objective here to explain why or how. That it is questioned is salutory to the extent that we are much more sensitive now to the psychological, social, and even economic conditions in which scientific thought appeared and developed as well as to the infinite diversity of the perspectives proposed by different scholars and sciences. On the other hand, it is harmful when particular states or individuals establish themselves as the heralds – and masters – of some militant truth. Militants, whether military or intellectual, band together everywhere around orders of the day, such as "Study the works of President X, follow his teachings, and obey his directives!" Yet wherever the master himself is on display, there can be no truth.

However such situations may have evolved, militant language, like poetry – albeit for different reasons – is fundamentally untranslatable and incommunicable: an order is comprehensible only to the persons addressed. In contrast, scientific language's distinctive feature is its accessibility to all those who have attempted to learn it as well as its translatability into every human dialect.

It is no reflection on the value of other human achievements – African, Chinese, or Amerindian – to recognize that scientific language, in the form in which it is most widely known today, originated in Greece, a Greece nurtured on a heritage far richer and more complex than any passed on by the "Indo-European" groups arriving on "Greek" soil at the end of the third millennium.

But even if reason was originally a Greek phenomenon, it must be historically contextualized. We must seek the fundamental factors in the history of Greek society, the history of the Greek people, to explain the *deliberate* abandonment of myth and the movement away from unconsciously organizational structures (by which I mean those that did not consciously recognize themselves as "logical," in Claude Lévi-Strauss's sense) in favor of a willful effort to describe first how the universe functions, then how human groups do. The reasoning of the "physicists" of Ionia and Italy grappled with the former problem, and the reasoning of historians such as Hecataeus, Herodotus, and Thucydides tackled the latter.

The transition from *myth to reason* remains a problem even for those who recognize that myth too contains reason. The difficulty has been apparent to several generations of scholars. In 1962, in *The Origins of Greek Thought*, Jean-Pierre Vernant established a framework that both Detienne and I share, one which I will assume is already familiar to the reader. To sum it up, "rational thought" arose within a specific political, economic, and social framework, namely, that of the city, which itself only appeared through a deci-

sive crisis of sovereignty, and within a social space unencumbered
by the dominating presence of a Minoan or Mycenaean monarch
modeled after Eastern "despots."

Before the appearance of reason itself, however, there was
its foundation, that is, man's (in this case Greek man's) representation of the truth, *Alētheia*. Detienne's book is not so much a
history of this word. Such a history would not be without interest, but Detienne is far too wary a philologist to surrender to
"proof through etymology." He defines his methodology clearly.
It consists in "determining the force lines of a lexical system
and identifying groups in opposition and association, in short
applying the method of structural lexicology and exploring the
theory of a *semantic field* within the domain of archaic Greece."
At the end of this journey we come to the remarkable imagery
opening Parmenides' poem and his meditation on Being: "a chariot journey guided by the daughters of the Sun, a way reserved
for the knowing man, a path that leads to the gates of Day and
Night, a goddess who reveals true knowledge," and the obligation to choose between the world of *being* and the world of
opinion.

In some sense, Detienne's aim is to write a prehistory of Parmenides' poem. That prehistory has turned out to be far richer
and more complex than he expected. Nevertheless, through the
maze of an erudition that can be almost overwhelmingly abundant,
the path he follows is, on the whole, extremely well defined.
Truth was initially speech, and Detienne captures the moment
when it was still a privilege reserved for certain persons: poets
and diviners, both trained in the long apprenticeship of "memory" or of the "muse" who alone knows "what was, what is,
and what will be"; speech when it constituted either praise or
blame and was capable of either glorifying or belittling, of being
either truthful or lying. In the Eastern societies of Egypt and

9

Mesopotamia, praising a king was no different from praising a
god. A poet's speech "strengthened" the "just king" by strength-
ening the god. His poem ensured that nature and society were
integrated in the king's royal person. There was no truth other
than that centered on the king.

By the time "Greek literature" emerged, the Mycenaean kings
had passed away. It is uncertain whether the mythical king, still
known to Pindar and Aeschylus in the fifth century B.C. and surviving in quasi-folkloric form in Hellenistic mythology, eventually to be resuscitated by Sir James Frazer, was really their direct
descendant. The fact that the king became mythical is perhaps
of even more crucial importance to me than it is to Detienne.
But in any event, as Detienne himself quite rightly notes, Hesiod's
Theogony is the only Greek poem that can really be compared to
the poems of the East; clearly, it is centered on a royal figure,
Zeus, just as the *Enuma Eliš* was centered on the god Marduk,
the prototype for the Babylonian king: "And again, this royal figure is only a god." This remark identifies what is essential: the god
has survived but the social support which gave him life, namely,
the king, has disappeared. Gods and men already have separate
destinies, and the time of the gods grows progressively more distant from the time of men. In one surviving tradition – signifi-
cantly, a poetic one – a "king of justice" holds the scales, at once
dispensing and accepting the true and the false. Similarly, we find
that all truth is enigma, as is the truth-teller himself, as depicted
for example by the figure of the Old Man of the Sea, Proteus or
Nereus, to whom Detienne devotes chapter 3 of this work.
There is no "opposition" or "contradiction" between the true and
the false, between truth (*Alētheia*) and oblivion (*Lēthē*): "Thus it
is not that *Alētheia* (+) stands on one side and *Lēthē* (−) on the
other. Rather, an intermediate zone develops between the poles,
in which *Alētheia* approaches *Lēthē* and vice versa. 'Negativity' is

thus not isolated from Being; it borders the truth and forms its inseparable shadow."

This ambivalence of efficacious speech in the most ancient works of Greek thought, however, was preceded in the classical city by an ambiguity of action.[1] Faced with the permanent risk involved in every collective decision (war or peace, a full colonial expedition or a simple operation of land clearance), the city slowly, progressively, elaborated a speech consisting of dialogue – dialogue between different social groups that clashed on the political terrain, dialogue between orators who favored one decision or another. From this point on efficacious speech lost its sovereignty, and dialogue could accommodate even the ambivalence of prophecy. At the time of the Second Persian War, when the Delphic oracle announced that Athens would be saved by a "rampart of wood," Themistocles saw fit to interpret this equivocal expression as the "Athenian fleet," although another, more obvious interpretation was also possible and indeed suggested. In the interstices of such interpretations, dialogue was established. "Truth" thus entered a world where things were relative. The wording of decrees ran, "It has pleased the people...," "it has seemed right to the people...." Detienne has marshaled his evidence around two poles. Adopting a classification whose essential features were established by Plato (although they largely predated him), Detienne contrasts the orator's and the Sophist's universal *competence* in the domain of the relative to the *knowledge* of the philosophical and religious sects. On the one hand, cunning and deceit (*apatē*) are knowingly accepted, on the other we find the possession of *Alētheia*, not to be bartered and only to be handed down by master to disciple. But, as the Pythagorean venture dramatically demonstrates, when such masters of truth tried to impose their truth on the whole city, they revealed themselves as insignificant groups who ended in failure. For the orator and the

Sophist, meanwhile, truth was *reality*, the good or bad argument that triumphed, the decision once it was put into practice.

The extraordinarily rapid evolution of historical thought testifies to the mutation studied by Detienne in this work. The writing of Herodotus — the "most Homeric" Herodotus, as he was later called — is still partly devoted to eulogy and even to the archaic function of memory: "What Herodotus the Halicarnassian has learnt by inquiry is here set forth, so that memory of the past may not be blotted out from among men by time and that great and marvelous deeds done by Greeks and Barbarians...may not lack renown." However, Herodotus also studies the "causes" of wars, that is, the accusations flung between the Greeks and the Barbarians, reconstructed in dialogue. Furthermore, Herodotus distinguishes between the time of the gods and the time of men, in other words, the time of confrontations. In Thucydides, there was to be nothing but dialogue. Lévi-Strauss's method of systematically uncovering binary structures concealed in myths is by now well known; in Thucydides' work, these binary structures are not concealed at all, and the appropriate pairs are in fact easily discerned: rational decision (*gnōmē*) and chance (*tychē*), speech (*logos*) and fact (*ergon*), law (*nomos*) and nature (*physis*), peace and war. History thus takes the form of a gigantic political argument: statesmen's plans are challenged by the plans of other statesmen, by reality, by *tychē*, by *ergon*, and by nature — nature, for which Thucydides, at the beginning of Book I, curiously claims a share in the upheaval of the human world, just as if the Peloponnesian War, that dialogue of arms that was also often a dialogue of words, had brought about the eruption of earthquakes. To what kind of universality could Thucydides lay claim, if not to that of dialogue?

Ambiguity had decidedly given way to contradiction. Or, to be more precise, the ambiguity that had characterized discourse in the archaic period now took refuge in facts. For the historian, however, ambiguity had disappeared. One was either at war or at peace: from the writer's perspective, this much was clear. Where Hesiod's logic is one of ambiguity – nobody is ever certain whether it is a matter of *Dikē* or of *Hubris*, whether he stands on the side of truth or lies – Thucydides' logic is one of contradiction.

Rather than be content simply to contrast efficacious speech and dialogic speech, as in a diptych, Detienne has also tried to explain how one led to the other. In a sense, the entire book pivots on chapter 5. Of course, he has not attempted the kind of total explanation that would involve all of Greek history but has instead made a number of extremely felicitous observations.

Since Aristotle, many historians have agreed that the first *politeia* consisted of warriors. It is often said that the city originates when disorganized warfare punctuated by individual exploits, such as that described by Homer, was superseded by the clash of two phalanxes composed of warriors clad in hoplite armor, acting in concert. The "equals" in the army became the "equals" in the city. We know that *Homoioi* was the name by which the citizens, *stricto sensu*, of Sparta were known. That is the traditional view of what, somewhat inaccurately, is called the "hoplite reform," which Detienne has also studied.[2] In that work, he analyzes certain procedures of military life – funeral games, distribution of booty, warrior assemblies, and councils – and shows how, within the army, a kind of prepolitical pattern was created out of which the procedures of city life later emerged. One example is the "vast assembly" convoked by Achilles before the funeral games held in honor of Patroclus. Even the word used for it (*agōn*) is significant in that it designates both the assembly and the games.

Of course, this "explanation" does not settle the problem, nor is it intended to, for other societies also experienced "military democracy" without ever evolving into cities or producing any political democracy. But Detienne's book makes it possible to set out the problem more cogently. *Solutions*, by definition, are always a matter for tomorrow.

Return to the Mouth of Truth

In archaic Greece, since the time sculptures first depicted walk-
ing figures, paths suddenly opened on to the "Meadow of Truth"
where the Plain of *Alētheia* came into view. Even more secret
tracks led to the Fountain of Oblivion or the icy waters of Memory. One day in Crete, the herb gatherer Epimenides fell into a
sleep so deep, without beginning or end, that he had all the time
in the world to speak in person with Truth. In the sixth century
B.C., Truth, *Alētheia*, figured as one of the intimate companions
of the goddess who greeted Parmenides and guided him to "the
unshakable heart of the perfect circle of Truth."

For inquirers of the archaic and of beginnings, Truth provides
a fascinating archaeology, ranging from Hesiod's Muses to the
daughters of the Sun, the guide of the man who knows. Two or
three earlier forays into the notion of the "demonic" and the adap-
tation of Homeric and Hesiodic themes in the philosophicoreligious circles of Pythagoreanism had already convinced me it was
productive to follow the paths leading from religious to philosophical thought.[1] I had begun to examine the subject in a brief
article published in 1960 and completed my inquiry in 1965 in
my Ph.D. dissertation at the Université de Liège.[2] Its starting
point was a simple observation: in archaic Greece, three figures –

the diviner, the bard, and the king of justice – share the privilege of dispensing truth purely by virtue of their characteristic qualities. The poet, the seer, and the king also share a similar type of speech. Through the religious power of Memory, *Mnēmosynē*, both poet and diviner have direct access to the Beyond; they can see what is invisible and declare "what has been, what is, and what will be." With this inspired knowledge, the poet uses his sung speech to celebrate human exploits and actions, which thus become glorious and illuminated, endowed with vital force and the fullness of being. Similarly, the king's speech, relying on test by ordeal, possesses an oracular power. It brings justice into being and establishes the order of law without recourse to either proof or investigation.

At the heart of this kind of speech as it issues from these three figures is *Alētheia*, a power belonging to the group of religious entities who are either associated with or opposed to her. *Alētheia*, who is close to Justice, *Dikē*, forms a pair with sung speech, *Moûsa*, as well as with Light and with Praise. On the other hand, *Alētheia* is opposed to Oblivion, *Lēthē*, who is the accomplice of Silence, Blame, and Obscurity. In the midst of their mythicoreligious configuration, *Alētheia* pronounces a performative truth. She is the power of efficacy and creates being. As Michel Foucault would later put it, true discourse is "discourse pronounced by men who spoke as a right, according to ritual."[3] *Alētheia* and *Lēthē* are not exclusive or contradictory in this way of thinking; they constitute two extremes of a single religious power. The negativity of silence and oblivion constitutes the inseparable shadow of Memory and *Alētheia*. In the name of this same power, the Muses, the daughters of Memory, possess not only the ability "to say many false things that seem like true sayings" but also the knowledge to "speak the truth."[4]

What place do the Sophist and the philosopher have in the lin-

eage of the "Masters of Truth? How does their speech differ from
the efficacious speech of the diviner, the poet, and the king of
justice, speech that conveys reality? How does the transition occur
between one type of thought where ambiguity is a central feature of both its mode of expression and its logic to another kind
of thought where argumentation, the principle of noncontradiction, and dialogue, with its distinctions between the sense and
the reference of propositions, apparently announce the advent of
a new intellectual regime?

It seemed to me that an understanding of the sociohistorical
context might contribute to this genealogy of the idea of truth.
During my research on the Pythagoreans, I gleaned signs of a process which set in motion the gradual secularization of speech. The
most important sign was to be found in the military assembly
since it conferred the equal right to speech on all members of
the warrior class, those whose very position allowed them to discuss communal affairs. The hoplite reform, introduced in the city
around 650 B.C., not only imposed a new type of weaponry and
behavior in battle, but also encouraged the emergence of "equal
and similar" soldier-citizens. At this point, dialogue — secular
speech that acts on others, that persuades and refers to the affairs
of the group — began to gain ground while the efficacious speech
conveying truth gradually became obsolete. Through its new function, which was fundamentally political and related to the *agora*,
logos — speech and language — became autonomous. Two major
trends now developed in thought about language. On the one
hand *logos* was seen as an instrument of social relations: How did
it act upon others? In this vein, rhetoric and sophistry began to
develop the grammatical and stylistic analysis of techniques of persuasion. Meanwhile, the other path, explored by philosophy, led
to reflections on *logos* as a means of knowing reality: Is speech
all of reality? If so, what about the reality expressed by numbers,

the reality discovered by mathematicians and geometricians?

I then began to study the rise and fall of *Alētheia*, particularly the way *Alētheia*, once devalued in sophistic thought, found itself linked in the discourse of Parmenides and early metaphysics with the immutable Being that is always self-identical and strictly governed by the principle of noncontradiction.

Thirty years later, with the publication of this careful translation by Janet Lloyd, whom I thank most warmly, I have the occasion to reexamine the assumptions and procedures of this early work as well as to consider a number of methodological problems. In 1958, at the Ecole Française de Rome in the Piazza Farnese, where my analysis of the "demonic" led me to consider various forms of mediation, Louis Gernet sent me his essay "Les Origines de la philosophie."[5] For many years already I had been reading the work of this Greek scholar who, in the 1980s, in the shrine on rue Monsieur-le-Prince was to become the object of some veneration by the devotees of the Centre de Recherches Comparées sur les Sociétés Anciennes and its left-wing historiographer, Riccardo Di Donato, who, with Marxist zeal, traveled from Pisa to organize the liturgy of its "founding heroes."[6] In that brief essay – which was very difficult to find until Jean-Pierre Vernant and I republished it in 1968, with other essays, in *The Anthropology of Ancient Greece* – Louis Gernet pointed out the importance of identifying how "mythical concepts, religious practice, and societal forms... were involved in philosophy's beginnings."[7] Gernet paid close attention to the figure of the philosopher, his way of behaving as if he had been "chosen," his view of his position and knowledge in the world and in the city. In the same year, 1958, in the Piazza Farnese, as I came to realize the fascination Greece exerted on ethnology, Claude Lévi-Strauss's *Structural Anthropology* revealed to me new ways of analyzing and theorizing "mythical thought," which Greek scholars hardly dared mention, even among themselves.[8] Underlying my inquiry into the religious configuration of truth was Ernst Cassirer's and Antoine Meillet's hypothesis that language guides ideas, vocabulary is more a conceptual system than a lexicon, and linguistic phenomena relate to institutions, that is, to influential schemata present in techniques, social relations, and the contexts of communicative exchange.

Speech and its use in the early city was my subject then, and my inquiry today continues along the same two general lines. The first concerns the practices of the assembly, which developed out of hundreds of experiments involving models of a political space. Closely linked to this is the nature of the environment in which the many reflections on speech, its effects, techniques, and relations with the world and with other people occurred. I am currently analyzing ways of using speech and modes of behavior in the assembly from a comparativist perspective, considering Ethiopian communities, Cossack societies, and the commune movement in Italy.[9]

The second line of study follows in the wake of *Thēmis*, examining schemata of creation and foundation ranging from oracular pronouncements, through the procedures for opening and closing assemblies, to the domain of decisions engraved on stones set up in the unfixed space of nascent cities.[10] Michel Foucault, in his 1970 inaugural lecture at the Collège de France, discovered in archaic Greece the province governing our own "will to knowledge" or, more precisely, our "will to truth."[11] To me he seemed to be referring to the landscape of truth sketched in my own inquiry. Once we jettison the poorly defined earlier identification of "power and knowledge," the desire to speak the truth seems, in retrospect, to have been very marked among the masters of truth in early Greece. Such a will or desire is expressed both by the Hesiodic Muses and by the Bee-Women of the young Apollo.[12] Similarly, in the political domain, a desire for practical effectiveness is always explicit: it is found across the board, from the ritual formula of the herald who opened the assembly with the question "Who wishes/desires to speak for the city?" to the formula repeated in thousands of decisions legibly carved in stone and carefully positioned where they could be read by "whoever had the will/desire to do so."[13] The philosophers wasted no time in attempting to monopolize this desire for truth. But the city was spared such a monopoly, thanks to its use of speech and the practices of the assembly – although this development was, at the same time, altogether in line with the will and desire of those who were obsessively establishing the forms for the government of men by men.

Such an inquiry into not only the semantic field of *Alētheia* but also the protohistory of philosophy and the changes in the archaic world was bound to evoke reactions, silent or vociferous, from the three academic disciplines in a position to judge the validity of the enterprise: philology and history, of course, but also anthropology, if it could overcome its complexes vis-à-vis those other two and their international prestige – in Europe, at least. One might have expected the historians to pay some attention to an essay on the "hoplite reform," but the potential of categories of thought constituted no part of any history program, modern or ancient.[14] Moses I. Finley was wary of anything outside the socioeconomic sphere, even politics in the strict sense of the term. Pierre Vidal-Naquet, working at that time with Pierre Levêque on Cleisthenes and the intellectual transformations accompanying his great political reforms, was the sole exception; I am now even more appreciative of his work than I already was at the time. But what about the philologists, the *littéraires*, as they are called on the Left Bank?

Observers of the intellectual scene have long recognized that the tribe of historians is divided into "nationalists" (about three quarters of the group) and the rest, of whom there are remarkably few in a "nation" such as present-day France.[15] The tribe of philologists – to which, as an archaeologist of the Truth, I am bound to return – has always fallen into two distinct species: the philologist who thinks and the one who dispenses with thinking. The latter, it must be said, is invariably the more prolific, regardless of climate or circumstances. However, the hermeneutic school of Lille, Germanic and philosophical in its inspiration, undoubtedly belongs to the first species.[16] Won over by a sociology of culture *à la française*, that is, by the works of Pierre Bourdieu, some members of this group have even manifested an interest in anthropological approaches that may illuminate certain important aspects of Greek culture. Examples of such areas include writing, considered a cognitive practice, and its effects on the modalities of certain types of knowledge; also earlier work in "mythology" or "mythical thought" as it relates to the practices of such an explicitly polytheist culture from the time of Homeric epic to almost the end of Antiquity.[17] A recent international colloquium on Hesiod, admirably organized by interpreters from the hermeneutic school, combined philosophy and anthropology with philology, that most eminent of all disciplines.[18] Since F.M. Cornford, Hesiod, author of the *Theogony*, has indeed been recognized as a precursor to philosophical discourse, but the inclusion of anthropology was not as predictable. This was especially so since, in the sociocultural context of this colloquium, what was labeled "anthropology" seemed to range from essays produced under the sign of a so-called historical psychology that was sometimes comparative as well; the works of historians of the *Annales* school, with their inventories of mentalities; and inquiries into the structures of myths, ranging from Georges Dumézil's studies to the ambitious work of Lévi-Strauss.[19] The "structural" analyses of the major narratives of Greece were obviously bound to irritate the more or less strict hermeneutists. Nevertheless, an important question had thankfully been raised: Do Hesiod and the truth of the Muses really fall into the province of a "science of literary works" as represented by the hermeneutists?

Heinz Wismann has addressed this question in his comments on studies of Hesiod.[20] Is it legitimate to apply to the author of the *Theogony* the modern hermeneutic principle on which the coherence of the work's meanings resides, in the last analysis, on the autonomous decision of a single individual?[21] The constraints of this principle involve accepting the work in its autonomy, the coherence of its meaning, a unitary project, an author at work, and a peerless interpreter responding to the appeal of a peerless author. Comparison is never even envisaged – which discourages from the outset any reference to anthropology, since anthropology was born comparativist. Out of loyalty to its own principles, elaborated between a reading of Plato and a reading of the New Testament at the end of the nineteenth century, philological exegesis cannot accommodate an analysis of historicoethnograhic context.[22] Institutional practices such as ordeals by water, prophecy via incubation, and Orphico-Dionysiac funerary rituals are barred from the magic hermeneutic circle, as are all the representations of memory and oblivion that throng the cultural field in which Hesiod belongs. On the grounds that they are "external" to the text – Hesiod's text – those "data" are considered to have no bearing on the literal meaning that alone gives access to the "sole meaning" of the work. "Structuralist school essayists" – as Jean Bollack has called them – are thus completely dismissed, along with their claims to understanding a Greek culture which is reduced to a certain number of great literary or philosophicoliterary texts.[23]

A great deal is certainly at stake here, as is demonstrated by the state of contemporary "classical studies" in the United States and its unceasing focus on "great texts" and their exegesis. In truth, classical studies devotes itself to maintaining certain privileged values, without the slightest concern for analyzing cultural systems as a way of understanding the mechanisms of human thought across different cultures. Yet for "structural essayists," as for members of the French school of hermeneutics, the subject of Hesiod's poem is clearly speech – not only its status and authority but also its representation by the poet and the Muses. We all recognize that from Homer to Hesiod the relationship between the bard and the daughters of Memory undergoes a transformation and becomes more complex. In the *Iliad*, the Muses are all-knowing, and, thanks to them, the poet can see perfectly into both the bards' and the daughters' camps. As the servant of the Muses, the bard can recount what happened when the Trojan horse entered the city of Apollo and Hector. Instructed by the Muses, he sings now for Odysseus, now for others, of what unfolded before his blind gaze, as though he himself were present in the days of the Trojan War.[24] But Hesiod of Acra speaks in the first person as well as the third. An author who is both poet and prophet is present and is chosen by the Muses, who now assume new modalities of speech. Wismann is right to emphasize this point: "They say that they know how to say false things [*pseudeis*, which I would translate as "deceptive" things] that seem to be real, but at the same time know how to make true things understood."[25]

Here the Muses are understood to be reflecting on the subject of narrative and its structures. The order of discourse, *logos*, thus has a double register: one of fine fiction, which is certainly by no means rejected, the other of "true understanding." According to Wismann, the latter means "seizing upon the structures of the narrative" or "the narrative of the true structures," and so on.[26] *Alētheia* thus designates the register of the intelligible, that of true understanding of the work produced by Hesiod and his

23

post-Homeric Muses. Both levels are in the province of the daughters of Memory, as is shown by comparing the representation of the three Bee-Women in the *Homeric Hymn to Hermes*. These Bee-Women instruct Apollo himself – in divination, no less – according to a double register: "From their home, they fly now here, now there, feeding on honeycomb and bringing all things to pass. And when they are inspired [*thuiôsin*, 'they leap,' like Thyiades possessed by Dionysus] through eating yellow honey, they are willing [*ethelein*] to speak the Truth [*Alētheia*]. But if they be deprived of the god's sweet food, they speak falsely [*pseūdesthai*] in the distress that assails them."[27] Here a comparison with the knowledge of a diviner is fundamental; fortunately for hermeneutics, it can be justified by the definition found in one of the "great texts":[28] the *Iliad* declares that Calchas is able to speak of the present, the future, and the past.[29] In both cases, there are thus two registers: with the Bee-Women for Apollo the diviner, and with the Muses, for Hesiod, there is both poet and prophet. The difference between them lies in the honey, the means of ecstasy. Hesiod's Muses, more down to earth despite being Olympians, feel no need for ecstasy, not even in the customary form of nectar and ambrosia. The "desire/will" of the Bee-Women, similar to that of Hesiod's Muses, diminishes the mechanical nature of the food of truth and thereby reduces the distance between the two groups.

While hermeneutics may successfully explore the double register of Hesiodic speech, it refuses to understand memory and oblivion in their ethnographic and religious contexts, as I myself have done in this book.[30] A hermeneutist must interpret literally, at the level of the words: *lēthē* must mean "a kind of unawareness," the counterpart to *alētheia*, "things of which we are no longer unaware" – and this, we are told, means we have "true comprehension of them."[31] *Mnēmosynē*, or Memory, a divine power married to Zeus as were first *Mētis*, then *Thēmis*, and finally Hera, dissolves into a platitude, a most ridiculous outcome. She becomes simply "good memory," because "we must remember what has already been said about perceiving *Alētheia*."[32] Yet the signs provided by Hesiod are certainly clear enough: on Mount Helicon, the Muses appear close to the altar of Zeus;[33] they "breathed a voice into" the poet (*empneuein*), as does Apollo when he gives the elect the knowledge of the present, past, and future.[34] In the *Theogony*, *Lēthē*, far from being simply "a kind of unawareness," is just as much a divine power as are the Words of Deception, the *Pseudeis Logoi*, who are listed among the Children of Night, along with Sleep and Death.[35] No thoughtful study of speech in Hesiod's poems could neglect the most immediate Hesiodic context, the work itself. Similarly, ignoring the Old Man of the Sea, who is listed among the Children of the Deep (*Pontus*), leads one to ignore another essential passage in the *Theogony* and to fail to ponder "the truth" implied by the king of justice, his prophetic knowledge, and his other powers.[36] What kind of *explication de texte* begins by sweeping under the rug whole chunks of the work, without the least explanation?

Interestingly enough, it is the American Hellenists at Harvard University, such as Gregory Nagy and Charles P. Segal, who have paid the most attention to the mythicoreligious aspects of memory and oblivion and their relation to blame and praise, no doubt because they recognized the paramount importance of wider horizons of knowledge and were disinclined to consider a cultural system simply as a more or less rich collection of separate and autonomous works.[37] In spite of all the philologists' skepticism, the most important recent discoveries have established the ancient and complex nature of the works and practices of philosophicoreligious circles. The first discovery was that of the oldest Greek book, the Derveni Papyrus of ca. 380 B.C., a scroll from the library of Orpheus containing rich philosophical commentaries on the Orphic poems.[38] Next came new gold tablets, from Hipponion in Magna Graecia and Pelinna in Thessaly, which establish both the "Bacchic" nature of the initiation reserved for the bearers of these engraved lamellae and the sacred path along which they were carried, at the end of which the dead man or woman accedes to life in all its plenitude.[39] A kind of Bacchic and Orphic ritual from the end of the fourth century B.C. in turn testifies to the importance of writing in philosophicoreligious circles fascinated by the interplay between memory, oblivion, and truth.[40] Finally, on the shores of the Black Sea at Olbia, a colony of Miletus, excavators from what was then the Soviet Union discovered bone tablets bearing graffiti from 500 B.C. Beneath the three terms *Life–Death–Life* and alongside the words *orphic* and *Dionysus* was *Truth* (*Alētheia*). On another slender tablet, parallel to the pair *Peace–War* stood the words *Truth–Deception* (*Alētheia–Pseudos*). Finally, on a third tablet, beneath a shortened version of the name Dionysus was inscribed *Soul* (*Psychē*), which was associated with *Alētheia*.[41]

The philosophicoreligious circles of the late sixth century were thus deeply involved with the subject of Truth, the very Truth which, rightly or wrongly, Martin Heidegger regarded as the essential element of Greek philosophy and which was at the heart of philosophical discussion during the "overthrow of metaphysics" between the time of the Greeks and "our own time."[42] Few scholars of Antiquity or educated readers are aware of how carefully Heideggerians and "deconstructionists" have built a veritable wall to separate themselves from the explorations of Greek scholars. The Hellenists are perhaps at fault in not realizing that the only real innovator in Greek thought is Heidegger; still, these scholars continue to publish and publicize documents, texts if not whole works, from the diverse world of archaic Greece. The barrier seems insuperable. Even lucid critics of successive interpretations of Heidegger's views on Truth seem to accept at face value his notion of the "unconcealed" or the "deconcealed," making no attempt to deconstruct it or set it alongside those archaic representations of *Alētheia*. André Doz, one of the boldest of those critics, as uninformed as the most obdurate of them about the discoveries at Olbia and Derveni, has written, "We ought to take a closer look at the word *alēthēs*."[43] On the other hand, many Greek scholars probably do not know that, for Heidegger and his disciples, the history of philosophy and hence the establishment of the meaning of *Alētheia* are part of the very history of being.[44] Clearly, this does not make it any easier to initiate a debate on the modalities of concealment, oblivion, and memory in Greek thought and culture.

From the perspective I have adopted from the start, no etymology can be singled out as infallible (thank God). At least from Parmenides on, Greek philosophers recognized that to think it was necessary to debate and argue. When an etymology seems bad or fantastic no appeal to higher grounds can confer authority on it. In the context of the same inquiry, it is important to remember that it is partly because of the etymology of the word *polis* that the field of politics is left out of the analyses offered by Heidegger and his followers, intent as they are on the "overthrow of metaphysics." During a seminar, Heidegger once said (and later wrote) that the word *polis* comes from *polein*, an ancient form of the verb meaning "to be." Such an etymology is entirely arbitrary; there is simply no convincing, verifiable "true meaning" for *polis*. Even so, there was no reason for such an elementary piece of information to inhibit thought on the *polis* from developing: if the city, or *polis*, is based on the verb "to be," that in itself demonstrates that the *polis* must be the site of a total unveiling of Being.[45] Thus, the city cannot have anything in common with "politics" in the trivial sense of *to politikon*. So, goodbye politics.[46] The "philosophicoreligious" aspect was not even mentioned in connection with either the mundane world or the world of the Beyond.

It is worth pausing to reflect on this matter since, for a non-debate, the fallout continues.[47] To my knowledge, not a single disciple of Heidegger's has ever questioned this feeble etymology. A few later insisted that, for Heidegger, politics is not a category or a field like ethics or ontology. Politics, with its foundation rituals, gods, and autonomy articulated through so many practices, does not exist. It vanishes into thin air, leaving no trace, useless and unknown. In fact, on closer examination, ever since Heidegger's *Being and Time* politics in the common sense of the word has been heaped with scorn. It constitutes an obstacle in the process of *Dasein*, the process of what is existent, which is determined by its concern for self and which can assume possession of itself only by turning away from the mundane social elements of life and from the city and its pointlessly loquacious public places. In this connection, only one philosopher, Dominique Janicaud, braver and more lucid than the rest, has sought to understand how Heidegger's thought laid itself open "to what happened to him."[48] I refer, of course, to the recent past, 1933: the philosopher of *Dasein* supported Adolf Hitler's national socialism, maintained a hermetic silence on the genocide of the Jews, and afterward failed to produce any philosophical critique of his "incidental" support of the Nazi party. It may not have had much to do with the so very Greek concept of truth, but it may not be totally unconnected with the equal scorn heaped on what Heidegger calls "Anthropology." For his disciples and devotees, the term incorporates the inquiries historians of archaic Greece have conducted both on the philosophicoreligious circles and on forms of thought discovered through methods that lead neither to familiar places nor to the heart of "great works."

Finally, two additional matters are worth raising here. The first concerns the "mythical thought" that, I maintain, possessed a true consistency yet also was "overthrown." The second deals with the "social and mental" conditions that made possible the deep changes I explore through the history of the concept of Truth.

In a grudging review of a work in which I considered the presuppositions of the essentially Greek category of "myth," Arnaldo Momigliano noted my disaffection toward studies of the transition from mythical to rational thought in Greece, an issue he considered well established by then.[49] Momigliano, usually a much more perceptive observer, believed that this disaffection indicated a break with the analyses Vernant had been working on ever since his *The Origins of Greek Thought*. But Momigliano was mistaken, as we all are at times. He had completely misunderstood the intentions of my book, *The Creation of Mythology*.[50] The aim of this book was to reflect on and provoke thought about the category of "myth" and its place in Lévi-Strauss's analytic methods – methods I myself had experimented with (the first to do so in a Greek context, I believe), in 1972 in *The Gardens of Adonis*.[51] Momigliano did not realize that I had been so successful in convincing Vernant of the need to rethink the category of narratives known as "myth" that Vernant himself had explained in the popular periodical *Sciences et Avenir*, with my *The Creation of Mythology* solely in mind, that "today Greek mythology is changing its meaning."[52] Unlike Momigliano, Vernant was not upset by this at all. In fact, at this point it even seemed to suit him.[53]

However, the question here concerns the "mythical thought" that was so important in the inquiry I began in 1960. At that time it was mediated through Louis Gernet, who from time to time referred to the ideas of Hermann Usener, yet spoke of them with all the conviction of a disciple of Emile Durkheim and possibly of Ernst Cassirer; Cassirer had devoted a whole volume of his 1924 *Philosophy of Symbolic Forms* to "Mythical Thought."[54] Following in Gernet's footsteps, Vernant set up a new "framework": "mythical thought"–"positivist, abstract thought," or, put another way, the transition "from myth to reason."[55] Lévi-Strauss, for his part, had not yet said enough on the subject. *The Raw and the Cooked*, the first volume of his *Mythologiques*, appeared in 1964, and it was not until I was prompted by the comparison between "alimentary codes" and Pythagorean sacrificial practices to try new methods of analyzing Greek myths that I saw how new meaning could be given to "mythical thought."[56]

Insofar as thought of a global nature incorporates a number of different types of experience, mythical thought or ancient religious thought made it possible to elaborate the most convincing configuration of poet, seer, and king around a single model of speech with shared gestures, practices, and institutions. Now, as then, an analysis of the trajectory of *Alētheia* from Hesiod to Parmenides provides a unique opportunity to observe the changes in the mechanisms of the intellect at work in the beginnings of philosophical thought. I am now planning to develop those religious and mythical representations of speech in the direction of *Thēmis*, positioned between the oracle, Apollo, and the assemblies.[57] I have no intention of writing the history of a "psychological function" such as memory; this is in no way the aim of an inquiry devoted to detecting traces of *Alētheia* in the many places where the tribe of philosophers do not venture.[58] Nor do I intend to seek what might intuitively seem to be "the" logic behind "mythical thought," for any such notion would be quite artificial. Rather than make the inquiry hang on a contrast between *a* principle of ambiguity and *the* principle of contradiction, I prefer now to emphasize the diversity of the configurations that include *Alētheia* and the comparison that should be made between the orientations of the various frameworks encountered during this first reconnoiter. Perhaps it is no longer enough to know that Truth also has a history and that, once Parmenides had depicted the Goddess as revealing the Way of Truth to him, Truth had to be proved, argued, and put to the test of refutation.[59]

From the time of my earlier inquiry into Truth and its double registers to my comparison between different ways of beginning – the central theme of "Transcrire les mythologies" – I chose to concentrate on instances of rupture and radical change.[60] My reasons for doing so were twofold. The first reason, explicit and factual, is that the Greek data are full of abortive beginnings and sudden impulses, which the Greeks are vibrantly aware of through the very force of reflection animating these new kinds of knowledge. The second reason has become clearer in the course of my comparative studies: conditions that involve profound change and abrupt breaks with the past make it easier to select apt comparisons between cultural systems. In the case of the *Masters of Truth*, the comparison remained internal: between two types of men, two successive configurations, two models of speech. Between Hesiod and Parmenides, the determining factors seem to have been the passage of time and the change of context. I wanted to analyze the social and mental conditions of the transformation of truth between Epimenides and Parmenides. Simply noting that there was a discontinuity seemed unacceptable, particularly since the contrast between two models of speech, the "magicoreligious" and the "dialogue-speech," became explicitly obvious in the earliest days of Greek culture and the Greek city. What I then called the "process of secularization" was first manifested in a social framework whose practices and representations, so important in the formation of the city, were found described by the time of Homer's poems, particularly in the *Iliad*. Now more than ever, the assembly practices and the representations of space that made for egalitarianism in warrior circles, which are described in epic, seem to me to be essential for an understanding of the increasing importance of the *agora* in the first Greek cities of the eighth century as well as for the development of the model of *isonomia* in the "political" world of the seventh and sixth centuries.

In the variegated landscape of the journeys from "mythical thought" to the "positivist and abstract thought" that found support in the mind of the city, a certain furrow was visible from the start. With this rift came a different kind of speech, a different framework, a different kind of thought, marked by temporal divisions (the eighth century for Homer; the midseventh century for the qualitative leap represented by the "hoplite reform"; between the two, the first circular *agora* laid out on the ground by the founders of the Magna Graecia cities from about 730 on). These matters are worth following up and keeping under observation, however difficult, even today. With the advantage of hindsight, I will avoid referring in the future to "undeniable relations" between a major phenomenon such as "the secularization of thought" and changes as rich and complex as "the emergence of new social relations and unprecedented political structures." Given the scarcity of evidence in archaic Greece, it was tempting to make too much of the coherence between widely differing aspects of the culture and to connect them boldly with a network of interrelations between a different kind of social and mental phenomena, which in many cases it was barely possible to glimpse.

In a careful and intelligent analysis of *The Masters of Truth*, Maurice Caveing has pointed out the large gap between a kind of egalitarian and secular scene and the formulation of, or at least insistence on, a principle of noncontradiction in the field of Parmenides' *Alētheia*.[61] Certainly, I was somewhat cavalier in pronouncing on what many earlier scholars had solemnly defined as "a great social fact."[62] Its importance could not be doubted, and

32

to simply sum it up as I did must have seemed quite incongruous. The juridical and political exercise of these two theses or two parties certainly deserves a study that takes account of their respective forms and procedures. However, it does seem more justifiable to stress the role which the technique of mathematical demonstration may have played in sixth-century Greece, together with the insistence on noncontradiction within this new kind of knowledge, as Caveing did in 1968. The debate on "common matters" (*ta koina*) within a space of equality is not necessarily directly related to the debate between intellectuals on the rules of reasoning, the forms of demonstration, and the criteria of conceptual analysis.[63] Indeed, the recent comparativist studies of Geoffrey Lloyd have revealed the complexity of this laboratory of new rational thought with all its various types of knowledge, its competitive frameworks of rivalry, its different types of proof, and its ways of distinguishing between discourse that is true and discourse that is not.[64] Still, in any project involving an increasingly refined comparison between modes of reasoning and ways of formulating or establishing the truth, there is even today a place for *The Masters of Truth*.

CHAPTER ONE

Truth and Society

In our scientific civilization, the idea of "truth" immediately summons up notions of objectivity, communicability, and unity.[1] *Truth* is defined at two levels: conformity with logical principles and conformity with reality.[2] Accordingly, truth is inseparable from concepts of demonstration, verification, and experimentation. Of all our commonsense notions, truth probably above all seems nowadays to have always existed, static as well as relatively simple. However, to undermine such impressions, we only have to recall that experimentation, for example, one of the underpinnings of our conception of what is true, only became mandatory in a society where it had become a traditional technique, that is, after physics and chemistry had already acquired an important place.

We may therefore wonder whether truth, as a mental category, cannot be dissociated from a whole system of thought as well as from material and social life.[3] By contrast, the Indo-Iranian word usually translated as *truth*, *Ṛta*, also means liturgical prayer, the power ensuring the continual return of the dawn, the order established by the cult of the gods, and law – in short, it comprises a collection of meanings that shatters our own image of truth.[4] What seems simple is replaced by complexity, and, moreover, complexity organized quite differently from our own.

35

If the Indo-Iranian world is so different from ours, what about the world of Greece? Is the place of "truth" the same as it is in our own conceptual system, and does it embrace the same semantic content? This question is not asked simply out of curiosity. Greece claims our attention for two interconnected reasons. First, the Western concept of objective and rational truth emerged historically from Greek thought. As is well known, in the wealth of thinking on truth produced by contemporary philosophers, Parmenides, Plato, and Aristotle are constantly invoked, studied, and challenged.[5] Second, in the Greek construction of reason from the sixth century B.C. on, a particular image of "truth" is fundamental. When philosophic thought discovered its own particular subject of inquiry, disentangled itself from the bases of mythological thought that still anchored Ionian cosmology, and deliberately set out to address the problems that would thereafter retain its attention, it became organized around a central concept that from then on would define a particular aspect of first philosophy (or metaphysics) and one aspect of a first philosopher (or metaphysician): that concept was *Alētheia*, or "truth."

When *Alētheia* appeared in the prelude to Parmenides' poem, it did not spring, fully developed, from the philosopher's brain. To judge by our historical documentation, it began with Homer. Although this fact may seem to suggest that the chronological development of the successive sources of evidence between Homer and Parmenides is required to illuminate "truth," the problem must be posed differently.[6] For many years, scholars have drawn attention to the strange features of Parmenides' setting: a chariot journey guided by the daughters of the Sun, a way reserved for the man who knows, a path that leads to the gates of Day and Night, a goddess who reveals true knowledge. In short, this mythical and religious imagery is singularly at odds with abstract philosophical thought focusing, for example, on Being itself. All

these features, whose religious character is undeniable, definitely
point us toward certain philosophicoreligious circles in which
a philosopher was still just a wise man, even a magus. And in
these circles we find a type of man and thought directed toward
Alētheia. Epimenides of Crete had the privilege of seeing *Alētheia*
with his own eyes; it was the "plain of *Alētheia*" that the soul of
the initiate aspired to contemplate.[7] Through Epimenides and the
philosophicoreligious sects, the prehistory of the rational *Alētheia*
is definitely oriented toward certain forms of religious thought
in which this same "power" played a fundamental role.

The prehistory of the philosophical *Alētheia* leads us to the
system of thought of the diviner, the poet, and the king of justice, three figures for whom a certain type of speech is defined
by *Alētheia*. Defining the prerational meaning of "truth" involves
answering a number of important questions.[8] How is *Alētheia* represented in mythical thought?[9] How and why was a type of efficacious speech replaced by another type of speech with its own
specific problems, such as the relation of speech to reality and
the relation between speech and other people? What is the relation between certain innovations in the social practice of the sixth
century B.C. and the development of thinking organized around
logos? Which values, even while undergoing a change in meaning,
remain important throughout the transition from one system of
thought (the mythical) to the other (that of reason)?[10] From the
opposite perspective, what constitutes the fundamental separation of religious and rational thought? The aim of this book is
not simply to examine the mental, social, and historical context
to define the prerational meaning of "truth" within the mythical system of thought and the beginnings of rational thought.[11]
The history of *Alētheia* provides us with an ideal field for two
further objectives. First, it allows us to consider the problem of
the religious origins of certain concepts in metaphysical philos-

37

ophy and thereby reveal one aspect of the type of man introduced through philosophy into the city. Second, this field allows us to pinpoint, in the very fabric of continuity between religious and philosophical thinking, the changes in meaning and the logical breaks that radically differentiate these two forms of thought.

CHAPTER TWO

The Memory of the Poet

At the beginning of a poem, the poet invokes the Muse whose task is to make past events known:[1]

> Tell me now, you Muses who have your homes on Olympus. For you, who are goddesses, are there, and you know all things, and we have heard only the rumour of it and know nothing. Who then of those were the chief men and the lords of the Danaans? I could not tell over the multitude of them nor name them, not if I had ten tongues and ten mouths, not if I had a voice never to be broken and a heart of bronze within me, not unless the Muses of Olympia, daughters of the aegis, remembered (*mnēsaiath'*) all those who came beneath Ilion.[2]

The poet's speech, as developed in the poetic tradition, is inseparable from two complementary concepts: the Muse and memory.[3] Together, these religious powers constitute the general configuration that confers on the *Alētheia* of poetry its true, deep meaning.

What is the meaning of the Muse and the function of memory? Scholars have noted the presence of deities in the Greek pantheon bearing the names of feelings, passions, mental attitudes, intellectual qualities, and so on. *Moūsa* is one of these religious powers that are outside man "even when he feels their presence within him."[4] Just as *mētis*, an intellectual faculty, is represented by Mētis, a wife of Zeus, and *thēmis*, a social concept, is represented by the great Thēmis, another of Zeus's wives, a common noun, *mousa*, is represented at the secular level by the Muse of the Greek pantheon. A number of classical texts suggest that *mousa* as a common noun means speech that is sung, or rhythmic speech.[5] This double significance of *mousa* (the common noun and the divine power) can be grasped particularly well from an "ancient discourse" (*palaios logos*) recorded by Philo of Alexandria:

> An old story is sometimes sung that was imagined by sages and, like so many others, committed to memory from one generation to the next.... It runs as follows: "When the creator had completed the whole world, he asked one of the prophets if there was anything that he wished did not exist amongst all the things that had been born on earth. The prophet replied that all things were absolutely perfect and complete, but there was just one thing lacking, laudatory speech (*ton epainetēn...logon*)."... The Father of All listened to what he had to say and, approving of his words, forthwith produced the lineage of singers full of harmonies, all born from one of the powers by whom he was surrounded, the Virgin *Memory* (*Mnēmē*) whose name the common people changed, calling her *Mnēmosynē*.[6]

In this context, a close link exists between the Muses and "sung speech," here described as "laudatory speech." This link is confirmed even more clearly by the extremely explicit names borne by the daughters of Memory, names that reflect a whole theology of "sung speech."[7] Clio, for example, denotes fame (*kleos*), the fame of the great exploits transmitted by the poet to future generations. Thalia alludes to festivity (*thallein*), the social condition for poetic creativity. Melpomene and Terpsichora both conjure up images of music and dancing. Others, such as Polymnia and Calliope, express the rich diversity of sung speech and the powerful voice that endows poems with life. The oldest invocations to the Muses are also revealing. Long before Hesiod, there were three Muses, Meletē, Mnēmē, and Aoidē, who were revered in an ancient sanctuary on the Helicon.[8] Each name referred to an essential aspect of the poetic function. *Meletē* designated the discipline indispensable to any bardic apprentice: attention, concentration, and mental exercise.[9] *Mnēmē* names the psychological function enabling recitation and improvisation. *Aoidē* is the product, the epic recitation, the completed poem, the end result of *meletē* and *mnēmē*.[10]

However, other nomenclatures are also cited. Cicero records one in which four Muses exist: Archē, Meletē, Aoidē, and Thelxinoē.[11] Two of these represent entirely new aspects: *archē* is the beginning, what is original; the poet's speech strives to discover the origins of things, primordial reality.[12] *Thelxinoē* is the seduction of the mind, the spell cast by sung speech on the listener.[13] These epithets for the Muse, through which a veritable theology of speech is developed, testify to the importance of the equivalence between the Muse and the notion of sung speech in circles of inspired bards and poets.[14]

However, sung speech is also inseparable from memory. In the Hesiodic tradition, the Muses are the daughters of *Mnēmosynē*.[15] In Chios they were called the "remembrances" (*mneiai*), since they made the poet "remember."[16] What is the meaning of memory, and how is it related to sung speech? First, the religious status of memory, its cult in bardic circles, and its importance in poetic thought can only be understood if one remembers that Greek civilization from the twelfth to the ninth centuries B.C. was based not on written, but on oral traditions:[17] "In those days men had to have a memory for many things. For many things were communicated to them, such as signs for recognizing places, favorable times for activities, sacrifices to be made to gods, and the secret burial places of heroes, hard to find for men setting forth on a distant voyage from Greece."[18] Memory is essential in an oral civilization, and specific mnemonic techniques must be perfected.[19] To understand the phenomenon of oral poetry, of which the *Iliad* and the *Odyssey* represent the culmination, we must postulate a veritable "mnemotechnique."[20] By analyzing formulary technique, Milman Parry and his followers shed much light on the composition procedures of these poets.[21] The bards created their poems as they recited them, "not with *words* but with *formulae*, groups of words ready made to be incorporated into the dactylic hexameter."[22] One senses that poetic inspiration is backed by long years of memory training. The Homeric poems provide a number of examples of these mnemotechnique exercises, which were designed to help young bards master the difficult skill of composing poetry.[23] One example occurs in the passages known as catalogs. A catalog exists of the best Achaean warriors and one of the best horses; the catalog of the Greek and Trojan armies takes up half of the second book of the *Iliad*, four hundred lines in all, and must have been a true feat of recitation for the bard.

But was the memory of these poets a psychological function like our own? Jean-Pierre Vernant's studies show that the ends achieved by the deified memory of the Greeks were, in fact, quite different from our own.[24] It did not aim to reconstruct the past according to a temporal perspective. Above all, sacralized memory was a privilege reserved for groups of men in fraternal orders. As such, it radically differs from the recollection of other individuals. Like mantic knowledge, the knowledge of these inspired poets was a form of divinatory omniscience. The formula defining their powers was the same; it was knowledge of "all things that were, things to come and things past."[25] For the poet, remembrance came through a personal vision that ensured direct access to the events his memory evoked. His privilege was to enter into contact with the other world, and his memory granted him the power to "decipher the invisible." Thus, memory was not simply the material basis for sung speech or the psychological function on which the formulary technique depended. It was also, and above all, a religious power that gave poetic pronouncements their status of magicoreligious speech.[26] Sung speech, delivered by a poet with the gift of second sight, was efficacious speech. Its peculiar power instituted a symbolicoreligious world that was indeed reality itself. In this context, what then was the function of the poet? What ends did his gift of second sight serve? On which scales did sung speech, rooted in memory, play? Finally, within these registers, what was the place and meaning of *Alētheia*?

Traditionally, the poet served two functions: "to hymn the immortals and the glorious deeds of heroes."[27] The example of Hermes illustrates the former: "While he played shrilly on his lyre, he lifted up his voice and sang. He sang (*krainōn*) [literally: through his praise he made real] the story of the deathless gods and of the dark earth, how at the first they came to be, and how each one received his portion."[28] This speech exists on the level of myths of emergence and order, cosmogonies and theogonies. However, alongside stories about the gods, we also find in the Greek tradition speech celebrating the individual exploits of warriors. The first important fact here, then, is the duality of poetry: it both celebrates human exploits and narrates the history of the gods. In turn, this double register of sung speech illuminates the fundamental characteristic of Mycenaean social organization. The palace system was apparently dominated by a royal figure in charge of religious, economic, and political functions.[29] Alongside this all-powerful king, however, was a "leader of the *laos*," who commanded the military.[30] In this centralized state, warriors constituted a privileged caste with a special status.[31]

The second register of poetry corresponds perfectly with this specialized warrior group. Nonetheless, we must still ask the question: What relation existed between theogonies and the figure of the king? An answer is offered in studies on the prehistory of Greek theogonies.[32] Although Hesiod was once viewed as the earliest author of theogonic literature, his work is now recognized as simply the last in a long line of accounts clarified through Eastern, Hittite, and Phoenician theogonies. F.M. Cornford, for example, saw in Zeus's battles against the Titans and Typhoeus important comparisons with Babylonian theogonies, in particular the battle between Marduk and Tiamat.[33] These comparisons proved most instructive, since story telling was still alive and was closely connected with ritual in Babylon. Every year, on the fourth day of the royal festival of the Creation of the New Year, the king mimed a ritual battle enacting Marduk's exploit against Tiamat. During this ritual, the *Enuma Eliš*, the poem of the creation, was recited. Vernant has since shown that the ordering of the world in the Greek cosmogonies and theogonies was inseparable from myths of sovereignty.[34] Furthermore, the myths of emergence, while recounting the story of the successive generations of the gods, foregrounded the determining role of a divine king who, after many struggles, triumphed over his enemies and once and for all established order in the cosmos. Hesiod's poem, the principal Greek example of this kind of account, marks the decline of the genre, for it was a written or dictated work and no longer an oral recitation pronounced on the occasion of a ritual festival. Nevertheless, Hesiod does appear to provide the final remaining example of sung speech praising the figure of the king, in a society centered on the type of sovereignty seemingly exemplified by Mycenaean civilization. In Hesiod's case, the royal figure is simply represented by Zeus.[35] At this level the poet's function was above all to "serve sovereignty":[36] by reciting the myth of emergence, he collaborated directly in setting the world in order.[37]

In Hesiod's poem we find the most ancient representation of a poetic and religious *Alētheia*. What is the Muses' function according to the theology of speech deployed in the *Theogony*? The Muses proudly claim the privilege of "speaking the truth" (*alēthea gērusasthai*).[38] The meaning of this *Alētheia* is revealed by its relation to the Muses and to memory, for the Muses are those who "tell of what is, and what is to be, and what was before now";[39] they are the words of memory. The very context of the *Theogony* thus already indicates a close connection between *Alētheia* and memory and even suggests that one should understand these two religious powers as a single representation. However, Hesiod's *Alētheia* achieves its full significance only when we locate the concepts dominating the poet's second register.

The second register of poetic speech is devoted entirely to praising the warriors' exploits. Though no direct evidence of the use of this type of sung speech in the Mycenaean civilization exists, it is possible to imagine its presence in an archaic Greek society such as ancient Sparta, where a group of warriors utterly devoted to warfare dominated. In ancient Sparta, society was ruled by two redoubtable powers, praise and blame.[40] This society, which established the principle of equality between all citizens, recognized only differences stemming from praise and criticism. At every level of society, individuals exercised the right to observe and be observed by others.[41] For example, in some festivals, such as the *Partheneia*, girls had the right to jeer at young men who had committed some misdeed; if, on the contrary, the young men had proved themselves worthy, the girls would sing their praises at length for everyone to hear.[42] On the strength of their authority in a society organized along age groups, the elders, who spent much of the day in the "speaking chamber," devoted most of their time to praising good actions and censuring bad ones.[43] In an agonistic society, which so highly valued a warrior's excellence, no domain was subjected more to praise or blame than military feats. In this domain, the poet was the supreme arbiter. His function, in this case, was no longer to serve sovereignty; instead, he was at the service of the community of "similar" and "equal" ones, those privileged to exercise the military profession.[44]

In a warrior society such as ancient Sparta, the Muses thus rightly occupied an important position. They were honored for two reasons. First, they were the protectresses of the players of flutes, lyres, and kitharas, since music was part of Spartan education and military marches and charges were accompanied by flutes and lyres.[45] However, their second function was of far greater importance. Kings offered a sacrifice to the Muses before each combat in order to remind the "equal ones" of the judgments they would receive, thus encouraging them to defy danger and accomplish feats "worthy of celebration,"[46] feats that would afford them a "glorious memory" (*mnēmē eukleēs*).[47]

It may seem paradoxical that, in such an agonistic society, recognition did not directly result from action. However, in warfare, the aristocratic warrior seems to have been obsessed by two essential values, *kleos* and *kudos*, both of them aspects of glory.[48] *Kudos* was the glory that shone on the victor, a kind of divine, instantaneous grace. The gods granted it to some and denied it to others.[49] *Kleos*, by contrast, was a glory that flourished as it passed by word of mouth, from generation to generation. *Kudos* came from the gods; *kleos* rose up to the gods. At no time could the warrior feel himself to be the agent, the source, of his actions: his victory was a pure favor from the gods and his feats, once completed, took form only through words of praise. A man was thus worth only as much as his *logos*.[50] A warrior's worth was decided by the masters of praise, the servants of the Muses.[51] They granted or denied him "memory."[52]

What was the status of praise? In aristocratic society, to praise another was, in principle, an obligation: "To be just," said the Sea's Ancient, "praise even a foe when he deserves it."[53] The poems of Pindar and Bacchylides demonstrate the impact of the injunction: they abound in praise for the strength of men's arms, the wealth of kings, and the courage of noble people.[54] However, a poet did not lavish praise indiscriminately. Praise was aristocratic: "We know of Nestor and of Lykian Sarpedon from resonant words, such as skilled craftsmen of songs have melded together. Radiant poetry makes virtue long-lived, but for few is the making easy."[55] Through the power of his speech, a poet made an ordinary mortal "equal in destiny to a king,"[56] conferring on him being and reality. His praise was called *etumos*.[57] However, like the Indian ideal of *samsa*, the poet's speech was double-edged, both good and bad.[58] As Pindar puts it: "Praise touches on Blame."[59] There is a negative aspect: "bitter speech" has a "crowding bite" and the face of *Mōmos*.[60] The field of poetic speech is polarized by these two religious powers. Between praise and blame stands the poet, the supreme arbiter: "I will praise the man I love, warding away lurid blame and bringing him true glory, like a stream of water."[61]

While in certain traditions blame is malevolent speech or positive criticism, it can also be defined as a lack of praise. In the most ancient religious thought, *Mōmos*, described as "shadowy," is one of the children of Night and a brother to *Lēthē*, oblivion.[62] Through its affinities with oblivion, blame is the negative aspect of praise; used simply as a doublet to *Lēthē*, its meaning is silence.[63] Oblivion, or silence, represents the rearing up of the power of death in the face of the power of life, Memory, the mother of the Muses.[64] Behind praise and blame is the fundamental pair of anti-

47

thetical powers, *Mnēmosynē* and *Lēthē*.[65] A warrior's life is played out between these two poles. The master of praise decides whether a man "should not be hidden beneath the black veil of darkness"[66] or, on the contrary, that silence and oblivion should be his lot;[67] whether his name should shine in dazzling light[68] or instead be consigned forever to darkness.[69]

The field of poetic speech is balanced by the tension between these two groups of powers. Each power is matched by another in the opposite group: in one group night, silence, and oblivion; in the other light, praise, and memory. Exploits that go unremarked die: "Mortal men forget whatever has not intermingled in the glorious streams of verses, and come to flower through a poet's skill."[70] Only through the bard's speech can silence and death be eluded. The positive values, the very existence of efficacious speech are manifested in the voice of this special man, the poet, and in the harmonious vibration in which his praise floats aloft, in this living speech that is the power of life.[71] A poet bestows through his praise a "memory" on man, who is not naturally endowed with it. Theocritus put the point bluntly: many wealthy people would have remained "without a memory" (*amnastoi*) had it not been for Simonides.[72] This does not mean they would have lacked the faculty of reconstructing their temporal past, but they would have never received the precious gift that Pindar calls a "memory" or a "memorial" (*mnamēion*).[73] Nor does it mean they would have lacked the vague, secular remembrance human beings always keep of the dead. Pindar's kind of "memory" is a privilege that a poet may confer even on the living.[74] The "memory" of a man is precisely "the eternal monument of the Muses," that is, the same religious reality as the speech of the poet, grafted on memory and actualized in praise.[75] At the level of sung speech, memory thus has two meanings. First, it is a gift of second sight allowing the poet to produce efficacious speech, to formulate sung speech. Second, memory is sung speech itself, speech that will never cease to be and that is identified with the being of the man whom the speech celebrates.

What place does *Alētheia* have in this system of thought whose balance depends on the tension between these antithetical powers? The triple opposition between memory and oblivion, praise and blame, and light and night neatly lays out the configuration wherein *Alētheia* finds its meaning. For Pindar, *Alētheia* is a power he calls "Zeus' daughter," one that he invokes, together with the Muse, when he is "remembering."[76] For Bacchylides, *Alētheia* is the "fellow citizen of the gods, the only one allowed to share the life of the Immortals."[77] *Alētheia* can conquer even the redoubtable *Mōmos*: "To be sure, the Blame of mortals attaches to all works, but *Alētheia* always triumphs."[78] Given the inseparability of praise and *Alētheia*, its function is identical to memory:[79] "The stone of Lydia condemns gold; amongst human beings, virtue has as its witness the Wisdom (of poets) and the omnipotence of *Alētheia*."[80] *Alētheia* is formally opposed to *Lēthē*, just as it is to *Mōmos*.[81] On the side of light, *Alētheia* brings brightness and brilliance; "it sheds luster on all things."[82] When the poet gives praise, he does so through *Alētheia* and in its name;[83] his speech is *alēthēs*, as is his mind (*nous*).[84] The poet has the power to see *Alētheia*;[85] he is a "master of Truth."

+	−
{ Praise { (*Epainos*)	{ Blame { (*Mōmos*)
Speech	Silence
Light	Darkness
Memory	Oblivion
Alētheia	*Lēthē*

In all likelihood this same relation between *Alētheia* and *Lēthē* organizes the representations of sung speech in cosmogonies. The affinities of *Alētheia* (of whom the Muses sing) and *Mnēmosynē* (who gave birth to them) lead one to postulate the second term in this basic pair, namely, *Lēthē*. Hesiod's *Works and Days*, different in subject from the *Theogony* but similar in spirit, partially compensates for the *Theogony*'s silence on this matter. The *Works and Days* obeys the same poetic ideology as the earlier *Theogony*. The Muses still inspire the poet; his poem is a marvelous hymn those goddesses cause him to hear.[86] Like the prophet-diviner, Hesiod claims the ability to reveal "the thought of aegis-bearing Zeus."[87] His words, described as *etētuma*, are religious in nature on two counts: both through the religious nature of Hesiod's own poetic function and also through the sacred character of the labors on the land that the poet explains to the farmer of Ascra.[88] In Hesiod's thought, to labor the land is an absolutely religious occupation. The gods have allotted these labors to men, and the days that divide these labors up over the year are those of "the counselor Zeus."[89] One who understands the ritual succession of labors and *remembers* each rite flawlessly, without any trace of forgetfulness, is a "divine man." Hesiod explicitly names the distribution of working and proscribed days *Alētheia*.[90]

In the *Works and Days*, we thus find a double instantiation of *Alētheia*. First, there is the *Alētheia* pronounced by the poet in the name of the Muses, which is manifested in his magicoreligious speech, and interacts with poetic memory. Second, we find the *Alētheia* possessed by the farmer of Ascra himself. In the latter case, "truth" is explicitly defined as a "nonforgetfulness" of the poet's precepts.[91] But no fundamental difference exists between these two cases of *Alētheia*. They are simply *Alētheia* considered from two different perspectives – in one case in its relation to the poet, in the other in relation to the farmer who listens.

The former possesses *Alētheia* purely through the privilege of his poetic functions; the latter can only acquire *Alētheia* by exerting his memory. In other words, knowledge of *Alētheia* is available to the peasant of Ascra only through exercising a memory prone to forgetfulness, which may suddenly darken his mind and deprive him of the "revelation" afforded by the *Works and Days*.

The complementarity between *Alētheia* and *Lēthē* thus becomes particularly obvious in the peasant-disciple relation. However, in addition to the partly "etymological" relation of the peasant's *Alētheia* to *Lēthē*, a second, similar, relation between *Alētheia* and *Lēthē* can be found vis-à-vis the master of truth. This second case is based not on *lēthē* in the sense of human forgetfulness but on *Lēthē*, the daughter of Night. Of these two relations between *Alētheia* and *Lēthē*, one religious, the other linguistic, the former is fundamental. In fact, this relation structures the representation of a sung speech that praises the figure of the king, just as it organizes the field of speech devoted to celebrating warrior's feats.

While the poet's religious function is attested to only in the last echoes of theogonical literature, his function of praising and blaming continued until the classical period. Pindar and Bacchylides exercised this function for the benefit of aristocratic minorities, fulfilling the role previously assumed by their predecessors. By the classical period, however, the system of thought that privileged sung speech as a religious power had become no more than an anachronism; its persistence simply reflected the tenacity of a particular elite. In reality, the poet's job now was to exalt the nobility and praise the rich landowners who were developing a luxury economy, spending large sums, glorying in their matrimonial alliances, and priding themselves on their horse-drawn chariots and athletic prowess.[92] The poet, serving a nobility all the more avid for praise now that its political prerogatives were challenged, reaffirmed all the more vigorously the essential

51

values of his own function, since poets were beginning to seem old-fashioned and the place in the Greek city for this type of magicoreligious speech no longer existed.[93] Classical democracy rejected this system of values once and for all. In the last analysis, the poet was now no more than a parasite whose task was to gratify the elite on whom he depended with an embellished image of its own past.

The contrast between this role and the poet's omnipotence in Greek society from the Mycenaean age to the end of the archaic period is striking. In Mycenaean society the poet seems to have played the role of an officiating priest or acolyte of the sovereign who collaborated in imposing order on the world. In the archaic period, even after this liturgical function disappeared along with the function of sovereignty, the poet remained an all-powerful figure for the warrior and aristocratic nobility. He alone could confer or withhold memory. It was in his speech that men could recognize themselves.

But whether as an official of the sovereign or as one who praised the warrior nobility, the poet was always a master of truth. His "truth" was a performative truth, never challenged or demonstrated, and fundamentally different from our own traditional concept of truth. Early *Alētheia* meant neither agreement between a proposition and its object nor agreement between judgments. It was not the opposite of "lies" or "falsehood." The only meaningful opposition involved *Alētheia* and *Lēthē*. If the poet was truly inspired, if what he had to say was based on his gift of second sight, then his speech tended to be identified with "truth."[94]

CHAPTER THREE

The Old Man of the Sea

Hesiod describes the negative powers of the children of Night, and then lists the descendants of Pontus, beginning with the eldest and most venerable, Nereus, the Sea's Ancient or the Old Man of the Sea:[1] "But Pontos, the great Sea, was Father of truthful (*apseudēs*) Nereus, who tells no lies (*alēthēs*), eldest of his sons. They call him the old Gentleman because he is trustworthy (*nēmertēs*), and gentle, and never forgetful of what is right (*oude themisteōn lēthetai*), but the thoughts of his mind are mild and righteous (*dikaia kai ēpia*)."[2] Three epithets, *alēthēs*, *apseudēs*, and *nēmertēs*, confer exceptional importance on Nereus. The association of these three epithets is in all likelihood traditional, since we also find them linked in this way in the description of the highest form of mantic speech, that of Apollo. In the *Homeric Hymn to Hermes*, when Hermes speaks before the gods, he claims in an *ad hominem* argument addressed to Apollo that he has the same virtues as those usually associated with his rival.[3] He declares that he will speak *Alētheia* and that he is *nēmertēs* and *apseudēs*.[4] The "truth" of the Old Man of the Sea thus seems to cover two domains: prophecy and justice. To understand the nature of this truth, we must first decipher the relations between *Alētheia* and both mantic speech and justice and then specify the modalities of justice dispensed by the Old Man of the Sea. To discover Nereus's "truth" it is necessary to investigate the institutions intimately connected, it seems, to the Old Man of the Sea.

In Hesiod's *Theogony*, Nereus administers justice. However, for an entire tradition he embodied a mantic power whose wisdom the Ancients always praised and whose "pronouncements" were carefully preserved and passed on.[5] The occasions on which he was consulted are famous.[6] Nereus was, moreover, at the head of a lineage of oracular deities: his daughter, Eidō, was called Theonoē because "she knew all divine things, the present and the future, a privilege she inherited from her forebear Nereus."[7] When Glaucus, a member of the same family of sea gods, appeared to the Argonauts, he declared himself to be the prophet of the Old Man of the Sea, the husband of Panteidyia, the All-Knowing One, and an *apseudēs* interpreter.[8] Nereus-like deities, such as Phorkys, Glaucus, and Pontus, the *Halios Gērōn*, were all related, or even identified, through their mantic function.[9]

Alētheia occupied a place of great importance in the realm of mantic speech (or prophecy). Evidence shows that the authority of mantic knowledge and pronouncements was derived from a particular concept of the truth. In the *Homeric Hymn to Hermes*, the ancient deities assigned to Hermes by Apollo are the Bee-Women who go everywhere, making all kinds of things "happen": endowed with a mantic knowledge, they speak *Alētheia*.[10] The oracle of the Ismenion is known as the *alēthēs* seat of diviners.[11] When Tiresias refers to his knowledge, he speaks of his *Alētheia*.[12] The nocturnal oracles summoned up by Gaia speak *Alēthosunē*.[13] Cassandra is *alēthomantis*.[14] Some dream visions also belong to *Alētheia*.[15] Finally, Olympia is "a queen of *Alētheia*," because there "men of prophecy, consulting Zeus' sacrificial fire, probe his will! God of the white-flashing bolt, what has he to say of the contenders, struggling for glory, breathless until they hold it?"[16] Furthermore, according to some traditions, *Alētheia* was the name of one of the nurses of the great oracular god Apollo.[17] Nereus, privileged by his possession of the most ancient oracular knowledge, is most certainly a rightful master of *Alētheia*.[18]

But the *Alētheia* of the Old Man of the Sea refers not only to his prophetic power; it is also why he is "never forgetful of what is right" and "the thoughts of his mind are mild and righteous":[19] in other words, his function as a purveyor of justice. Like his daughter Theonoē, Nereus is "a living sanctuary, an august temple of *Dikē.*"[20] In religious thought a distinction does not exist between the domains of justice and truth. The many affinities between *Dikē* and *Alētheia* are well attested. When Epimenides goes in broad daylight to the cave of Zeus Diktaios, where he then dreams for many years, he converses with the gods and speaks with *Alētheia* and *Dikē*.[21] This association is so natural that Hesychius defines *Alētheia* as *dikaia*, "things of *Dikē.*"[22] Furthermore, through a play on the words *Chronos* and *Cronos*, Plutarch tells us that Cronos is said to be the father of *Alētheia*, no doubt because he is naturally "the most just one" (*dikaiotatos*).[23] *Alētheia* is in effect the "most just" of all things.[24] *Alētheia*'s power is basically the same as *Dikē*'s:[25] *Alētheia*, "who knows in silence what is going to happen and what has happened," corresponds to *Dikē*, who knows "all things divine, the present and the future."[26] At this level of thought no distinction exists between truth and justice. The power of *Alētheia* thus encompasses the twofold domain of prophecy and justice.

The double field in which the *Alētheia* of the Old Man of the Sea operates makes it possible to define the forms of justice over which he presides: to wit, judicial procedures that involve and, to a point, are confused with forms of divination. This type of judgment was not unusual and was still current in the sixth century B.C. in Megara, where Theognis declares, "I must judge this case as exactly as with a line and a ruler, and give both parties their just due by consulting the diviners, the birds, and the burning altars, so as to spare myself the shame of making a mistake."[27] However, gods such as Nereus, Proteus, and Glaucus live in the depths of the sea, from which they dispense a special kind of justice. To consult Glaucus, one had to set out in a boat; the god would rise from the waves when he was ready to prophesy.[28]

These gods were patrons of a sea justice involving ritual ordeals who harkened back to the earliest Mediterranean civilizations. Sumerian documentation published by Georges Dossin, with commentaries by Charles Picard that compare it with certain Greek traditions, enables us to explain how these ordeals worked.[29] As early as the third millennium, forms of river ordeals are clearly attested in Sumer. The message from the young Carchemish to his father Zimrilim proves that ordeals were imposed at the Upper Euphrates and at Mari according to a procedure identical to that described in paragraph 2 of the code of Hammurabi.[30]

The Mari letters detail the circumstances and modes of immersion. First, such rituals seem to have been designed to decide conflicting territorial claims of two rival princes. Whereas in certain traditions this kind of altercation was sometimes resolved through puzzles and riddles, in Mesopotamia water tests were used.[31] Each party was represented by a team of two men and two women who were obliged to plunge in turn into the middle of the river to justify the claim made to the disputed territory. At an institutional level, it is noteworthy that the king of Mari, as sovereign over his two disputing vassals, established the conditions of the ordeal and appointed a high official to preside in his place over its correct performance. Justice was thus dispensed by the royal figure, even if the decision stemmed from the will of the river god.

This institutional evidence from the Sumerian world is important for Greek civilization. Some mythical Greek traditions seem to indicate that the Achaeo-Mycenaeans who established themselves in the area of the Colophon were aware as early as the fourteenth century B.C. of certain Asiatic practices and beliefs, which the Hittites were probably instrumental in bringing to the attention of the Aegean archipelago.[32] But as Picard points out, these ritual ordeals underwent a slight but significant geographical deformation when they were transmitted to the Greeks: it was no longer a river that provided the means for the ordeal but instead the sea surrounding the coasts and islands. For example, when a conflict arose between Minos, guilty of violating a virgin, and Theseus, who defended the girl, the matter was decided by a "miracle duel."[33] Theseus dove into the waves and recovered the ring he had just hurled to the bottom of the ocean. He thus penetrated the world of the gods and proved his own divinity by surfacing in the waters, safe and in possession of the ring. For the Greeks, the sea was a kind of Beyond, just as the river had been for the Sumerians. To return from these waters, one needed the assent of the gods.

Among these sea ordeals, one episode emphasizes even more strongly its nature as ordeal by immersion.[34] In Book IV of the *Histories*, Herodotus recounts the tale of Phronimē, the wise virgin, slandered by her stepmother and given by her father to the merchant Themison, the dispenser of justice. Once at sea, he attached a rope to the girl, flung her into the waves, then pulled her out alive. The sea had pronounced its verdict.[35] Solon's contemporaries still believed that the undisturbed sea represented "justice for all."[36] This same historical and religious context nurtured and strengthened the belief that a safe sea crossing stood for innocence. The belief was taken seriously enough that a fifth-century B.C. Greek accused of murder did not hesitate in claiming the opportunity to prove his innocence.[37] The Old Man of the

Sea most likely embodied the gravest and most solemn form of justice because he assumed the role in the Greek world that the river gods had played in Anatolia and Mesopotamia.[38]

However, justice by ordeal was not unique. There were many other ordeals; among those associated with the Old Man of the Sea, the ordeal by the scales is worth mentioning. This ordeal is doubly interesting in that first, a royal figure often presided over it and, second, it was placed under the aegis of *Alētheia*. In his *Sur le travail poétique d'Homère*, Picard has shown how a strange misunderstanding of the famous judgment scene concerning the shield of Achilles has misled commentators, particularly historians of Greek law.[39] As is well known, the Ancients, seated in a circle, individually declared their opinion regarding compensation for a murder: "Two talents of gold to be given to that judge who in this case spoke the straightest opinion."[40] But what was actually involved was not a measure of metal but a golden pair of scales, for *talanta* initially meant a pair of scales or the plates of the scales; only later did it come to mean a measuring unit.[41] No doubt the poet who described this work of art did not have it before his eyes and confused *talanta*, "scales," with the same word meaning a measure of metal. The scales of justice thus disappeared from this ancient source of evidence. As the *Homeric Hymn to Hermes* proves, the scales are certainly present when Zeus presides over a judgment.[42] Zeus, the overseer, holds them when deciding the outcome of a battle or a warrior's fate.[43]

The use of scales in juridicoreligious procedures dates to earliest Greek times, the Mycenaean civilization. In that time – as we know from the tablets – everything was weighed, and the overseer and the scales represented the eye of the king and his justice, respectively.[44] Even in the mid-sixth century, the bowl of Arcesilas of Cyrene depicted an accounting king. Seated on his throne and clad in ceremonial garb, Arcesilas II watches the delivery of his revenues. In front of him stands a tall pair of scales surrounded by bustling officials. Assisted by two officials, the king is checking to see that each of the Libyans has delivered his tribute of silphion.[45] The scales thus had an economic as well as judicial function. Indeed, it was probably because the Creto-Mycenaean palace overseer used the scales to measure tribute that it assumed the role of the royal instrument of divine justice, just as in certain Eastern civilizations.[46]

Here again, mythical thought sheds light on social and institutional factors, for it preserved the memory of Minos, the king of Crete, who dispensed justice through the scales and was later commemorated as presiding over judgment in Hades.[47] Traditionally, however, he was enthroned on the "plain of *Alētheia*"; this was not the plain of the philosophicoreligious sects but the natural and fully justified seat of a king who was a master of justice and, like Nereus, a master of *Alētheia*.[48] This particular example is revealing, for the same King Minos personally practiced ordeals by water.[49] In this figure of a mythical king, justice through water and justice through the scales thus converge, both under the sign of *Alētheia*.[50]

Through these forms of justice associated with the Old Man of the Sea, the function of sovereignty begins to emerge. There are further indications that the Old Man of the Sea is a model of sovereignty, especially in his "political" aspects. Of his fifty daughters, most bearing names associated with navigation and sea trading, a dozen or so bear the names of "political virtues" (e.g., Leagorē, Evagorē, Laomedeia, Polynoē, Autonoē, Lysianassa, Themistō, Pronoē).[51] The *Theogony* provides even more information about Nereus. He is given two telling epithets. First, he is the Old One, the *presbutatos* par excellence.[52] In contrast to *Gēras*, accursed Old Age, Nereus symbolizes the beneficent side to agedness. To a society divided into age groups, he embodies the principle of authority that elderly men naturally receive. Furthermore, Hesiod's other epithet for Nereus, "gentle," "kindly" (ēpios), reinforces and expands on the first.[53] This epithet is normally used for the father of a family, as opposed to the young children, the nēpioi, for in archaic Greek society a child was defined negatively against an adolescent or adult man.[54] In Greek the verb ēpuein connotes the impact of the voice, the authority emanating from a leader.[55] As such this epithet is traditionally given to a royal figure:[56] in contrast to the nēputios, who is incapable of participating in the deliberations in the Agora, the king is par excellence the voice of authority.[57] It is he who makes wise decisions for the greatest good of his "flock," those who submit to his authority the way children do to their father's. In mythical thought, the Old Man of the Sea thus represents one aspect of the function of sovereignty:[58] the just king in his benevolent and paternal guise.[59]

Since Nereus is a master of "truth" and his Alētheia incorporates the power of justice as well as oracular knowledge, we may be able to elucidate the meaning of Alētheia by examining more deeply these complementary aspects of the royal function. The characteristics of the Old Man of the Sea help define the function of sovereignty; mythical and legendary traditions provide the essential information for this definition and in turn illuminate certain aspects of Nereus by providing them with a context in the overall picture of the mythical king.[60] There are hints that early on the sovereign's function in Greece was comparable to that in the great Near Eastern civilizations. In a society that conceived of sovereignty through a pastoral vocabulary, the king was the "shepherd of men." His power shone forth through his role as the holder and dispenser of wealth. He possessed such mythical objects as the ram with the golden fleece, the slip of the golden vine, and the precious necklace, all sources of prestige and talismans that testified to his functional relation to the gods, guaranteeing his power to multiply wealth.[61] Through his own virtue, the king encouraged the fertility of the earth and the flocks, and generously dispenses goods. His function was to treat his people to gifts and plenty.[62] Some mythical traditions go even further: the king is a magician, the master of the seasons and atmospheric phenomena.[63] The glimpses we have of the Mycenaean civilization suggest that the type of king whose memory is perpetuated in legend corresponds, on the mythical level, to the Mycenaean status of sovereignty. In the palace system, the *anax* was the central source of all powers, dominating economic, political, and religious life. In this period, the function of sovereignty was inseparable from the organization of the world, and every aspect of the royal person was a dimension of his cosmic power.

On this mythical level, justice was in no way differentiated from the all-embracing function of sovereignty; it is inseparable from the sovereign's other activities. When the king forgot about justice or erred in ritual the community became automatically afflicted by calamities, famine, and sterility among the women and the herds: the world was consigned to disorder and returned to anarchy.[64] Still, this undifferentiated justice was nevertheless closely associated with certain forms of prophecy. The king held the scepter, the guarantee and instrument of his authority.[65] Through the power of this rod, he announced *themistes*, oracular decrees and judgments.[66] The term *themistes* denoted words of justice as well as the oracular words of Apollo; the power of the goddess Themis extended to the domain of prophecy as well as to justice and political life.[67] The complementarity of justice and and prophecy is even more positively confirmed by the mythical image of Minos,[68] who perpetuated the imaginary figure of the type of king from whom judgments were expected. But Minos simultaneously maintained a personal relationship with the father of the gods, in a cave on Mount Ida: Minos, a master

61

of *Alētheia*, was a king who practiced incubatory prophecy.[69]

For an entire mythical tradition, the exercise of justice was indissociable from certain forms of divination, particularly incubatory consultation. When sovereignty as an absolute function disappeared with the decline of the palace system, the *basileus* who succeeded the *anax* retained a number of the latter's privileges.[70] In particular, he remained a master of justice. In his description of Troezene, Pausanias reports that the tomb of Pittheus, the king of the region, stood near a temple of the Muses. On the tomb, the king was represented as dispensing justice, seated on a throne and flanked by his two assessors.[71] But this king of justice was also a diviner-king. Known as the "chresmologue," he was considered an authority on oracles.[72] He also founded the altar of the Themidae.[73]

Such affinities between political power and forms or procedures of divination were very common. In Thebes and Sparta, the royal houses carefully guarded the oracles, for these played an important role in the conduct of affairs.[74] In Athens, even at the end of the sixth century B.C., Athena, who had once resided in the domestic chapel of the palace of Erechtheus, seems to have continued in her post as adviser.[75] In fact, during his expedition to bring aid to Isagoras, the Spartan Cleomenes went up to the Acropolis to consult the incubatory oracle of Athena.[76] Shortly after, when he found himself lodged in the fortress of Athens, he seized a series of oracles deposited there by the Pisistridae.[77] Even after the figure of the king had been definitively replaced by official appointees, it remained customary to resort at times to divinatory procedures. An archaic inscription from Argos refers clearly to a privilege of oracular consultation, "an exceptional favor" granted to magistrates explicitly qualified as officials.[78] Another inscription from the sanctuary of Thalamai tells us that the earliest magistrates of Sparta received inspiration from Pasiphae while they slept.[79] For an entire tradition, various forms of political power and certain judicial practices were in essence based on prophetic knowledge.

Both mythically and historically, the divinatory procedure of incubation, "the most ancient form of divination," seems to have been especially highly valued.[80] How did it operate, and what kind of mental representations were associated with this religious institution?

Of all the oracles in which divination through sleep was practiced, none was more famous or widely known than that of Trophonius at Labadaea.[81] Trophonius the Nurturer delivered his oracles in an ancient sanctuary. It has been suggested that this sanctuary may formerly have been a *tholos*, a beehive-shaped tomb, where a Boeotian king was buried.[82] The consultation took the form of a descent into Hades. After several days in retreat and under strict dietary prohibitions, the individual wishing to consult the oracle was admitted inside to make sacrifices to Trophonius and the other deities. Having sacrificed a ram, whose entrails were supposed to indicate whether Trophonius was disposed to deliver his oracles, the person requesting help was led to the nearby river, where two young children, known as the "two Hermes," washed and anointed him with oil. Soon after, he was taken to the oracle. Before entering, however, he paused at two neighboring springs, called *Lēthē* and *Mnēmosynē* after the two religious powers that dominated the inspired poets' system of thought.[83] The water from the first spring obliterated the memory of human life, while the water from the second allowed the individual to remember everything he saw and heard in the otherworld. After drinking from both springs, he slipped feetfirst into the "mouth" of the oracle's cave. Once his legs were in as far as his knees, the rest of his body, it was said, was pulled violently inside. Pausanias tells us he was swallowed up as though a fast-flowing river were sweeping him away. After a spell of unconsciousness, the patient was retrieved by those who tended the oracle and was seated on the throne of memory, not far from the oracle's "mouth."[84] Gradually, he emerged from his unconsciousness and recovered his ability to laugh.[85]

It has been frequently pointed out that this type of oracular consultation resembles an initiation. The alimentary taboos and period of confinement prepare for the entry into a different world from that of human beings;[86] the burst of laughter at the end marks the break with the period of tension and the return to normal daily life after the journey to the Beyond. This was no doubt a matter of a journey in the supernatural and invisible world. By drinking the water of *Lēthē*, that is, the water of death that opened the gates to Hades, the individual consulting the oracle became like one of the dead; he assumed the mask of the deceased and slipped into the bosom of Mother Earth. Through the water's potency, he entered the "plain of Oblivion."[87] However, before leaving the human world, he had been careful to drink from the second spring as well. From it he garnered the resources that would let him contact the powers of the Beyond and return enriched with knowledge extending to the past and the future.[88] The descent into Hades by one consulting Trophonius was thus the ritual corresponding to the religious experience through which a diviner or an inspired poet penetrated the invisible world. In both cases, Memory and Oblivion were essential. On emergence from his incubatory consultation, the initiate was endowed with a memory, the same gift of second sight as that of the poets and diviners. Through the water of memory, one consulting Trophonius enjoyed a status equivalent to that of a diviner. Like Tiresias and Amphiarus, he became one of the living among the dead.

In this context the judicial and divinatory *Alētheia* acquires its full meaning. *Alētheia* is a kind of double to *Mnēmosynē*. The equivalence between the two powers is borne out on three counts: equivalent meanings (*Alētheia* and *Mnēmosynē* stand for the same thing); equivalent positions (in religious thought *Alētheia*, like *Mnēmosynē*, is associated with experiences of incubatory prophecy); and equivalent relationships (both are complementary to *Lēthē*). The most obvious equivalence concerns meaning. Like *Mnēmosynē*, *Alētheia* is the gift of second sight: an omniscience, like memory, encompassing the past, present, and future.[89] The nocturnal visions of dreams, called *Alēthosynē*, cover "the past, the present, and all that must be for many mortals, during their dark slumber,"[90] and the *Alētheia* of the Old Man of the Sea is knowledge "of all divine things, the present and the future."[91] As a power of prophecy, *Alētheia* sometimes replaces *Mnēmosynē* in certain experiences of incubatory prophecy, as in the story of Epimenides.[92] This magus spoke with *Alētheia*, accompanied by *Dikē*, during his years of retreat, in the cave of Zeus Diktaios, the same cave where Minos consulted Zeus and where Pythagoras, in his turn, visited. Elsewhere, in Philostratus's description of the cavern where Amphiarus delivered his prophecies and "told the truth," he mentions a young woman, robed in white, in front of the oracle. Her name is Alētheia.[93] Finally, the complementarity between *Mnēmosynē* and *Lēthē* is found between *Alētheia* and *Lēthē*. Lucian, for example, tells how he saw on the Island of Dreams two temples close to the site of an incubatory oracle: the temple of *Alētheia* and the temple of *Apatē*. The former was consecrated to a positive power and the latter to a negative one, a child of Night, who held striking affinities with *Lēthē*.[94]

Even more significant, the passage in Hesiod dealing with the Old Man of the Sea is constructed entirely around the complementarity of *Alētheia* and *Lēthē*. This complementarity operates at two levels, one etymological and conscious, the other mythical and unconscious. The Old Man of the Sea is truthful (*alēthēs*) because he does not forget (*oude lēthetai*) the *themistes*, a connection confirmed by Hesychius when he notes that *alēthea* things "are those that do not fall into Oblivion."[95] Furthermore, Nereus, the *alēthēs* one, is symmetrically opposed to *Lēthē*, the child of Night.[96] The same complementarity exists between the *alēthēs* Old Man and Oblivion as is found between the epithet applied to him, *apseudēs*, and the "lying words" (*logoi pseudeis*), associated with *Lēthē*, and even between his image as the "benevolent" (*ēpios*) Old Man and the image of accursed Old Age (*gēras oulomenon*).

Behind the Old Man of the Sea – the mythical vicar of the king of justice, a master of *Alētheia* endowed with prophetic powers – and Minos – a combination, like Nereus, of royalty, justice, prophetic knowledge, and the privilege of *Alētheia* – stands a particular type of man: the royal figure endowed with the gift of second sight. When the king presides over an ordeal and pronounces words of justice, he, like the poet and the diviner, enjoys the privilege of memory, and thus is able to communicate with the invisible world. At this level of thought, where politics and religion, divination and justice, are intermingled, *Alētheia* is defined – as in poetry – by its fundamental complementarity with *Lēthē*. *Alētheia* represents not sung speech, pronounced by virtue of a gift of prophecy, but the processes of divination and justice. However, the efficacy of these processes relies all the same on a form of knowledge analogous to that of inspired poets.

The *Alētheia* of the Old Man of the Sea is no more a "historical" type of "truth" than that of the poet. The king of justice is not concerned with reconstructing the past qua past. "Proof" of justice here consists in ordeals; in other words, we have no indication of the concept of a real proof.[97] To submit oneself to justice meant entering into the domain of the most redoubtable religious forces. "Truth" was established by the correct application of a procedure duly carried out according to ritual. When the king presided in the name of the gods over a judgment by ordeal, he "told the truth," or rather conveyed the "truth." Like the poet and the diviner, the king was also a master of truth. In such thought, truth is thus always linked with certain social functions. It cannot be separated from specific types of individuals and their qualities or from a reality defined by their particular function in archaic Greek society.

We can distinguish three different domains in archaic thought: poetry, prophecy, and justice. These correspond to three social functions in which speech played an important role, and they predate the notion of the autonomy of speech and the elaboration of a theory of language by philosophers or Sophists. In this ancient period, these three domains were no doubt interconnected, since poets and diviners shared the same gift of prophecy and diviners and kings possessed the same power and used the same techniques.[98] However, all three – poet, diviner, and king of justice – were certainly masters of speech, speech defined by the same concept of *Alētheia*. Without losing sight of the various activities and institutions constituting the context for this type of speech, let us now attempt to determine its fundamental characteristics: the status of speech in religious thought and the form assumed by the configuration of *Alētheia*.[99]

CHAPTER FOUR

The Ambiguity of Speech

"Truth," as we have seen, is not intelligible outside a system of religious representations. There is no *Alētheia* without its complementary relationship with *Lēthē*, no *Alētheia* without the Muses, memory, and justice. In this system of thought where a concept of truth is absent, *Alētheia* cannot be dissociated from praise, liturgical recitation, or the function of sovereignty; it is simply one aspect or dimension of these three. While truth may be essentially expressed through ritual acts and gestures in the domain of justice, in the other domains it qualifies for the most part as a particular type of speech, pronounced under particular circumstances, by a figure invested with particular functions. We will now attempt to define this type of speech.

However, one preliminary point should be made. I have used the expression "poetic (or sung) speech" simply as a matter of convenience to distinguish, at this level of religious thought, what is apparently its most enduring quality. In this period of Greek history, one must recognize the presence of the Muse, or Muses, as religious powers, themselves inseparable from other powers such as the Charites, Mōmos, Hypnos, and so on. In mythical thought, where the oldest manifestations of truth are found, speech is clearly not a distinct aspect of reality demarcated through some particular feature and defined by specific qualities. Speech is not really considered in itself but as part of a pattern of behavior whose symbolic meanings converge.[1] For example, when Achilles swears a great oath, his speech is inseparable from a particular action and type of behavior. It is indissociable from the power of the scepter, which assimilates the oath to oracular pronouncements.[2] The language of words is constantly intermeshed with the language of actions: Althaia's cursing of her son takes the form of both words and gestures. She crouches on the ground, "beating with her hands on the earth abundant" to summon up the avenging Erinys. Her posture gives her speech, already identified with the dark figure of the Erinys, its force.[3]

In supplication, the voice falls silent, leaving the body to speak through a kind of polysemic prostration. It might denote mourning or the attitude assumed by the dead in the underworld, by condemned men, or by candidates for purification or initiation.[4] When the voice does break through, its force stems from body language. All these modes of social behavior are efficacious symbols. Their own inherent power allows them to make a direct impact:[5] the gesture of the hand, the scepter, the olive branch festooned with wool are all endowed with a religious power. The same applies to speech: like the hand that offers, receives, or seizes something, like the scepter that affirms the king's power, or gestures of imprecation, speech is a religious force operating through its own efficacy. The act of the diviner, the poet, or the king of justice making a pronouncement does not differ fundamentally from the declaration of the avenger or the imprecations a dying man addresses to his murderers.[6] Both are magicoreligious speech.

The principal and most important aspect of this type of speech is efficacy, expressed in Greek by the verb *krainein*, a word invariably applied to all modalities of such speech.[7] The application of an adjective such as *theokrantos* is defined in the world of the gods: they can "realize" or "accomplish" their own desires, just as they can "realize" a wish expressed by mortals.[8] The gods possess the privilege to "devise and accomplish" (*noēsai te krēnai te*):[9] Apollo "realizes through his speech,"[10] and Zeus "realizes" everything.[11] This is the domain of the irrevocable – as well as the immediate, for "swift is the doing and short the road when a god sets his mind to a thing."[12] Once articulated, this kind of speech becomes power, force, action.

The divine world may be preeminently the place where decisions are never made in vain and speech is never gratuitous, but in the poetic world speech is equally efficacious.[13] When Hermes plays the part of an inspired poet who, with skill and knowledge, can draw harmonious sounds from the lyre, far from pronouncing "vain, useless" words, he "realizes" the immortal gods and the dark earth (i.e., "makes them real").[14] Through the power of his poetic language, he establishes the powers of the invisible world, and exposes in detail the theory of the gods, wherein each is assigned his proper place in the hierarchy and accorded the appropriate "honor" due. Poetic praise establishes the same order of reality.[15] Here, speech is even a living thing, a natural reality that develops and grows; as it does so, the man praised also grows in stature, for he is no more than what he is praised as. A myth from the *Mahābhārata* conveys this idea perfectly:[16]

> When Indra, the king of the gods, in order to save the three worlds, killed the demon Vṛtra, he seemed at first to be annihilated, wiped out by the shock that assailed him following his exploit. He disappeared and lived for a long time reduced to the size of an atom, in the hollow stem of a lotus, on an island in the Ocean that is at the end of the world.

71

The gods sent Agni to find him, and, after a long search over the earth and through the air, he at last discovered in the water the lotus

> where the shrunken god was sheltering. When his scout told him this, Bṛhaspati, in his turn, went to this lotus and sang to the god... praising his past exploits: "Arise Indra! See how the divine Sages have gathered around you. Great Indra, great lord,...it is through you, Indra, that all beings continue to exist! It is you who have made the gods great! Protect the gods and the worlds, great Indra; recover your strength!"... Thus showered with praise, Indra began, gradually, to grow.

In Greek thought as well, a hymn of praise is something that makes human beings grow and expand in stature. The Muse "swell[s] the breath of songs" and "fosters delight in glory."[17] Speech, praise, glory: these are a shoot, a jet rising up to the light: "Like a tree fed by fresh dews, virtue soars into the air, raised among the good and the just toward the shimmering ether."[18] Thus, when Pindar and Bacchylides write of fame growing or taking root, it is no mere literary image.[19] Speech is truly conceived as natural reality, a part of *physis*. A man's *logos* may grow, just as it may shrink and shrivel away. The Erinyes boast that they, like *Mōmos*, have the power to diminish the fame of human beings: "Men's illusions in their pride, under the sky, melt down and are diminished into the ground, gone before the onset of our black robes, the pulsing of our vindictive feet against them."[20] In this malevolent role, the Erinyes are the reverse of the white Charites, the powers of fecundity that give the poet's *logos* its luminous brilliance.[21] Speech, in its association with both the Erinyes and the Charites, is always subject to the laws of *physis* and human fecundity or sterility.[22]

72

The speech of the diviner and of oracular powers, like a poetic pronouncement, defines a particular level of reality: when Apollo prophesies, he "realizes" (*krainei*).[23] Oracular speech does not reflect an event that has already occurred; it is part of its realization.[24] One spoke of the "realizations of the Pythian" (*puthokranta*),[25] while the visions of dreams in which words were not realized (*akraanta*) were opposed to dreams that did "accomplish the truth" or "realize reality" (*etuma krainousin*).[26]

The three winged virgins, the Bee-Women who taught Apollo divination, are described as creators of reality: "They fly now here, now there, feeding on honeycombs and bringing all things to pass" (*kai te krainousin hekasta*).[27] This establishment of reality seems no different from the formulation of the truth to which the three sisters give their consent "after having fed upon golden honey."[28]

As a master of truth, a king of justice has the same powers of efficacy: his pronouncements of justice, his *themistes*, are themselves types of oracles.[29] The chorus of the *Suppliant Maidens*, lauding anachronistically the power of the king of Argos ("your hearth is the center of the city!"), addresses him forthrightly as "you who realize everything" (*pan epikraineis*).[30] His power is symbolized by the chieftain's scepter he carries, which is also a magician's wand, no doubt the same one Apollo gave to Hermes: "it...will [accomplish] every task, whether of words or deeds that are good, which I claim to know through the utterance of Zeus."[31] The "splendid staff of riches and wealth" is an expression of royal power, its fecundity, and the efficacy of its pronouncements of justice. Until the midclassical period, such judgments retained traces of that efficacy. *Dikē*, for instance, continued to be described as *telos echousa*.[32]

Speech with the power of "realization" contrasted with "words without realization," words lacking efficacy, *epe' akraanta*. But at this level, words "without realization" did not belong to the secular domain. They fell into a particular class within the magico-religious field, that of everything "vain" or "useless."[33] Pindar scornfully contrasts those who have only learnt the love of Song and one who speaks the truth. The former, with their endless noise, are like crows who "chatter in vain."[34] There are sometimes dreams that are deceptive and without realization,[35] divinatory procedures that are not efficacious,[36] and curses that "fall to the ground, without result;"[37] and certain diviners, like Halitherses, do speak "what will not happen."[38] These, however, would seem to be just accidents.

Magicoreligious speech is above all efficacious, but its partic-ular kind of religious power comprises other aspects as well. First, such speech is indistinguishable from action; at this level noth-ing separates speech from action. Furthermore, magicoreligious speech is not subject to temporality. Last, it is always a privilege resulting from a socioreligious function.

Speech endowed with efficacy is indissociable from its reali-zation. Such speech immediately takes effect, is realized, becomes action.[39] This aspect is forcefully conveyed by the substitution of *prattein* and *praxis* for the Greek verb conveying efficacy, *krainein*: Zeus *ekprattei*;[40] one spoke of the *praxis* of oracles;[41] and the Erinyes, who executed the high works of justice, were the *Prax-itheai*, the goddesses of justice "in action."[42] The use of *prattein* was limited to a natural action whose effect was not external or foreign to the action but simply the accomplishment of the action itself.[43] Furthermore, such actions seem to occur outside time. At this level, there is no suggestion of a temporal aspect to action or speech. Magicoreligious speech is pronounced in the absolute present, with no before or after, a present that, like memory, incorporates "that which has been, that which is, and that which will be." This kind of speech eludes temporality because it is at one with forces beyond human ones, forces that are completely

74

autonomous and lay claim to an absolute power.[44]

The poet's speech never solicits agreement from its listeners or assent from a social group, no more than does a king of justice: it is deployed with all the majesty of oracular speech. It does not attempt to establish a chain of words in real time that would gather force from human approval or disagreement. To the extent that magicoreligious speech transcends human time, it also transcends human beings. It is not the manifestation of an individual's will or thought, nor does it constitute the expression of any particular agent or individual. It is the attribute and privilege of a social function.

This same efficacy characterizes the words of those privileged with truth. However, the articulation of *Alētheia* and the verb *krainein* is particularly noticeable in the case of the Erinyes. The Erinyes are venerable goddesses with unassailable powers of memory.[45] They never suffer from forgetfulness, since they somehow predate time and are as old as the Old Man of the Sea. But the Erinyes are not merely those who do not forget (*mnēmones*);[46] they are also called the "truthful ones" that "accomplish."[47] They are sometimes called *Praxidikai*, "the workers of justice." They are identified with speech that brings down curses, the kind of speech Oedipus uses in his blindness, the kind that can destroy a whole house. Their "truth" is the efficacious curse that unleashes sterility and annihilates all forms of life.[48]

Truth is thus established by the deployment of magicoreligious speech and is based on memory and complemented by oblivion. But the configuration of *Alētheia*, expressed by the fundamental opposition between memory and oblivion, also involves the contribution of other powers, including *Dikē*, *Pistis*, and *Peithō*. Justice, like *Alētheia*, is a modality of magicoreligious speech, for *Dikē* too has the power to "realize."[49] When the king makes a "pronouncement of justice," his speech is regarded as decisive.

75

In the domain of justice, *Alētheia* is, of course, inseparable from *Dikē*, but *Dikē* is no less indispensable in the poetic world.[50] Praise is given with "justice," as in Adrastus's praise of the diviner Amphiarus.[51] To "praise [the memory of] the noble" is in line with the strictest justice. The Old Man of the Sea's precept is: "Praise even a foe when he deserves it."[52] In fact, praise is, in a way, a form of justice.[53] When the poet sings a person's praises, he is following the path of justice.[54] Poets are "men who love the song and who love the right";[55] their *Alētheia* is reinforced by *Dikē*.[56] In the system of religious thought in which efficacious speech is triumphant, there is no separation between truth and justice.[57] This type of speech always conforms with the cosmic order; it both creates and is the necessary instrument of this order.

While *Dikē* underlines and reinforces this aspect of "realization" in magicoreligious thought, *Pistis* reveals the relation of this type of speech to others, a dimension that the complementary power of *Peithō* will help to define. Traditionally, *Pistis* meant faith in a god or in the speech of a god, confidence in the Muses, or faith in the oracle.[58] But the concept of *Pistis* is also frequently linked with promises or oaths, and it has been pointed out in this connection that it strictly paralleled the Roman *Fides* and thus corresponded to the Indo-European concept of *credo*.[59] When Theseus and Pirithoüs swear an oath of friendship, they engrave their mutual promise on the side of a crater containing the blood of sacrificial victims that they then bury.[60] But their *pistis* is not just the mutual commitment and reciprocal trust that forms the basis of this contractual bond; it is also faith in the efficacy of magicoreligious speech.[61] In the divine world, *Pistis*, a "powerful goddess," represents a psychological pattern of human behavior.[62] It seems to stand for a kind of intimate individual commitment, an act of faith that authenticates the power speech holds over others. Moreover, *Pistis* is also a necessary and binding agreement, the assent required by the power of *Alētheia*, as by all efficacious speech. *Pistis* is thus close to *Peithō*, which without question represents the power of speech over others, its magical and seductive effect on listeners.

Peithō is a necessary aspect of *Alētheia* on the same grounds as *Pistis*. The example of Cassandra demonstrates its importance to the functioning of magicoreligious speech. Cassandra is a "truthful prophetess" (*alēthomantis*);[63] she is not a diviner who "seeks to deceive."[64] However, since she has broken a promise, betrayed *pistis*, Apollo has deprived her of her persuasive powers.[65] Her speech has no power over others. This defect is so serious that, even if her speech is efficacious, Cassandra seems capable of producing only "vain" (*akranta*) or even "untrustworthy" words.[66] Deprived of *peithō*, she is by the same token deprived of *pistis*. Incapable of persuasive speech, Cassandra's *Alētheia* is, so to speak, condemned to "nonreality." Her *Alētheia* as a prophet is fundamentally undermined.

What, then, is "persuasion"? In mythical thought, *Peithō* is an all-powerful deity, not only for men but also for the gods. Only death can resist her.[67] *Peithō* casts "spells of honeyed words."[68] She has the power of enchantment, gives words a magic sweetness, and lives on the lips of the orator.[69] In the Greek pantheon, *Peithō* stands for the power of speech over others. Mythically, she represents the charm of the voice, the seduction of speech, and the magic of words. She is defined by the verbs *thelgein* and *terpein* and the words *thelktērion*, *philtron*, and *pharmakon*.[70] Wearing the mask of Thelxinoē, she is one of the Muses; when disguised as Thelxiēpeia, she is one of the Sirens.[71] However, like the Sirens, she is fundamentally ambivalent, both beneficent and harmful.[72] Alongside the good *Peithō* who walks with wise kings stands another *Peithō*, who "exerts violence," the "strong daughter of designing Ruin," of *Atē*, who, "caressing and gentle," "leads men astray in her snares."[73] The bad *Peithō* is indissociable from the "caressing words" (*haimulioi logoi*), the tools of deception and the snares of *Apatē*.[74] In one respect, *Peithō*, so strongly connected with *Alētheia*, is also linked with such negative powers as *Lēthē*.[75]

Peithō's ambiguity can be apprehended particularly well on the level of myth, through the relationship between this power and other equally ambiguous religious forces. In mythical thought, *Peithō*, "who never suffered a rejection,"[76] was associated, like Pothos and Himeros, with Aphrodite, the goddess "of subtle thoughts" (*aiolomētis*).[77] Aphrodite had the power to deceive at will both mortal men and immortal gods. She thus played the principal role in Hera's famous Deception of Zeus.[78] When Hera wanted to arouse Zeus's amorous desire and plunge him into a sweet sleep, she did not depend solely on her own *Charis*, manifested in her ambrosia-washed body, in the brilliance of the fragrant, shining oil in her hair which was carefully combed into "ambrosial curls," in the robe of Athena she wore, and in her jewels, veil, and gleaming feet. To ensure the invincibility of her vitality-charged body, Hera asked Aphrodite to grant the "loveliness" and "desirability"[79] Aphrodite used to overcome both mortals and immortals. She begged her for the all-powerful charm that she said (disguising the real purpose of her ploy) would enable her to "win over with persuasion" and thereby win over Tethys and Ocean "since now for a long time they [had] stayed apart from each other and from the bed of love, since rancour [had] entered their feelings."[80]

For this task of persuasion, Aphrodite "the laughing" detached from her bosom the ribbon embroidered with varied designs in which every charm was lodged: "loveliness (*philotēs*) . . . and passion of sex (*himeros*) is there, and the whispered endearment (*oaristus*) that steals the heart away even from the thoughtful."[81] The whole scene unfolds under the sign of the good *Peithō*, who accompanies

Aphrodite with whispers and smiles, and the sign of "caressing" *Apatē* with "the delight, and the sweetness of love, and the flattery."[82] However, the positive combination in which Aphrodite, the smiling woman with seductive speech, is associated with *Peithō* and *Apatē* in their beneficent guises, is matched by a combination in which each term corresponds to a negative member within the same framework of mythical thought. The counterpart to the *Apatē* of Aphrodite is another Deceit, a child of Night, a negative power who is the sister of *Lēthē* and of words of deceit (*logoi pseudeis*).[83] These words of deceit, the flip side of "whispered endearments," are under the patronage of the nocturnal Hermes, the master of the *Peithō* of "cunning" (*dolia*), the negative aspect of Aphrodite's *Peithō*.[84] These words of deceit are given by Hermes to Pandora, the femme fatale who is the shadow of the woman of "gentle pleasure."[85]

+	Aphrodite	Light	Loving talk	Beneficent woman	*Peithō* gentle	*Apatē* – seduction
—	Hermes	Night	Words of deception	Harmful woman	*Peithō* violent	*Apatē* – duplicity

To the degree that speech is *Peithō* or *Apatē*, in mythical thought it is a double power, both positive and negative, and analogous to other ambiguous mythical powers. In a sense, they are all equivalent: ambivalent speech is a woman, it is the god Proteus, and it is a many-colored web. In poetic thought, still sensitive to these mythical associations, this equivalence is remembered. Pindar compares his poem to a "Lydian fabric, intertwined with whistling strains of the flute."[86] Later, Dionysius of Halicarnassus declares that a poem is a precious fabric created by the hand of the poet when he combines several kinds of language into a single one: the noble and the simple, the extraordinary and the natural, the concise and the more expansive, the gentle and the mordant.[87] But this many-colored fabric, in which opposites are harmoniously intermingled, is itself like Proteus, the multiple, undulating god who is at once water, fire, tree, and lion – the god who combines all forms.[88] Similarly, the seductive power of poetic speech, expressing itself through the pleasures of "song, meters, and rhythms," is like a woman's seduction through the "charm of her gaze" (*charis opseōs*), the persuasive sweetness of her voice (*phōnēs pithanotēs*), and the attraction of her physical beauty (*morphēs epagōgon eidos*).[89] The correlation between the various levels of mythical thought is even reflected in the vocabulary: Aphrodite's embroidered ribbon and "whispered endearments" (*oaristus*) are closely connected with *Parphasis* and "seductive words."[90]

Parphasis is another power that gives a just king's speech its seductive force and its ability to "lightly turn back ... actions to the right direction" by "talking them over with gentle arguments (*paraiphamenoi*)."[91] Pindar has *Parphasis* appear in *Nemean* 8.32ff.: she is the "partner of flattering tales" (*haimulioi muthoi*), "hatcher of schemes," and "doer of evil."[92] Although beneficent for the just king, in Pindar's account she is a harmful power. He accuses her of "reproach that overwhelms the brilliant" and of lifting "into view the spurious glory of the obscure." *Parphasis* is also Homer's "charm" (*haduepēs*), which Pindar denounces as a deceit, a power of illusion, and claims that art deceives by seducing us with fables.[93] Attempting to define this power, both *Peithō* and *Charis*, Pindar describes it as "going beyond" *Alētheia*.[94] "Going beyond" in this manner is a deception, *Apatē*. At this moment, under the influence of "deception woven cunningly," even "what is unbelievable," or "past belief," is believed, and contraries become confused and synthetically intertwined.[95] At such moments, *Alētheia* takes on meanings that dim her brilliance and luminosity: she is concealed by *Apatē* and darkened by *Lēthē*.[96]

$$\begin{bmatrix} + \\ - \end{bmatrix} Peith\bar{o} \begin{cases} \text{Woman} \\ \text{Poem} \\ \text{Proteus} \end{cases} = Parphasis \begin{cases} \text{Aphrodite} \\ \text{Poet} \\ \text{King} \end{cases} = \begin{cases} \textit{Alētheia} \text{ and } \textit{Lēthē} \\ \textit{Alētheia} \text{ and } \textit{Apatē} \\ \textit{Alētheia} \text{ and } \textit{Pseudēs} \end{cases}$$

This relation can be stated even more strongly: there can be no *Alētheia* without a measure of *Lēthē*. When the Muses tell the truth, they simultaneously bring "a forgetting of ills and a rest from sorrow" (*lēsmosunēn te kakōn ampauma te mermēraōn*).[97] Through their charm and the pleasure they provoke, a mortal can escape everyday time, the time of wretchedness and troubles. He becomes overwhelmed by forgetfulness: "When a man has sorrow fresh in the troublement of his spirit and is struck to wonder over the grief in his heart, the singer, the servant of the Muses singing the glories of ancient men, and the blessed gods who have their homes on Olympus, makes him presently forget his cares, he no longer remembers sorrow."[98] The poet's memory is oblivion for others. The poet's speech is like the song of the Sirens, the Muses' sisters.[99] Its power to bring oblivion is the same as that diffused by Phidias's Zeus: "In his presence a man forgets all the sufferings and terrors that human life brings."[100] This power acts like the drug Helen tosses into a crater; "she cast a medicine of heartsease, free of gall, to make one forget all sorrows."[101]

What is the nature of Oblivion? It is not the negative power, the child of Night who stands opposed to the luminous *Alētheia*. Here, *Lēthē* is not thick darkness; it is the shadow that surrounds a light, the shadow of *Alētheia*. It is important to distinguish between two kinds of Oblivion that pair as twins, as Thanatos and

81

Hypnos do. The former is *black*, with a heart of iron, "and brazen feelings without pity are inside his breast," and the latter is *white*, "quiet," and "kind to mortals."[102] The counterpart to the negative Oblivion-Death is the positive Oblivion-Sleep. Apollo declares that the sung speech that calms "desperate cares" (*mousa amēchaneōn meledōnōn*) contains three pleasures: "mirth and love and sweet sleep."[103] The good Oblivion is the slumber that overtakes the eagle of Zeus, the "darkening cloud" that is a "soft seal upon his eyelids."[104] It is the softening slumber that makes Ares forget the harsh iron of spears, the slumber dispensed by songs and wine.[105] This *Lēthē* is not the child of Night but the mother of the Charites, of "brilliant visions," the joy of banquets and the "glittering (*ganos*) liquid that flows at sumptuous feasts":[106] the *Lēthē* accompanying Eros and the sweet pleasure of women.[107]

		Night
—	*Thanatos* (black)	*Lēthē* (*Mōmos-Atē*)
+	*Hypnos* (white)	*Lēthē* (Eros-Aphrodite)
		Charites

Thus, *Alētheia* (+) does not stand on one side and *Lēthē* (–) on the other. Rather, an intermediate zone develops between the poles, in which *Alētheia* approaches *Lēthē* and vice versa. "Negativity" is not isolated from Being. It borders the truth and forms its inseparable shadow.[108] The two antithetical powers are thus not contradictory but tend toward each other. The positive tends toward the negative, which, in a way, "denies" it but cannot maintain itself in its absence.

We must therefore qualify what has been suggested above and show that neither the king of justice nor the poet is purely and simply a master of truth. Rather, their *Alētheia* is always edged with *Lēthē* and lined with *Apatē*. The Old Man of the Sea appeared to embody truth itself. However, Nereus, like Proteus and other marine deities, is also a god of enigmas. When Heracles tries to question him, he elusively changes into water, fire, and a thousand other forms; he is undulating, impossible to grasp.[109] His case is not unique. Pittheus is a king of justice mythically represented as exercising his judicial function and possessing great prophetic powers, but he is also closely associated with the Muses, in whose temple he is said to have taught "the art of words" (*logōn technēn*).[110] He is the inventor of "rhetoric," the art of persuasion and of using "lying words that resemble reality." Furthermore, the typical judge-king, associated with the Muses and an expert in persuasion, is one of the predominant figures in the Prologue to Hesiod's *Theogony*. When Hesiod praises human sovereignty, which interacts closely with the sovereign power of Zeus, he portrays an ideal king who dispenses justice by delivering fair sentences. This king has received from the Muses a particular gift of speech: "from his mouth the words run blandishing," and his language is a "distillation of sweetness." While he fittingly knows how to speak the truth, he also knows how to charm and win others over, like the poet. Again like the poet, he furthermore knows how to set matters right with ease, by wooing hearts "with gentle arguments."[111] He is a master of truth skilled in deception as well.

The same ambiguity characterizes dreams that seem to bring contact solely with *Alētheia*. In the oracle of Amphiarus, "truth" is accompanied by *Oneiros* but is clad in a white garment over a black one.[112] As Plutarch observes, some dreams contain what is "deceptive and many-colored" (*to apatēlon kai poikilon*) as well as the simple and true (*to haploun kai alēthes*).[113] For this reason, on the Island of Dreams *Apatē* faces *Alētheia*.[114] There can be no prophetic *Alētheia* without a dose of the *Apatē* contained in "sweet and deceptive" dreams.[115] As early as in the *Odyssey*, truthful and deceptive dreams are closely associated. The latter emerge from the ivory gate, bringing "words without realization" (*epe' akraanta*), while the former come from the gate of horn and "realize reality" or "accomplish the truth" (*etuma krainousi*).[116] The Bee-Women of the *Homeric Hymn to Hermes* are oracular powers that consent to tell the truth when they are fed gold honey, but when refused, they try to prevaricate and lead one astray:[117] *Apatē* obliterates *Alētheia*.

In ritual, this ambiguity is conveyed particularly well by the procedure for a consultation with Trophonius at Lebadaea, where *Mnēmosynē* assumes the role taken by *Alētheia* elsewhere. Before entering the oracle's cave, the person who has come to consult it drinks from the springs of *Lēthē* and *Mnēmosynē*. When he drinks the water of *Lēthē*, he becomes like a dead person, but through the water of *Mnēmosynē*, which works as an antidote to *Lēthē*, he retains the privilege of remembering everything and thus acquires the ability to see and hear in a world where ordinary mortals can no longer do so. An initiate of Trophonius thereby acquires the same ambiguous double status as the diviners Tiresias and Amphiarus, who remain "living" in the world of the dead and retain "memory" in the world of oblivion.[118]

The divine world is fundamentally ambiguous, and even the most positive gods are tinged with ambiguity. Apollo is the Shining One (*Phoibos*), but at times, as Plutarch notes, he is also the Dark One (*Skotios*). While for some he is flanked by the Muses and memory, for others oblivion (*Lēthē*) and silence (*Siōpē*) stand at his side.[119] The gods know the truth but can also deceive:[120] their appearances are traps for men, and their words are always enigmatic, concealing as much as they reveal. The oracle "reveals itself through a veil, like a young bride."[121] The gods' ambiguity is matched by human duality. Although some can recognize the gods' appearance even in their most deceptive guises and can understand the secret meaning of their words, all others are misled by the gods' disguises and fall into the traps designed to fool them.[122]

In the Prologue to the *Theogony*, the Muses forthrightly declare their ambiguity:[123] "We know how to say many false things (*pseudea*) that seem like true sayings (*etumoisin homoia*), but we know also how to speak the truth (*alēthea*) when we wish to."[124] The Muses are capable of speaking *Alētheia* but may also speak words of *Apatē* that are almost indistinguishable from *Alētheia*. The wording of the Muses' declaration is remarkable: first, it represents an intermediate stage between the mythical level of a double *Apatē* and the rational level of *alēthēs* and *pseudēs*, and second, it conveys both the ambiguity of deception and the deception of ambiguity. The phenomenon of *Apatē* entails the fundamental idea of a presence within absence and the complementary absence within presence.[125] Patroclus's *psychē* is in every respect "like him," but when Achilles tries to clutch it, he grasps nothing but air. Patroclus is there, Achilles can see him, but at the same time he is not there and Achilles knows it.[126] The formula "false things that seem like true sayings" (*pseudea...etumoisin homoia*) is designed to express the fallacious character of ambiguity. As early as the *Odyssey*, this formula defines the power of "rhetoric," whether that of Odysseus or Nestor, two masters of *mētis*.[127] The same formula is used in the *Dissoi Logoi* to clarify the nature of tragedy and painting. In both these *technai*, the most adept artist is "one who knows how to deceive (*exapatan*) by making things that for the most part resemble the truth (*homoia...tois alēthinois poieōn*)."[128]

In all these expressions the connection between *Alētheia* and

Lēthē is conveyed through "resemblance," an almost rational notion. Although at a certain level archaic Greek thought posits a veritable equivalence or at least a "sharing" between the two terms of the comparison, it increasingly tends toward a basic theory of *mimēsis*.[129] In the expression *pseudea…etumoisin homoia*, the ambiguity of fallacious things is clearly conveyed, for the *etuma* are of the same reality as the *alēthea* and, by the same token, the *pseudea*, through resemblance, are founded in the *alēthea*. However, this fundamental ambiguity, left unanalyzed in mythical thought because it consists of the same, simultaneously becomes the object of rational analysis predicated on imitation, or *mimēsis*.[130] In such formulae, in which *pseudēs* resembles *alēthēs*, the religious power *Apatē* is as out of place as the concept of the "double" or the *eidōlon* in figurative representation, which is conceived in the classical period as a simple image.[131] This type of thinking, in the process of freeing itself from its roots in myth, thus prefigures the formula of the *Cratylus*. *Logos* is "something double" (*diplous*); it is at once *alēthēs* and *pseudēs*.[132]

Ambiguity	Kings	Dreams	Muses	Logos
Alētheia and *Apatē*	*alēthēs* Nereus and God with *mētis*	*Alētheia* and Dreams { white / black	*Alētheia* and *pseudēa* (-ētumoisin homoia)	*Alēthēs* and *Pseudēs*

We can draw two conclusions from this fundamental ambiguity. First, the master of truth is also a master of deception. To possess the truth entails the capability to deceive. Second, the antithetical powers *Alētheia* and *Lēthē* are not contradictory: in

86

mythical thought, opposites are complementary.[133] This particular configuration thus confirms a general characteristic of the
logic of myth.

Alētheia is thus at the center of a configuration structured
around the major opposition between memory and oblivion. This
fundamental pair matches up with specific pairs such as praise and
blame, as well as more general ones like day and night. But in
magicoreligious speech in which the *Alētheia-Lēthē* opposition
operates, *Alētheia* interacts with *Dikē* and two complementary
powers, *Pistis* and *Peithō*, and *Peithō* introduces the ambiguity
bridging the gap between the positive and the negative. In mythical thought, ambiguity is not a problem, since all such thought
obeys a logic of oppositions with ambiguity as an essential, oper-
ative mechanism. In Hesiod, for example, the reason we find a
sort of conceptual translation of such ambiguity is that ambiguity has begun to present a problem for the kind of thought that is
no longer mythical but not yet rational, still intermediate between
religion and philosophy. By definition, speech is one aspect of
reality, an efficacious power. But the power of speech is not directed solely toward reality; it inevitably affects other people.
There can be no *Alētheia* without *Peithō*. This second power of
speech is dangerous, since it may produce an illusion of reality.
Before long a sense of unease creeps in: the seductive powers of
speech allow it to pass itself off as reality. *Logos* can impress on
the mind objects that convincingly resemble reality but are actually only vain images. But this unease, detectable in certain lines
of Hesiod and Pindar, only becomes a fundamental difficulty in
the form of thought capable of posing the new, as yet untackled
problem of the relation between speech and reality.

When we attempt to formulate the problem inherent to a concept of speech characterized by ambiguity, we find that this ambiguity provides the origins of the notion of instrumental language,

which rational thought would develop in two directions. On the one hand, it would pursue the problem of the power speech has over reality, an essential issue in earliest philosophic thought. On the other, it formulated the problem of the power speech had over other people, a fundamentally important matter to rhetorical and sophistic speech. *Alētheia* is thus at the heart of all archaic Greek thought on speech. Both major tendencies defined themselves in relation to *Alētheia*, either by rejecting it or by making it essential.

Such problems do not spontaneously arise simply through the interplay of ideas. The history of ideas never "has an autonomous principle of intelligibility."[134] For such questions to arise, for philosophy to pose the problem of the relation between speech and reality, and for sophistry and rhetoric to construct a theory of language as an instrument of persuasion, it was first necessary for the Greeks to supersede the system of thought in which speech was intermeshed in a network of symbolic values and was itself regarded as a natural power or dynamic reality acting spontaneously on its listeners. In other words, problems such as these could only be posed within a new conceptual framework, illuminated by new mental techniques, and in new social and political conditions.

CHAPTER FIVE

The Process of Secularization

However absolute the dominion of magicoreligious speech may have been, some social groups seem to have eluded it.[1] Since the earliest times, these groups had possessed a different type of speech: the speech of dialogue. The two types of speech were opposed to one another on a whole series of points. Magicoreligious speech was efficacious, atemporal, and indissociable from symbolic behavior and meaning; moreover, it was limited to an exceptional type of person. Dialogue-speech, in contrast, was secular, complemented action, operated within a temporal context, and possessed a unique autonomy that extended to one whole social group. This group was composed of those specializing in the warrior function, who apparently enjoyed a special status from the Mycenaean period to the hoplite reform that extended the warrior's privileges to the citizen of the city.[2]

Warriors occupied a central, exceptional position in both social and mental structures. First, this group coincided with neither the family nor the territorial group. Warriors were divided into age groups and belonged to fraternities. They were linked by contractual relations rather than blood or kinship. Furthermore, the warrior group was exceptional because of certain patterns of behavior and educational techniques. As demonstrated by Dorian societies, warriors underwent initiatory trials guaranteeing their professional qualities, sanctioning their social standing, and expressing their vocation for death, which radically distinguished them from others. The warriors' special status was also indicated by a number of institutional practices:[3] funerary games, the distribution of booty, and deliberative assemblies that, through the solidarity they expressed, demarcated a kind of ideological field peculiar to the group. Identifying the essential features of dialogue-speech — which stands in absolute opposition to magico-religious speech — involves examining these various institutions, showing how they mutually clarify each other, constructing a representation of a new kind of space from their interrelations, and elucidating certain new mental structures.

Funerary games present a strongly structured context in which both gestures and words carry special meanings.[4] Not only do we find extremely ancient customs and states of thought, but also a terrain that anticipates law, "an exceptional moment in collective life" that witnessed the development of procedures later adopted in institutionalized law.[5] These games were not improvised; they obeyed certain rules. When the funeral pyre of Patroclus was consumed by the flames, Achilles told his troops to "sit down in a wide assembly, and he brought prizes for games out of his ships, cauldrons and tripods, and horses and mules and the powerful high heads of cattle and fair-girdled women and grey iron."[6] The assembly of warriors marked off the material space for the games, the site of the major contests. This space contained a precise center. When Achilles brought out the prizes offered out of princely generosity for the competitions, he set them down in the middle (*es messon ethēke*).[7] Such placement is not a matter of chance but a well-attested custom. After the funeral of Achilles, when the Achaeans had raised "a grave mound that was both great and perfect," Thetis personally organized the funeral games. She set down in the middle of the assembly (*thēke mesōi en agōni*) "the beautiful prizes for the best of the Achaeans."[8] Other examples abound. In the description of the chariot race in the pseudo-Hesiodic *Shield*, the author notes that "a great tripod of gold, the splendid work of cunning Hephaestus was set out for them within the course [or 'within the assembly place'; *entos agōnos*]."[9] When Cyrus declares that the very wealth of the Persians is at stake in the war, he uses the expression "For now all these good things are offered as prizes [set down in the middle]" (*en mesōi gar ēdē keitai tauta ta agatha*).[10] When Theognis describes a match in which he is paired against a friend, the prize (*athlon*), a young man in the flower of his youth, is placed "in the middle" (*en messōi*).[11] Finally, Demosthenes metaphorically refers as well to "prizes set down in the middle" (*athla keimena en mesōi*).[12]

In epic, we thus find an image of an assembly of warriors seated in a circle. To define the significance of the *middle* in this context of athletic games, we must digress and examine another important warrior-group institution, the division of the spoils of war. In most cases, each warrior strove to seize his opponent's arms and thus to win his own "personal" booty. But along with such direct, personal seizure of possessions that increase a warrior's own riches, which he will carry to his tomb, another custom is suggested: the possessions seized from the enemy are set down "in the middle."[13] When Theognis of Megara describes the misfortunes of the great landowners, the woes of the city, and the wrecking of order, he laments that he is surrounded by nothing but disaster and looting: "By brute force, [the wicked] pillage riches, all order has vanished...who knows even whether booty is still shared out equally?"[14] The distribution of booty is *dasmos es to meson*, since booty is specifically "that which is set down in the middle." When Odysseus captures the diviner Helenus in the course of a nighttime raid, he takes him "to the middle" (*es meson*), for two reasons.[15] It is the most visible site for the assembled crowd, and it is the spot reserved for a "fine capture" that is part of the Achaean war booty. Like the prizes distributed in the athletic games, the warriors' booty is set down *es meson*. From the account of the quarrel between Achilles and Agamemnon we know that all loot to be divided up was known as "things held in common" (*xunēia keimena*).[16]

This digression demonstrates that the middle may be equated with whatever is held in common. This equivalence is confirmed by everything else we know about the *meson*.[17] After each victory or pillaging raid, the booty was delivered to the leader, the representative of the group.[18] Through this warrior chief, the group as a whole exercised its right to oversee these riches, a right it retained until the moment of distribution. We have no direct knowledge of the details of distribution. Achilles' incensed protestations simply convey that "the king distributes very little, but keeps a great deal." However, the scene presented by the athletic games compensates for this dearth of information, for the distribution of booty and the allocation of prizes in the games seem to follow the same institutional plan.[19]

Each time Achilles "brings into play" an object of value, he sets it down *es meson*, and it is here that the victor comes to collect it or, more precisely, to "pick it up." One of the gestures best characterizing the episode of the athletic games is this laying hold of the prizes.[20] However, the particular nature of such acquisition is only clearly revealed when it is contrasted with another form of appropriation repeatedly mentioned in this context, an action combining giving and receiving, namely "placing in the hand" or "handing out" (*en chersi tithenai*).[21] To unlucky participants – for example, Nestor, who is too old to participate in the race – Achilles "hands out" some object, a tripod or a breastplate, which he takes from his reserve stock. In both instances the riches in question no doubt belong to Achilles. However, in the first instance, given that Achilles' own possessions, his *ktēmata*, have been set down *at the center*, they become booty objects, "things that are common" (*xunēia*). Through this action they are no longer private property. They are now *res nullius*.[22] A victor may lay his hand on them without more ado. In contrast, when Achilles hands Nestor the bowl he has himself picked up "from the middle," it is a personal gift, just as when he rewards Eumelos by ordering a breastplate to be brought from his tent and placing it in his hands.[23] This personal gift, which forges a link between the two men and obliges the beneficiary to reciprocate, is clearly opposed to a proprietorial right involving no reciprocity.[24] Setting one's hand on booty could thus only be effected through the intermediary of the *meson*, whose powers expunged the "personal property" relations binding Achilles to his share of the *ktēmata*. Once set down "at the center," Achilles' possessions reentered circulation and could be reapportioned. The same procedure likely governed the distribution of booty. Every object seized by a warrior during a pillaging raid was "placed in common," that is, "set down at the center." There the man selected by destiny – just as a victor was designated by the gods – came to "pick it up" (*aeirein, anaeirein*) in full view of all.[25] The gesture of laying hands on it sealed the "right of immutable ownership" to which Achilles refers.[26]

Book XIX presents a remarkable example of this practice. When Agamemnon honorably confesses he was a victim of Error (*Atē*), he offers to return to Achilles his possessions, his "choice share." But Agamemnon does not personally place them in Achilles' hands, since that would necessarily make Achilles indebted to Agamemnon. Odysseus, acting as a skillful arbiter, suggests the solution they then adopt: "As for the gifts, let the lord of men Agamemnon bring them to the middle of our Assembly (*oisetō es messēn agorēn*)."[27] Odysseus justifies this procedure by insisting on the publicity it will involve, which is essential in such a legal contest and in warrior circles. "[In this way] all the Achaians can see them before their eyes, so your own heart may be pleasured."[28] But what follows in this episode demonstrates another equally imperious reason for the decision. At Agamemnon's invitation, Odysseus and the young Achaean *kouroi* go off to Agamemnon's hut:

> No sooner was the order given than the thing had been done. They brought back seven tripods from the shelter, those Agamemnon had promised, and twenty shining cauldrons, and twelve horses. They brought back immediately the seven women, the work of whose hands was blameless, and the eighth of them was Briseis of the fair cheeks. Odysseus weighed out ten talents of gold and led them back, and the young Achaians carried the other gifts. They brought these into the midst of the assembly (*kai ta men en messēi agorēi thesan*).[29]

After Agamemnon's great oath, which solemnly guarantees his reconciliation with Achilles, and the sacrifice of a boar, whose carcass Talthybius casts into "the great reach of the gray sea," the gathering disperses. Only then do "the great-hearted Myrmidons dispose...of the presents": they come to pick them up *at the center of the Assembly*, at the spot where Odysseus and his followers had set them down.[30] The Myrmidons exercise the same proprietorial rights over these objects, which have become "common property" as a result of being set down *es meson*, as those of a victor over prizes in the athletic games. The procedure recommended by Odysseus thus makes it possible to re-create the conditions of a distribution. In this way the operation Achilles himself apparently refers to in Book I, when faced with Agamemnon's claims ("It is unbecoming for the people to call back things once given" [*palilloga taut' epageirein*][31]) is eventually completed. Aga-

94

memnon has not made a gift to Achilles; instead, he has restored the circulation of riches he had earlier seized for himself.

For an entire tradition, to put things *es meson* is to set them "in common." Herodotus remarks: "This, however, I know – that if every nation were to bring all its evil deeds (*ta oikēia kaka*) to [the middle] (*es meson*) in order to make an exchange with other nations when they had all looked carefully at their neighbours' faults, they would be truly glad to carry their own back again."[32] Whether it concerns leaving property undivided or making it common before proceeding to a new distribution, the same expression, *es meson*, is always used.[33] The significance of the center emerges clearly from the institutional forms operating both in the allocation of prizes and in the distribution of booty: the center means both "that which is held in common" and "that which is public."

The expression *es meson* contains the same meaning at other levels too, but always in a similarly social context. In military assemblies, claiming the right to speak involves following specific rules that give the deliberations in the *Iliad* a highly institutional form. Before speaking, one must first move to the center and then take hold of the scepter. To address the assembly, there is a strict rule that one move into position at the *meson*. When Idaeus, the Trojans' herald, goes to the hollow ships and find the Danaans gathered in assembly around the stern of Agamemnon's ship, he does not speak until he has arrived "in their midst."[34] When he returns to Troy, he delivers his message standing "in the midst" of the Trojans and Dardanians, who are likewise gathered in assembly.[35] The same rule applies to any orator. For example, when Telemachus speaks in the assembly, the same expression is used: "He stood in the middle of the assembly (*stē de mesēi agorēi*)."[36] When someone disregards the rule, the poet notes it as an exception. For example, in Book XIX, when Agamemnon responds to Achilles' conciliatory words, he speaks "from the place where he was sitting, and did not stand up among them."[37]

Once an orator had reached the middle of the assembly, the herald would hand him the scepter, which conferred on him the necessary authority to speak.[38] An essential affinity existed between the scepter and the center point, for the scepter appears to have symbolized in this custom the impersonal sovereignty of the group rather than an "emanation of royal power." To speak *at the center* in a military assembly was to speak on behalf of the group or at least about something important to the group as such: matters of common interest, particularly military matters. When Telemachus orders his criers to summon the Achaeans of Ithaca to the Agora, old Aegyptius, the senior elder, is alarmed and exclaims:

> Never has there been an assembly of us or any session since great Odysseus went away in the hollow vessels. Now who has gathered us, in this way? What need has befallen which of the younger men, or one of us who are older? Has he been hearing some message about the return of the army which, having heard it first, he could now explain to us? Or has he some other public matter (*dēmion*) to set forth and argue?[39]

When Telemachus replies, he begins by apologizing for not discoursing on the army or some other matter of concern to the group at large. The entire scene shows that to speak of one's personal affairs in the assembly was quite unusual, even incongruous. The central point where the orator stood, scepter in hand, was thus strictly homologous to the spot where the prizes for athletic games as well as booty were set down. Such objects were *xunēia*, and the central point was already the *koinon* or the *xunon*.[40] In the *Argonautica*, when Jason wants to remind his companions that the expedition is a matter concerning them all, he says, "Sharing the danger as we do (*xunē chreiō*) we share the right of speech (*xunoi muthoi*)."[41] Although this expression appears only in Apollonius of Rhodes, it is postulated by the context of deliberatory assemblies throughout epic.

A single spatial model dominates the interplay of all these institutions – deliberative assemblies, booty distributions, funeral games: a circular and centered space within which, ideally, each individual stands in reciprocal and reversible relationship to everyone else. From the time of epic on, this representation of space went hand in hand with two complementary ideas: publicity and community. The *meson* was the common point for all those gathered in a circle around it. All the riches set down there were common, *xunēia*, as opposed to *ktēmata*, possessions owned individually. The same held for words spoken from this spot: they concerned matters of common interest.

As a commonly shared point, the *meson* was the public place par excellence: its geographical position was synonymous with all that was public. Given that anything said *es meson* concerned the group interests, it was necessarily addressed to every member of the assembly. The division of booty also occurred in the public domain: each man stepped forward to take his share in full view of the rest. As Odysseus noted, all the Achaeans could see it with their own eyes. Moreover, within the warrior group, publicity operated at every level. It pervaded the scene of the games. · The results of the contests were solemnly proclaimed before the assembly, which took note of the decision, thereby conferring a veritable legality on it.[42] The competitions themselves were held in front of everyone. Most contests took place *es meson* and, when the time came for the chariot race, Achilles sent Phoenix to the boundary post that marked the racetrack so that the public nature of the race would be recognized even beyond the circle around the central point. At every level, in the athletic games, in the booty distribution, and in the assembly, what was central was always both submitted to the public gaze and shared in common. The complementary characteristics of centrality were publicity and common sharing.

This institutional context and mental framework help us grasp the essential features of dialogue-speech. In epic, when one wishes to praise a young warrior, like Thoas in the *Iliad*, one says he was "far the best of the Aitolians, skilled in the spear's throw and brave in close fight. In assembly few Achaians when the young men contended in debate could outdo him."[43] A perfect warrior not only does great deeds but is also ready with good advice.[44] One warrior privilege is the right to hold forth. In this context, then, speech is not the privilege solely of an exceptional man possessing religious powers. Assemblies are open to all warriors, all who fully exercise the profession of arms.[45] This indivisibility of the warrior function and the right of speech, as attested in epic, is also confirmed by the urban customs of the archaic period, in which the army assembly acted as a permanent substitute for the people, as well as by the conservative practices of the Macedonian assembly.[46] Such customs provide valuable evidence, since they illuminate one particular, essential aspect of the privilege of speech in warrior circles. When Polybius wishes to refer to this privilege among Macedonian warriors, he speaks of their equality of speech, their *isēgoria*.[47] He thus employs a political vocabulary closely allied, in Herodotus's *Histories*, to *isokratia* and *isonomia*.[48] However it is also the word Philodemus spontaneously uses to specify the privileges of comrades in their communal meetings and in their collective banquets.[49] The term is perhaps anachronistic, but it conveys perfectly a fundamental feature of the social relationship binding warriors: *equality*. This equality marks the military institution of "equal banquets" (*daïs eïsē*), in which the men of the *laos* gather, and the warrior assemblies in which each participant holds an equal right to speech.[50] Even as early as in epic times, the warrior group tended to define itself as a group of equals (*homoioi*).[51]

In warrior assemblies, speech was a common right, a *koinon* set down "in the middle." Each individual could exercise this right when his turn came, with the agreement of his peers. Standing at the center of the assembly, an orator found himself equally distant from all his listeners, and each listener found himself, ideally at least, in a position of equality and reciprocity vis-à-vis the speaker.

The language of warrior dialogue-speech was not only egalitarian; it was also secular. It was language that belonged to human time, unlike the magicoreligious speech that coincided with the action it promoted in a world of nonhuman forces and powers. Dialogue-speech, by contrast, preceded human action and was an indispensable complement to it. The Achaeans met to deliberate before every military engagement. When the Argonauts prepared the next stage of their expedition, they never failed to discuss it among themselves. By its very subject matter, this type of speech is immediately subject to human time. It is directly concerned with human affairs, affairs that concern every member of the group in his relations with his comrades.[52]

This type of speech is an instrument of dialogue. It no longer depends on the interplay of transcendental religious forces for its efficacy. It is founded in essence on social agreement manifested as either approval or disapproval.[53] In such military assemblies, the value of speech for the first time depended on the judgment of the social group as a whole. It was here that preparations for the future status of legal or philosophical speech were made, speech that submitted itself to "publicity" and drew its strength from the approbation of a social group.[54]

Within these same circles concepts such as *parēgoros, oaristus,*

99

and *paraiphasis*, which defined the field of persuasion, emerged. A skillful purveyor of advice knew how to gain his audience's attention. He knew which words elicited assent, softened hearts, and won support.[55] In Homeric vocabulary, *paraiphasis* (which, like *Peithō*, could be either good or bad) means a persuasion born of reassuring familiarity;[56] *oaristus* means mutual influence arising out of the intimate social life of a brotherhood;[57] and *parēgoros* refers to exhortatory speech used to encourage a comrade-in-arms.[58] However, these three notions represent religious powers that form part of Aphrodite's following and are tokens of the omnipotence of *Peithō*.[59] In military assemblies, speech was already an instrument of power over others, an early form of "rhetoric." Thus, early on in warrior circles, a kind of speech operated specifically concerning man, with his human problems, activities, and relations.

As Greek society developed, the warrior class, initially a closed social group, opened up to incorporate the newest and most influential institution: the city, itself a system of institutions as well as a spiritual framework. Within these circles of professional warriors a number of concepts essential to the earliest Greek political thinking took shape, such as the ideal of *isonomia*, the vision of a centered and symmetrical space, and the distinction between personal and collective interests. When Polycrates of Samos died, his successor, Maiandrios, made a public declaration whose terms harmonized with political thought of the late sixth century B.C.: " 'I never approved the ambition of Polycrates to lord it over men as good as himself (*homoiōn*) nor looked with favour on any of those who have done the like. Now therefore, since he has fulfilled his destiny, I lay down my office (*egō de es meson tēn archēn titheis*) [literally, I set my power down in the middle], and proclaim equal rights (*isonomia*).' "[60] Sameness, centrality, and a rejection of domination by a single individual are the three essential aspects of *isonomia*.[61] They encompass the image of a human world in which "those who participate in public life do so as equals."[62] Given that the ideal of *isonomia*, as soon as it appears as a concept, is seen as inseparable from sameness and centrality, it is *virtually* present in the characteristic institutions and patterns of behavior of the warrior group.

Funerary games, the division of war booty, and deliberative assemblies are institutions that represent a level of *prepolitical* thought. The circular, symmetrical space favored by such institutions found its purely political expression in the social space of the city, centered on the *Agora*. A seventh-century poem by Alceus tells of the existence of a "great sanctuary" described as *xunon*, a federal sanctuary "common to all the people of Lesbos."[63] Louis Robert identifies this sanctuary as one called *Messon* and known to us from two inscriptions of the second century B.C.; it is the ancient place name for the *Mesa* excavated by Robert Koldewey. The name conveys perfectly the geographical position of the temple since, as Robert remarks, "it is situated near the center of the island, close to the innermost point of the gulf of Kallonia, which cuts into Lesbos as if to divide the island in two."[64] All this suggests that the name is simply derived from the expression *es meson*, which suits the meetings and deliberations bringing the men of Lesbos together at the center of the island to discuss their common affairs.

By the seventh century B.C., the political solution of the people of Lesbos anticipated Thales' suggestion to the Ionians a century later. At the general assembly of the *Panionion*, "He counselled them to establish a single seat of government [*bouleuterion*], and pointed out Teos as the fittest place for it, 'for that,' he said, 'was the centre of Ionia. Their other cities might still continue to enjoy their own laws, just as if they were independent states [*demes*]."[65] As the geometric center of the Ionian world, Teos thus became the "common hearth" of the city, its political center, the place for "communal affairs," the *xunon*. Teos occupied the same position as the "town" in Cleisthenes' "isonomic" Athens of the sixth century.[66] There is no tidy continuity between epic times and these forms of political thought; nevertheless, a transition somehow occurred between a prepolitical and a specifically political situation.

Thus, in the deliberations of the warrior class an opposition was forged between collective and personal interests, a crucially important opposition for the language of political assemblies. The expression "to deliberate on the course of behavior to be adopted" is rendered in Greek as "to set the matter down in the middle" (*es meson protithenai* or *katatithenai* or *tithenai to prēgma*).[67] In the same way as power was set down "in the middle," so was any business requiring discussion and any question concerning the interests of the group as a whole. More precisely, to express one's opinion in a political assembly was to "take one's opinion to the middle" (*pherein gnōmēn es meson*) or "speak in the middle" (*legein es meson*).[68] The expression "to speak in the middle" (*legein es meson*) is counterbalanced by the symmetrical expression "to withdraw from the middle" (*ek mesou katēmenos*).[69] Once he had withdrawn from the middle, the speaker became a private citizen again. All these expressions help define a political space whose importance in Greek thought is conveyed by the ancient formula pronounced by the herald at the beginning of the assembly: "What man has good advice for the city and wishes to make it known [at the center] (*tis thelei polei chrēston ti bouleum' es meson pherein echōn*)?"[70] By distinguishing so clearly between public and private, and by opposing speech relating to group interests to that of private matters, political thought set forth a distinction that was fundamental to the deliberations of professional warriors. Those egalitarian gatherings prepared the way for the future political assemblies of Greece. Those same social circles likewise elaborated the speech–action dichotomy that would make it easier to distinguish the domains of speech and reality.[71]

Among the professional warriors, dialogue-speech, with its own specific features, nevertheless remained a privilege, belonging to the "best" men, the *aristoi* of the *laos*. This elite contrasted with the "crowd," the *dēmos*, that is, the territorial constituency and by extension its inhabitants.[72] The *dēmos* did not give orders, pass judgments, or deliberate. It had yet to become either "the people" or the state.[73] Odysseus's treatment of Thersites, the epitome of the man of the *dēmos*, reflects the limits of egalitarian speech. When Thersites raises his voice in dissent, Odysseus does not bother to attempt to win him over but simply belabors him with blows of the scepter. Thersites is a common man, lacking the right to speak because he is not a fighting man. A major transformation had to occur before those like Thersites could participate in the dialogue and the barrier between *laos* and *dēmos* could crumble. That transformation would involve extending warrior privileges to every member of a larger social group. The phalanx formation of hoplites, in which each fighting man had a particular place in the ranks and each soldier-citizen was regarded as an interchangeable unit, made the democratization of the warrior function possible and, by the same token, extended political privileges from the aristocracy or a group of "chosen ones" to a far greater number of men.

Although the hoplite reform was based on technological progress, it was simultaneously a product and an agent of new mental structures that would create the model of the Greek city. The interconnected hoplite reform and the birth of the Greek city were indissociable from a crucial intellectual mutation in the development of Greek thought: namely, the construction of a system of rational thought that dramatically broke with the old, religious, all-encompassing type of thought in which a single form of expression sufficed for different types of experience.

Many scholars — above all Louis Gernet and Jean-Pierre Vernant — have shown that the transition from myth to reason was not the miracle hailed by John Burnet, nor was it the progressive replacement of mythical thought by philosophical conceptualization imagined by F.M. Cornford. Rather, during the seventh and sixth centuries B.C., a secularization in thinking occurred in the context of political and legal practices. Both the conceptual framework and the mental techniques favoring the emergence of rational thought developed in social life. Within this general framework, with its constant interplay between the social and mental levels, the secularization of speech came about. It occurred on several different levels: through the elaboration of rhetoric and philosophy, of course, but also through law and history.

Regarding the whole question of speech in Greek thought, this phenomenon had two consequences. First, it sealed the decline of the magicoreligious speech that accompanied the old system of thought. Second, it determined the emergence of an autonomous world of speech and thought about language as an instrument.

A particular moment in the history of law strikingly illustrates the decline of magicoreligious thought.[74] Prelegal thinking offered a mode of thought in which efficacious words and gestures determined the course of all action. Proof was not offered for the benefit of a judge's assessment but was instead aimed at an opponent who had to be overcome. No use was made of witnesses who might produce proof. Procedures in the form of ordeals solely and automatically determined the "truth." The function of the judge was simply to confirm these "decisive proofs."[75] But the emergence of the Greek city marked the end of this system. It is a moment recalled by Athena when she declares to the Eumenides during the trial of Orestes, "I say the wrong must not win by use of oaths." That is a crucial statement, endorsed by the citizens as follows: "Examine him then yourself. Decide it and be fair."[76] The technicality of the swearing of oaths, which carried a definite religious force, gave way to discussion that allowed reason to put forward its arguments and thereby gave the judge a chance to form an opinion based on these arguments.[77]

In this way dialogue triumphed and the old kind of speech was devalued, as Aeschylus's *The Suppliant Maidens* clearly demonstrates. When the chorus praises Pelasgus, the king of Argos, it tells him: "You are, yes, the city, the people. A prince is not judged. You rule the land, the hearth, the altar."[78] However, the king rejects these trappings of a bygone prestige and declares himself the servant of the people: "I said before that never would I act alone, apart from the people, though I am ruler."[79] To protect the "suppliants" he uses persuasion, as would any ordinary orator. Instead of speaking from his high seat of authority, he addresses an assembly in which decision is reached through a majority vote.[80] His former privilege is thus converted into collective decision: "Thus unanimous the [city] vote decreed" (*krainei*).[81] By this time the people deliver *decisive* decrees (*pantelē psēphismata*); the citizens as a whole "create reality" (*krainei*). The old concepts of *telos* and *krainein* have become mere metaphors. The magicoreligious power has been converted into social ratification; it is the deathblow for efficacious speech.[82]

From this point on dialogue-speech was what mattered. Once the city was born, dialogue-speech was paramount, the "political instrument" par excellence, the most highly prized tool in social relations.[83] Through speech men were effective in assemblies, established their command, and dominated others.[84] Speech was no longer enmeshed in a symbolicoreligious network; it now became autonomous. It engendered its own world in the interplay of a dialogue that created a particular kind of space; that is, an enclosure where one discourse confronted another.[85] Through its political function, *logos* became an autonomous reality and obeyed its own laws.[86] Thought about language began to be elaborated along two major lines: as an instrument of social relations and as a means of knowing reality. Rhetoric and sophistry explored the former path, forging techniques of persuasion and developing the grammatical and stylistic analysis of this instrument.[87] The latter path was the subject of one current of philosophical reflection: Was speech reality, all of reality? The problem seemed even more urgent given that mathematical thought was beginning to posit that reality could be expressed by numbers.[88]

These new problems and two-pronged reflection on language as an instrument evolved within the general framework of rational thought. Here another question arose: What mental structures link mythical and rational thought? Or, more plainly, what becomes of the configuration and semantic content of *Alētheia* once speech becomes secularized? Greek thought produced two antithetical and complementary answers to this question: the solution of the philosophicoreligious sects and that of sophistry and rhetoric. The two were antithetical in that the former made *Alētheia* the central concept in their thought, while the latter valued *Apatē* above all, which played a capital role in *their* thought. Yet the two were at the same time complementary: in the one case, *Alētheia* regressed, melted away, and disappeared, while in the other it stood firm, was confirmed, and became consolidated. The way this took place empirically proved, so to speak, that *Alētheia* was truly the center of a configuration of necessarily interlinked religious powers.

CHAPTER SIX

A Choice between *Alētheia* and *Apatē*

In the history of mental categories, historians usually only manage to detect different states; "transformations and their mechanisms have to be reconstructed."[1] But in some cases the mutation takes place before the very eyes of the historian, like a chemical reaction observed by an experimental scientist. If our only evidence was either sophistic or philosophical thought, the transition from religious to rational thought would elude us and we should indeed be reduced to reconstructing it. As it so happens, however, we are fortunate enough to have excellent evidence provided by Simonides of Ceos, on the one hand, and by the philosophicoreligious sects, on the other.[2]

Through Simonides' thought and work we can see exactly how *Alētheia* came to be devalued.[3] Simonides of Ceos, born circa 557–556 B.C., marks a turning point in the poetic tradition both with respect to the new type of man he represents and through his concept of his art. Simonides was the first to treat poetry as a profession. He composed poems for a fee, as the virtuously scandalized Pindar informs us: the sweet songs of Terpsichorus, so gentle and lulling, were up for sale.[4] With Simonides, the Muse became greedy (*philokerdēs*) and mercenary (*ergatis*).[5] Simonides forced his contemporaries to recognize the commercial value of his art, and they, in turn, took their revenge by treating him as a greedy man.[6] For a long tradition from Xenophanes down to Aelian, Simonides' cupidity was proverbial.[7] However, by the same token Simonides shed new light on the poetic function: the shift was accompanied by a deliberate effort to reflect on the nature of poetry. Antiquity ascribed to him the famous remark, "Painting is silent poetry and poetry is painting that speaks."[8] This is a stimulating comparison, for painting is a technique that calls on the intellectual quality Empedocles calls *mētis*, professional know-how and an indissociable magical kind of skill.[9] A painter brings together various colors, and from these inert materials he creates figures the Greeks describe as *poikila*, flickering, many-colored, living things.[10] For an entire tradition, painting was an art of illusion, "trickery." The author of the *Dissoi Logoi* defines painting as an art in which the best artist is one who can deceive (*exapatēi*) "by making most things appear to be real" (*pleista...homoia tois alēthinois poieōn*).[11] Simonides' analogy between painting and poetry thus fully confirms an anecdote detecting a predecessor to Gorgias in this poet.[12] When Simonides was asked, "How is it that it is only the Thessalians that you do not manage to deceive (*exapatas*)?" the poet supposedly replied, "It is because they are too ignorant to be deceived by me." This anecdote, which is sometimes connected with Gorgias rather than Simonides, clearly indicates that the Ancients regarded Simonides' poetry as an art of trickery, a form of expression in which *apatē* was valued positively. Through painting, which at that time was acquiring an increasingly important role in Greek society as a form of expression, Simonides discovered one of the characteristic features of his art.[13] However, he simultaneously discovered the *artificial* nature of poetic speech. This discovery is seemingly conveyed by the remark attributed to him by Michael Psellos: "Speech is the image (*eikōn*) of reality."[14] *Eikōn* is the technical term denoting painted or sculpted figurative representation, the "image" created by a painter or a sculptor.[15] Simonides was roughly contemporary to a change in the meaning of statuary and in the traditional relationship between artist and work of art. By the end of the seventh century, a statue was no longer a religious sign; it was an "image," a figurative sign functioning to evoke some external reality. One aspect of the change in meaning was the appearance of the artist's signature on the base of his statue or close to his painting.[16] In his new relationship to the work of art, the artist discovered himself as an agent, a creator, situated midway between reality and its image. On the level of sculpture and painting, the artist's discovery of himself was intimately associated with the invention of the image. Simonides identifies the very moment when the poet, in turn, came to recognize himself through his speech, whose specific character he discovered through the intermediary of painting and sculpture.[17]

Not only did Simonides' thinking recognize a desire to practice poetry as a profession, but his reflection on poetry, its function, and its particular object confirmed as well the break from the tradition of the inspired poet, for whom speaking *Alētheia* came as naturally as breathing.[18] By declaring himself to be a master of *Apatē*, Simonides seems to be categorically rejecting the old religious concept of a poet, prophet of the Muses and master of *Alētheia*. One fragment declares so unequivocally: *to dokein kai tan Alatheian biatai.*[19] *Alētheia* no longer ruled; it had been usurped by *dokein*, or *doxa*. However, the devaluation of *Alētheia* can only be understood in relation to a technical innovation representing another fundamental aspect of Simonides' secularization of poetry. An entire tradition attributes to him the invention of techniques of memorization.[20] At a poetic level, what was significant about the elaboration of procedures of memorization? Until Simonides' time, memory had been a fundamental tool for any poet. It was a religious function enabling him to know the past, present, and future. Through a direct vision or through memory, the poet entered the Beyond, gaining access to the Invisible. Memory was the basis of poetic speech as well as the poet's special status. But with Simonides, memory became a secularized technique, a psychological faculty available to all via definite rules that brought it within everyone's reach. It was no longer a form of privileged knowledge, nor was it an exercise for salvation, as the Pythagoreans' notion of memory had been. It was simply an instrument that helped one learn a profession. The same purpose prompted the invention of memorization techniques as another technical improvement, also attributed to Simonides: the invention of letters of the alphabet to facilitate written notation.[21] The lyric poets, it is worth noting here, did resort to writing, and not solely to recitation, to make their works known.[22] By the seventh century B.C., writing had become the necessary form to make works public. It was no longer limited, as in the Mycenaean world, to socioeconomic structures connected with the storage of possessions.[23] Its essential purpose was no longer simply to reinforce the strength of rulers; now it was an instrument of publicity.[24] But for Simonides the new function of memory could not be separated from a new attitude toward time, an attitude diametrically opposed to the religious sects and the philosophicoreligious circles. Whereas the Pythagorean Paron saw time as a power of oblivion, from which the only possible escape was memory, an ascetic and spiritual exercise, for Simonides, time was, on the contrary, "the best of things," not because all-powerful Chronos never aged but because "it is in time that one learns and that one memorizes."[25] By turning memory into a positive technique and considering time as the framework for secular activity, Simonides dissociated himself from the entire religious tradition, the tradition of both the inspired poets as well as the sects and philosophicoreligious circles. Here again technical innovation served the same purpose of secularizing poetry. Practicing poetry as a profession, defining the poetic art as a work of illusion (*apatē*), making memory a secularized technique, and rejecting *Alētheia* as the cardinal virtue were all aspects of one and the same project. Here one can also detect an inevitable link between the secularization of memory and the decline of *Alētheia*. Cut off from its source, *Alētheia* abruptly lost its value. Simonides rejected it as a symbol of the old kind of poetry. To take its place, he recommended *to dokein*, *doxa*.

This seems to be the first time *Alētheia* was directly opposed to *doxa*; at this point an important conflict arose that would overshadow the entire history of Greek philosophy. Thus, it is important to elucidate the meaning of *doxa*. There are several possible ways to do so. We no longer know the context of the poem containing Simonides' line, but we do know the context of his thought on poetry. We can therefore adopt as a starting point what we know of this thought and then compare it with both the meaning ascribed to the fragment by the principal "citer" and the various meanings emerging from the semantic history of *doxa*.

Our starting point is Simonides' analogy between poetry and an art of *Apatē*, such as painting. Frag. 55D opposes the power of *Alētheia* – which here seems to mean poetic truth – with what Simonides calls *to dokein*. It seems reasonable to suppose that, against the old *Alētheia* of the traditional poet, Simonides would champion the superiority of his own notion of poetic art. *Doxa* would thus belong to the order of *Apatē*.[26] This inference would be entirely gratuitous, were it not for its impressive confirmation in the text of the principal "citer," who incorporates Simonides' line in a commentary opposing *Apatē* and *Dikē*. In the *Republic*, Plato imagines the choice in front of an adolescent at a crossroads: "Is it by justice (*dikai*) or by crooked deceit (*skoliais apatais*) that

I shall scale the higher tower and so live my life out in fenced and guarded security?" He has two options: the way of *Dikē* and the way of *Apatē*. To Plato, it seems obvious that, in a city where poets openly criticize the gods and spur men toward injustice, the adolescent will reason as follows: "Since it is the 'seeming' (*to dokein*) as wise men show me [the intervention by the *Schol. Eur. Or.* 235 (1.122 Schw.) allows us to recognize Simonides behind those "wise men"] *that 'masters the reality'* (*Alētheia*) and is lord of happiness, to this I must devote myself without reserve. For a front and a show I must draw about myself a shadow-outline (*skiagraphian*) of virtue, but trail behind me the fox of the most sage Archilochus, shifty and bent on gain (*kerdalean kai poikilēn*)."[27] The terms of the alternative are then restated in forms that pinpoint their significance. The world of ambiguity is symbolized by the fox, which always embodies *apatē*, two-faced and ambiguous behavior, in Greek thought.[28] It is further represented by the *skiagraphia*, which, for Plato, meant *trompe l'oeil*, the conjuror's art (*thaumatopoiikē*) and a highly developed form of *apatē*.[29] Alternatively, there is the world of *Dikē*, which is also the world of *Alētheia*.[30]

The affinities between *doxa* and *apatē* and the various forms of ambiguity are borne out by a number of the fundamental meanings of *doxa*.[31] For Gorgias and rhetorical thought, *doxa* was fragile and unstable (*sphalera kai abebaios*); it would only sustain precarious positions. Functionally speaking, *doxa* was subjected to *Peithō*, which could substitute one *doxa* for another.[32] Far from belonging to the order of *Epistēmē*, *doxa* was associated with *kairos*, "the time of possible human action," that is, the time of contingency and ambiguity.[33] Instability was one of the fundamental characteristics of *doxa*. *Doxai* were of the same nature as the statues of Daedalus: "they run away and escape."[34] No one more carefully noted their ambiguous aspects than Plato.

He remarked that Philodoxoi were people "who loved and regarded tones and beautiful colors and the like," people concerned with intermediate things that partook of both Being and
Non-Being. To specify more precisely the nature of such things,
Plato resorts to the following comparison: "They are like those
jesters who palter with us in a double sense at banquets...and
resemble the children's riddle about the eunuch and his hitting
of the bat – with what and as it sat on what they signify that he
struck it." Such betwixt-and-between things, described as both
"bright and dark" are enigmatic, just like the following riddle:
"A man who is not a man, seeing yet not seeing a bird that was
not a bird, perched on wood that was not wood, threw yet did
not throw a stone that was not a stone."[35] Each term is flanked
by its opposite, and their synthesis produces a kind of dizziness,
a flashing in which darkness and light intermingle and become
confused.

In rational thought, one thus finds in *doxa* the principal feature
that, in myth, characterizes the Muses, Sirens, and Bee-Women,
in short, all the powers that are both "true and false" (*alētheis* and
pseudeis). Indeed, Plato in the *Theaetetus* even explicitly describes
doxa as "*alēthēs* and *pseudēs*": opinion (*doxa*) "turns and twists
about and proves false (*pseudēs*) or true (*alēthēs*) (*doxa strephetai
kai helittetai...pseudēs kai alēthēs gignomenē*)."[36] The whole mythical world of ambiguity is conjured up by the verb *strephein*, which
refers to the action of the fetters that bind the *poikilomētis* Hermes,
the fox's wheeling about with its multifaceted *mētis*, and the
movements of the athlete and the Sophist as they twist and turn.[37]
Plato combines *strephein* and *helittein* to express the permanent
movement characterizing ambiguity in Greek thought. Gorgias and
Plato are echoed by Aristotle, for whom *doxa* is also both *alēthēs*
and *pseudēs*.[38] It is "the only authentic way of approaching things
that are born and then perish."[39]

113

Doxa is the appropriate form of knowledge for a world of change and movement, a world of ambiguity and contingency. It is "imprecise knowledge, but imprecise knowledge of whatever is imprecise."[40] The agreement among these three sources, which so often disagree elsewhere, suggests that the affinity between *doxa* and the world of ambiguity is by no means fortuitous. Analysis of the Indo-European root **dek-* makes the proposal even more positive: Georges Redard has demonstrated that this root means "to confirm with what one considers to be a norm" and that the family *dokos*, *dokein*, and so on revolves around the basic meaning "to decide to do whatever one judges to best suit the situation."[41] *Doxa* thus conveys two indissociable ideas: the idea of choice, but a choice that varies according to the situation.[42] This fundamental meaning not only shows that *doxa* has always been associated with ambiguity; it also leads one to detect again, in the choice of *dokein*, this same process of secularization apparently accounting for a number of the traditions surrounding Simonides.

Simonides is the first writer in the history of choral lyric not only to compose hymns to the gods but also to sing the praises of men and celebrate the victors in the games. He is also among the first to praise citizens who have risked their lives for the city. It is he who sings of the fame of the heroes of Marathon and the "victors" of Thermopylae.[43] Although he is often regarded as a court poet whose salary was provided by the great families of Thessaly, the Scopadae and the Aleuadae, Simonides was in fact one of the first poets "committed" to the city.[44] One of his poems, addressed to Scopas, is entirely devoted to criticizing the aristocratic ideal of the *agathos* or the *esthlos anēr*.[45] Simonides replaces that ideal, of Homeric origin, with the ideal of the "healthy man" (*hugiēs anēr*), whose virtue is defined by reference to the *Polis* (*eidōs g' onēsipolin dikan*).[46] Simonides was also responsible for coining the famous expression "The city makes the man" (*polis andra didaskei*).[47] This political context gives Simonides' choice of a verb such as *dokein* its full significance, since *dokein* is a technical term in the vocabulary of the *polis*, the verb used par excellence for political "decision."[48] Thus, when Simonides declares that *dokein* is more important than *Alētheia*, he is both clearly breaking with the entire poetic tradition in which *Alētheia* represents the essential value and unequivocally announcing his desire to secularize poetry. He is replacing an exceptional and privileged mode of understanding with the most "political" and the least religious type of knowledge imaginable.[49]

Simonides marks the moment in the history of *Alētheia* when ambiguity broke away and took refuge in *doxa*. However, it is important to note that Simonides' insistence on the superiority of *doxa* over *Alētheia* does not result from the perspective defined by Parmenides, as the context of the *Republic* might have us believe. For one thing, in this context *doxa* does not mean opinion in the philosophical sense: "it has nothing to do with problems concerning Being and Seeming."[50] It does not carry the derogative sense of uncertain knowledge that fifth-century philosophical thought would give it (in opposition to *epistēmē* or certitude). Second, the opposition between *Alētheia* and *doxa* relates to a problem internal to poetic thought: the *Alētheia* condemned by Simonides is not the *Alētheia* of the philosophers but that of the poets. Indeed, one might even say that for Simonides a choice between *Alētheia* and *doxa* did not really arise, for once poetry had become secularized, "poetic revelation" gave way to a technique of fascination. By turning memory into a secular technique, Simonides rejected *Alētheia* and committed himself to *Apatē*. Thus Simonides testifies not simply to the decline of *Alētheia* but, even more important, to a current of thinking that regarded

Apatē more highly. When he defined poetry as an art of illusion whose function was to deceive by conjuring up "images," elusive beings that were at once themselves and something other than themselves, Simonides anticipated one of the two major developments that would define the history of the whole problem of speech.

Thanks to certain stylistic characteristics and personality traits, Simonides has often been seen as prefiguring the Sophist.[51] In his poems, he cultivates antitheses and delights in playing on the ambiguity of words. To his contemporaries he was a man who sold his poetry and boasted of "deceiving" people. But Simonides and the early Sophists share more in common than mere anecdote. Both sophistry and rhetoric, which appeared with the advent of the Greek city, were forms of thought founded on ambiguity. This is so not only because they developed in the political sphere, the particular world of ambiguity, but also because they defined themselves as instruments that formulated the theory and logic of ambiguity and made effective action on that same level of ambiguity possible. The earliest Sophists, the forerunners of the brilliant generation of the fifth century, claimed to be specialists in political action. They possessed a kind of wisdom akin to that of the Seven Wise Men, "a political skill and a practical intelligence."[52] Mnesiphilus, a man of *praxis* in whom the Greeks saw the very model of ancient sophistry, first appears in Greek history on the eve of the battle of Salamis, disguised as the "wise counsellor" in a particularly difficult moment.[53] At a crucial point – truly a moment of *kairos* – Mnesiphilus helped Themistocles, whose shadow or double he had to some extent become, to control a shifting situation.[54] Thanks to Mnesiphilus, the most resourceful of the Greeks was able to turn a manifestly unpromising situation to his own advantage. A Sophist was thus remarkably close to a "statesman," one whom the Greeks called "prudent" (*phronimos*): they shared the same domain of action and a similar cast of intelligence.[55] Both were directly involved in human affairs, the domain "where nothing is stable" and where, in Aristotle's words, "the agents themselves must in each case consider what is appropriate to the occasion, as happens also in the art of medicine or of navigation."[56] The domain of politics and sophistry thus belongs to a level of thought that is completely opposed to that of the philosopher in Plato's *Parmenides*. Their domain is on the level of contingency, the sphere of *kairos*, which belongs not to the order of *epistēmē* but *doxa*.[57] This is the domain of ambiguity.[58]

In this respect, sophistry is indissociable from rhetoric. The latter first appeared in Magna Graecia, also in a political context – either in relation to deliberations on early "democracy" or in association with the workings of argued justice.[59] In Plato's words, rhetoric was "the occupation of a shrewd and enterprising spirit, and of one naturally skilled in its dealings with men."[60] It therefore requires the same intellectual qualities as the "prudent man," for it becomes established in the same ambience of human affairs, where nothing is stable and everything is shifting, double, and ambiguous. Sophistry and rhetoric, products of the same political culture, thus encouraged indissociable mental techniques. In a world where social relations were controlled by speech, both the Sophist and the orator were technical experts on *logos*. Both helped to elaborate a line of thought on *logos* as an instrument and a means of affecting human beings. For the Sophist, the field of speech was limited by the tension between the two opposite views expressed on every matter, the contradiction between the two theses advanced on every question.[61] At this level of thought ruled by the "principle of contradiction," the Sophist is a theorist able to impose logic on ambiguity and who can transform this logic into an instrument with the power to fascinate one's opponent and make the weaker triumph over the greater.[62] The aim of sophistry, like rhetoric, is persuasion (*peithō*), trickery (*apatē*).[63] In a fundamentally ambiguous world, these mental techniques allowed the domination of men through the power of ambiguity itself. Both Sophists and orators were thus very much men of *doxa*. Plato was correct to regard them as masters of illusion who presented men not with the truth but with fictions, images, and "idols," which they persuaded others to accept as reality.[64]

For Sophists and orators, the supreme art was to speak *pseudea … etumoisin homoia*.[65] At this level of thought *Alētheia* has no place. After all, what was speech for a Sophist?[66] Discourse was certainly an instrument, but not a way to know reality. *Logos* was a reality in itself, but not a signifier pointing to the signified. In this type of speech there was no distance between words and things. For Gorgias, who drew his ultimate conclusions from this notion, discourse did not reveal the things it touched upon and had nothing to communicate. In fact, it was impossible for discourse to constitute communication with others. It was "a great lord with a tiny, invisible body," curiously resembling the infant Hermes of the *Homeric Hymn*, the child with a magic wand (given to him by Apollo to control the flocks) who becomes an instrument of persuasion or "psychagogia."[67]

The power of *logos* is immense: it brings pleasure, dispels worries, fascinates, persuades, and changes things as though by magic.[68] At this level, *logos* never attempts to tell *Alētheia*.[69] Clement of Alexandria studied the aims of sophistic, rhetoric, and eristic language, noting that sophistry acted on the imagination through the interplay of words, rhetoric operated in the domain of the specious and aimed at persuasion, and eristic found its starting point in the *Agora* and its fulfilment in victory. Clement therefore remarked that *Alētheia* "had nothing to do with all this," in effect repeating Plato's conclusion in relation to rhetoric: "Nobody cares for truth...but for that which is convincing."[70] Sophistry and rhetoric were thus beyond the scope of *Alētheia*. Furthermore, as in the case of Simonides, the old relationship between *Alētheia* and memory as a religious function is definitely severed on this level. For the Sophists, memory is simply a secularized function whose development is essential to the kind of intelligence at work in both sophistry and politics.[71]

An examination of the Sophists' and the orators' thought on language as an instrument produces two conclusions. First, Greek thought delimits a specific zone for the ambiguous, a level of reality that is the exclusive preserve of *Apatē*, of *Doxa*, of both "the *alēthēs* and the *pseudēs*" at once. Second, at this level of thought, the secularization of memory and the devaluation of *Alētheia* are perfectly correlated. The relation between the two is necessary. So far as mental structures are concerned, what is essential is that we are entering a new system of thought, different because ambiguity is no longer an aspect of *Alētheia*. At this level of reality there is, in a sense, no room for *Alētheia*. Another reason for the difference is that ambiguity is no longer a combination of complementary contraries; instead, the synthesis now involves "contradictory" contraries.[72] The consequences of this mental and logical change are abundantly illustrated by a second development.

Toward the end of the sixth century, certain circles in Greece witnessed the birth of a type of philosophical and religious thought absolutely opposed to that of the Sophists.[73] The thought of the Sophists was secularized, directed toward the external world, and founded on *praxis*, while the other was religious, introverted, and concerned with individual salvation. Whereas the Sophists, as a particular type of individual and as representative of a certain form of thought, were the sons of the city, and their aim, within an essentially political framework, was to influence others, the magi and initiates lived on the periphery of the city, aspiring only to an altogether internal transformation.[74] The diametrically opposed aims of the two groups were matched by their radically different techniques. While the mental techniques of sophistry and rhetoric marked an abrupt break with the forms of religious thought that preceded the emergence of Greek reason, the philosophico-religious sects, in contrast, adopted procedures and modes of thought that directly prolonged earlier religious thought. At this level, among the values that *mutatis mutandis* continued to play the same important role as in earlier thought, memory and *Alētheia* held a recognized position.

In a myth whose cosmological framework is borrowed directly from the Pythagorean Petron of Himerus, Plutarch describes a plain of *Alētheia*:

> The worlds are not infinite in number, nor one, nor five, but one hundred and eighty-three, arranged in the form of a triangle, each side of the triangle having sixty worlds; of the three left over, each is placed at an angle and those that are next to one another are in contact and revolve gently as in a dance. The inner area of the triangle is the common hearth of all and is called the plain of Truth, in which the accounts, the forms, and the patterns of all things that have come to pass and of all that shall come to pass rest undisturbed; and round about them lies Eternity, whence Time, like an everflowing stream, is conveyed to the worlds. Opportunity to see and to contemplate these things is vouchsafed to human souls once in ten thousand years if they have lived goodly lives; and the best of the initiatory rites here are but a dream of that highest rite and initiation; and the words of our philosophic inquiry are framed to recall these fair sights there — else our labor is vain.[75]

Although Plutarch may not be a source of irreproachable antiquity, his myth is particularly interesting in that, in a religious context, it strongly associates the act of memory and the vision of the plain of *Alētheia*.[76] In this fundamental respect, it echoes the myth of the *Phaedrus* in which Plato describes the heavenly procession of souls to the region above the heavens.[77] In their desperate rush to contemplate "the regions without," the souls strive to follow the gods as perfectly as possible. Only a few of them succeed in beholding the Realities:[78] "The reason wherefore the souls are fair and eager to behold the plain of Truth, and discover it, lies herein – to wit, that the pasturage that is proper to their noblest part comes from that meadow, and the plumage by which they are borne aloft is nourished thereby."[79] But the plain of *Alētheia* is only one part of a mythical landscape we can reconstruct. According to the terms of the decree of Adrastus: "whatsoever soul has followed in the train of a god, and discerned something of truth (*tōn alēthōn*), shall be kept from sorrow until a new revolution shall begin.... But when she is not able so to follow, and sees none of it, but meeting with some mischance comes to be burdened with a load of forgetfulness (*lēthēs*) and wrongdoing, and because of that burden sheds her wings and falls to the earth," then she is caught in the cycle of births.[80] The opposition between *Alētheia* and *Lēthē* is thus explicitly confirmed. Proclus's commentary notes the correlation between the plain of *Alētheia* and the plain of *Lēthē* in Plato's *Republic*.[81] The soul "gorged with forgetfulness" to which the *Phaedrus* refers is a thirsty soul that failed to heed the advice of the *Republic* and has drunk deeply the water no receptacle can hold, the water of the river Amelēs that runs through the plain of *Lēthē*.[82] In the Platonic theory of knowledge, the opposition between the plain of *Alētheia* and the plain of *Lēthē* mythically represents the opposition between the act of *anamnēsis* – an escape from time, a revelation of immutable and eternal being — and the error of *Lēthē* — human ignorance and forgetfulness of the eternal truths.[83]

These various sources show the opposition of *Alētheia* and *Lēthē* as well as the association of *Alētheia* and memory. These two essential factors prompt a comparison with a series of mystical texts that inform us of eschatological doctrines in which *Mnēmosynē* is a complementary power to *Lēthē*.[84] Such a comparison is further legitimized by the fact that the opposition between the plain of *Alētheia* and the plain of *Lēthē* is not a fable purely inspired by Platonism.[85] According to one tradition this mythological representation is also attested in Empedocles, and it also belongs to an "ideological field" suggested by the opposition between *Alētheia* and *Lēthē* in both poetic and mantic thought.[86] The mythical geography of the two plains, along with the eschatological representation of the sources of *Mnēmosynē* and *Lēthē*, of figures in imagery peculiar to the circles intermediate between philosophy and religion, that is, philosophicoreligious circles. Both representations are connected with the doctrine of the reincarnation of souls. They are intelligible only in the context of thought obsessed by individual salvation and the problem of the soul in relation to time. At this level of thought, memory is not simply a gift of second sight that allows one to grasp the totality of past, present, and future; even more important, it is the terminus of the chain of reincarnations.[87] Memory's powers are twofold. As a religious power, it is the water of Life, which marks the end of the cycle of "metensomatoses"; as an intellectual faculty, it constitutes the discipline of salvation that results in victory over time and death and makes it possible to acquire the most complete kind of knowledge.[88]

According to the dichotomatic view of the philosophicoreligious sects, earthly life was corrupted by time, which was synonymous with death and oblivion. Man was cast into the world of *Lēthē*, where he wandered in the meadow of *Atē*.[89] To transcend human time and purge themselves of oblivion, these sects elaborated a technique of salvation that constituted a rule for living, a "recipe for sanctity." It involved psychophysiological techniques that, through a cataleptic experience, aimed to free the soul from the body.[90] A rhythm of life composed of obligations and taboos allowed the initiate, at the end of his ascetic exercise, to appear before the guardians of the spring of Memory; there he could drink the water that would purge temporality and forever consecrate his divine status. To "remember," to "separate the soul from the body," to "drink the water of *Mnēmosynē*" – all these expressions, at different levels, conveyed the same way of life.

In this context the vision of the plain of *Alētheia* assumes its full significance. On this point, Epimenides' experience is crucial: "During the day Epimenides lay down in the cave of Zeus Diktaios and he slumbered in a deep sleep for many years; he conversed in his dreams with the gods and spoke with *Alētheia* and *Dikē*."[91] Epimenides' experience belongs on the same social and mental level as that of the philosophicoreligious sects. The setting is that of the magi, inspired men, individuals with an exceptional pattern of behavior, men on the periphery of the social group organized within the *Polis*: this level of thought is the same as the ecstatic movement of specialists of the soul. Epimenides was a magus who ate mallow and asphodel, a purifier and a diviner. He knew the past, the present, and the future. Like others inspired in this way, he was subject to cataleptic slumber. His soul could escape from his body at will. Such behavior incontestably emulated incubatory mantic procedures, for sleep represented a special moment when the soul, "enmeshed with the body" during the day, could contemplate pure *Alētheia* after being delivered from the body.[92] Then it could "recall the past, discern the present, and foresee the future."[93] While the conversation with *Alētheia* signified Epimenides' gift of second sight, similar to that of a diviner, it also confirmed a *meletē* whose goal was to escape time and attain a level of reality characterized by its opposition to *Lēthē*.[94] Once he entered into contact with *Alētheia*, Epimenides acceded to an intimacy with the gods strictly analogous to the divine status of the initiate of the "tablets of gold," when he is able to drink the fresh water of Lake Memory.[95] The level of *Alētheia* is divine: it is characterized by intemporality and stability. This is the level of Being, immutable and permanent, which stands in opposition to the level of human existence, which is subject to generation, death, and oblivion.

For the philosophicoreligious sects, *Alētheia* is at the center of a configuration of powers and concepts similar to those that attend it in religious thought. Based on the religious function of Memory, *Alētheia* is associated with *Dikē*, which indicates its identification with the order of things. *Alētheia* is also supported by *Pistis*, which here, as in the religious thought of diviners and inspired poets, represents faith in Being and harmony with a superior power whose revelations man accepts: namely, the Muse of Empedocles, who speaks what is *Alētheia* and produces "trustworthy words" (*pistōmata*).[96] However, that is where the resemblance ends between the *Alētheia* of the philosophicoreligious sects and the *Alētheia* of the poets, diviners, and kings of justice. Whereas *Alētheia* as a religious power is inseparable from *Peithō* to the latter group, for the philosophicoreligious sects the level of *Alētheia*/ *Dikē*/*Pistis* is radically dissociated from that of *Peithō*. In the *Gorgias* myth, the men of *Peithō* are characterized by their *apistia*. They are the unfortunate victims of oblivion – pleasure's prey, carried along in the ceaseless flow of things.[97] *Peithō* is on the side of *Lēthē* and the sister of *Hēdonē*, while *Atē* is her double.[98]

Peithō symbolizes the humid world of generation, the soft sweetness of the pleasure of speech, but also the pleasure provided by women and physical delight. Because of this inward-looking thought, obsessed by wrongdoing and yearning for purity, the human condition, committed to Oblivion and sunk in Night, is placed under the sign of *Peithō*.[99] In the archaic tradition, while man felt himself to be subject to Oblivion and possessed of a wavering memory, he felt that the memory of the gods could also be faulty. But in times of religious crisis, with men separated from the gods by an unbridgeable chasm, unwavering Memory became the property of the gods alone, something lacked most definitely by man. For the philosophicoreligious sects, then, the Immutable, Being, Memory, and *Alētheia* were on one side, and Fluidity, Non-Being, Oblivion, *Lēthē* on the other. The division between the two was clear-cut, as was proved by the *theios anēr*: his whole effort of "asceticism" was directed toward passing from the level of *Lēthē* to that of *Alētheia*. The spiritual universe of the philosophicoreligious sects was a split world in which ambiguity had given way to contradiction. Even though the *Alētheia-Lēthē* pair, despite their change in values, reflected a continuity with mythical thought, the relationship between those two powers was now radically different. One logic had been abandoned for another.

Some curious correspondences are detectable between this level of thought, radically split between *Alētheia* and *Lēthē*, and certain representations that refer to the same spiritual universe. A number of disparate documents from different periods demonstrate the fundamental importance of a problem of choice in these circles. Man no longer lived in an ambivalent world in which "contraries" were complementary and oppositions were ambiguous. He was now cast into a dualist world with clear-cut oppositions. Choice thus became an urgent matter. In the Pythagorean society, which held an important place in these philosophicoreligious circles, a marked dualism distinguished these two different paths: the left path was *Hēdonē*, the right path *Ponos*. Some evidence suggests that for these circles Heracles' exemplary decision at the crossing of the ways represented the need to make a fundamental choice, the same choice faced by an adolescent on the threshold of adult human existence.[100] The path of salvation involves effort; it is the way of *Meletē*, a long *askēsis*, and the exercise of memory. The other is the path of pleasure, vice, and oblivion. The former is rough and steep, the latter level and easy; furthermore, given man's taste for pleasure, this is the path he naturally follows.[101] The crossroads at the beginning of existence corresponds to the bifurcation of paths in the Beyond, since the soul comes to a branching fork in the otherworld as well, with one leg leading to the Islands of the Blessed, the other to Tartarus.[102] In the "tablets of gold," each path leads to a spring, one to the left, the other to the right of the waters of the Lake of Memory. However, in the Beyond there is in reality no real choice: the tablets accompanying the initiate to his tomb clearly indicate the path he is bound to follow, the path he has a right to take. One tablet states explicitly that the souls of the elect follow the right-hand path, and most tablets give the initiate the password that will allow him to drink the water of Life.[103]

Thus, choice in the Beyond is predetermined by the one made on earth. The earthly level corresponds exactly to the eschatological level. This whole current of dichotomic thought, which opposes right and left, *Ponos* and *Hēdonē*, Memory and Oblivion; and *Alētheia* and *Lēthē*, is a way of thinking in terms of alternatives. The choice that is obligatory in the philosophicoreligious sects is a clear sign of the contradiction ruling this thought. Nevertheless, even though ambiguity, in the sense of an intermediate zone between antithetical terms, has disappeared, it has not been totally expunged from the reality of the human world. Empedocles presents his disciple, Pausanias, with a choice between two kinds of life. One follows the way of *Meletē*, the path of "divine *prapides*," which will enable him through strict *prapides* to acquire a solid grasp of the teachings of the Muse and, based on these, to master others as well. The other follows the path of "dark *doxa*," where man is left to his own devices, free to explore countless base things.[104] For the philosophicoreligious sects, stability and solidity are opposed by fluidity and flow: it is natural for man to live in the world of *Peithō*, the world of *doxa*, in which everything is shifting and perpetually mobile. In other words, this world's very essence, for the Greeks, is ambiguity.

The evolution of *Alētheia* in the philosophicoreligious circles was thus both antithetical and complementary to that which can be traced from Simonides through the Sophists. It is antithetical since *Alētheia* plays the same absolute role for the former that *Apatē* takes in the thought of the latter. But it is also complementary because, in positive fashion for one group and negatively for the other, *Alētheia*'s relationship to memory as a religious function proves both necessary and structural. On one essential point, the history of the sects completes what was already indicated by sophistry and rhetoric. In the latter, given that *Alētheia* became marginalized, in effect elevating *Apatē*, it was impossible for us to define the logical relation between the two. In contrast, to the philosophicoreligious sects, the predominance of *Alētheia* does not rule out the world of ambiguity: the world of the philosophicoreligious sects demands choice. On this level of thought, whether in the form of *Lēthē*, *Peithō*, *Apatē*, or *Doxa*, ambiguity is always the contrary of *Alētheia*. There is no third term: the choice is between *Alētheia* and *Apatē*.

+	−
Plain of *Alētheia*	Plain of *Lēthē*
Mnēmosynē	*Lēthē*
Meletē Thanatou	*Amelēs*
Memory { Soul / Time	Oblivion
Ponos	*Hēdonē*
Right	Left
Intemporality	Time
Alētheia { *Dikē* / *Pistis*	*Peithō* { *Lēthē* / *Hēdonē* / *Atē*
Light	Night

Should we, from our diachronic perspective, speak of a break in continuity or of a continuity in the break? Despite the split radically separating the logic of ambiguity and the logic of contradiction, in a number of essential respects there is a perfect continuity between the two: in the thought of the philosophico-religious sects as in the thought of the poet, diviner, and king of justice, memory remains fundamental. The magus is as much a master of truth as the seer and the king of justice.

All the same, between these types of masters of truth and between these different truths, striking differences stand out among the resemblances. Within a system of thought featuring problems of time and soul, memory is not simply a gift of second sight, a "decoding" of the invisible that constantly interacts with the visible. Instead, it becomes a means of transcending time and separating the soul from the body, hence a method of acceding to something radically different from the visible world. Simul-

taneously, the meaning of *Alētheia* changes. It is no longer an efficacious power established by the speech of the diviner or the
poet. In the system of thought that emerged at least from the
logic of myth, if not from its forms, *Alētheia* became a power that
was more strictly defined and more abstractly conceived. It still
symbolized a level of reality, but that level took the form of an
intemporal reality, identified with stable and immutable Being
to the extent that *Alētheia* was radically opposed to the level of
reality associated wtih Time, Death, and *Lēthē*. Furthermore,
the level of reality that *Alētheia* now symbolized was not simply
defined by the religious qualities of a type of man from which it
seemed indissociable. Now it became objectivized and conceived
more abstractly.[105] It was radically differentiated from other levels of reality, for which it established a standard. It increasingly
tended to become a religious prefiguration of Being or even of the
One, in that it was irreducibly opposed to whatever was changing, multiform, or double. Thus, not only the logical relationship between the two terms underwent a change, but also the
terms themselves.

This change in meaning inevitably led to a difference between
the two types of "master of truth." To the extent that *Alētheia* was
felt to represent a value radically separated from other levels of
reality and to the degree that it stood for Being over against the
vacillating and ambiguous world of *Doxa*, the master of truth of
the philosophicoreligious sects was more conscious of the distance between him – one who knew, one who recognized and
told *Alētheia* – and other men who knew nothing, unfortunate
creatures swept about by the ceaseless flow of things. On the
mythical level, the seer, whether a poet or a diviner, was a natural "master of truth": *Alētheia* was part of the essential order of
things, an aspect of a social function, but not totally dissociated
from *Apatē*. In contrast, in the world of the philosophicoreli-

gious sects, where the gap between gods and men yawned wider, *Alētheia*, radically separate from *Apatē*, was no longer connected with any social function: the magus was an individual. This new master of truth was thus bound to be aware of what set him apart from other men and made him a quite exceptional individual.

Between Epimendes of Crete and Parmenides of Elea, between the ecstatic magus and the philosopher of Being, the gap seems unbridgeable. Parmenides replaced Epimenides' concerns about salvation, his thought on the soul, and insistence on purification with the problem of the One and the Many and thought about language and logical necessities.[106] The two men's vocabulary, problems, and level of thought were altogether different. However, despite the unquestionable divergences which underline the very originality of philosophical thought, a network of affinities links Epimenides with Parmenides on a whole series of points centered around *Alētheia*. First, the whole setting of the *Proem* to the *Treatise on Nature* refers back to attitudes peculiar to the diviner, the poet, and the magus.[107] When Parmenides sets out to define the nature of his spiritual activity and to pinpoint the aim of his research, he resorts to the religious vocabulary of the sects and brotherhoods. He uses, for example, the theme of the chariot journey: the chariot, an aristocratic vehicle, is the means of transport for his eschatological voyage. He also adopts the theme of deities who conduct souls to the place of the dead. Leaving the abode of the Night, the daughters of the Sun give him access to the path of Light. On his galloping "mares of eloquence," Parmenides is transported into a kind of Beyond.[108] He passes from Night into Day, Darkness into Light. Behind the heavy doors guarded by justice, he is granted a direct vision of the Goddess, who reveals *Alētheia* to him, just as the Muses did to Hesiod. In all these respects, Parmenides presents himself in the guise of an elect, exceptional man, for he is one who knows. *Alētheia* is his privilege. As a master of truth, he is different from "those who know nothing," "men with two heads, who are deaf and blind."[109] The way of truth is distinct from the path followed by men "with wandering eyes and buzzing ears."[110]

Indissociable from a gift of second sight like that of the diviners and inspired poets, Parmenides' *Alētheia* furthermore operates surrounded by a configuration of powers that completely resembles that in the most ancient religious thought. Like Hesiod's and Epimenides' *Alētheia*, Parmenides' *Alētheia* acts in association with *Dikē*, which here means not only the order of the world but also strict rectitude of thought.[111] *Pistis* accompanies this *Alētheia* with all the force required for the revelation of a goddess, and *Apatē* challenges it with apparently equal determination.[112] The discourse on *Alētheia* is countered by the *kosmos apatēlos epeōn*.[113] The path of *Doxai* opens up opposite the path of *Alētheia*. Through its religious context and configuration, Parmenides' *Alētheia* fits in with a tradition extending back beyond Epimenides and the sects as far as Hesiod and the religious thought for which he provides the most authentic testimony.

There are also affinities in a third respect, which affect the very essence of Parmenidean philosophy. Through its entire history, *Alētheia* is at the heart of the problem of Being. Behind the *Alētheia* of the diviner and the inspired poet we have glimpsed the idea of "speech-reality" and the idea that the *Alētheia* of the philosophicoreligious sects constitutes an early version of Being – that is, the One.[114] For Parmenides, the question of Being is central. Indeed, the role of *Alētheia* is so crucial in his system of thought because Parmenidean philosophy is a philosophy of Being. In Parmenides, the question of Being arises out of the problem of the relations between speech and reality, a problem posed in terms of *Alētheia* and *Apatē*.[115] Where a gap appears between words and things, the philosopher in search of Being tries to differentiate what is stable and unstable in language, the permanent and the fluid, the "true" and the "deceptive."[116] He persists in trying to sift Being from what he calls words or names (*epea, onomata*), which he regards as a ceaseless flow of things at the level of language.[117] Parmenides' entire thought on language as an instrument for knowing reality develops around the little Greek word *esti*, the verb "to be."

In this thought, which parallels Sophist thought on language as an instrument for acting on others, it is important to distinguish between two levels: the properties of the Greek language and the problems philosophy is led to express through those properties. First, Greek possesses a verb "to be," which, as Emile Benveniste points out, is by no means necessary for every language.[118] Second, Greek uses this verb in a number of remarkable ways: it is endowed with the logical function of a copula. The verb "to be" is a verb that extends further than others; it can become a nominal concept or even its own predicate.[119] Against these particularities of Greek, the question of the relationship between speech and reality arises. To address whether the *logos* is reality, all of reality, and what is the fixed point in the flow of words, Parmenides replied: "It is" or, more expansively, "Being is, Non-Being is not." "Being is": that is *Alētheia*.[120] Parmenides' entire philosophy is fascinated by Being: given that it can be expressed in a single word, Being has a unique, irreducible meaning. Since it is a single noun, it necessarily means one single thing.[121] Its singularity rules out any diversity of meanings or plurality of predicates. In Parmenidean Being, all aspirations to the One, the Permanent, and the Intemporal are satisfied in one stroke. In another language and level of thought, Parmenides' Being solves the same problem as the Orphics' Chronos, namely, how to reconcile the One and the Many.[122] For Parmenides, as well as a whole tradition not directly inspired by his philosophy,

Alētheia is defined as what is "simple," as opposed to what is "double," ambiguous, "two-headed."[123]

In one final respect, there are noticeable affinities between Epimenides and Parmenides in that, like the world of the philosophicoreligious sects, Parmenides' world entails choice. The pronouncement of the goddess in the *Proem* is clear: there is the way of *Alētheia* and that of *Doxai*. The choice is between *Alētheia* and *Apatē*. However, in contrast to the preceding list of affinities, this similarity confirms the break between the logic of mythical thought and rational thought.

However, there are also differences between Epimenides, who sees *Alētheia*, and the philosopher, who speaks the truth. One crucial difference indicates a turning point in the meaning of truth. For the man who knows, the one who is elect and privileged with memory, Oblivion is evil, pure negativity; there is a gap between *Alētheia* and *Lēthē*. By contrast, although in a whole number of respects Parmenides is one of those who know, he nevertheless devotes at least half his poem to *Apatē* and the *Doxai* of mortal men.[124] When one possesses Being, why speak of what is not *Alētheia*? Because between the time of Epimenides and Parmenides the social context had changed. The magus had lived apart from the *polis*, on the periphery of society, but the philosopher, by contrast, was subject to the urban regime and therefore to the demands of publicity. He was obliged to leave the sanctuary of revelation: the gods gave him *Alētheia*, but at the same time, his truth was open to challenge if not to verification.[125] Parmenides takes account of *Doxai*, discoursing on "words of deception." Faced with *Alētheia* and based on Being, *Apatē* displays its powers: it establishes a level of reality where *parphasis* reigns and where Day is mixed with Night.[126] This is the world of the plurality of *Doxai*, the world Parmenides describes when speaking of men who have sought to name two things when even naming one did not seem necessary to them. Here, thought is ruled by contradiction, but contraries are introduced simultaneously in language.[127] Thus, *Apatē* is no longer pure negativity; here, light is intermingled with the Night. The scene could almost be described as simultaneously *alēthēs* and *pseudēs*. The philosopher can discover traces of *Alētheia* even at the heart of the "deceptive" world. Accordingly, choice no longer carries the same meaning as it did for the philosophicoreligious sects. Whereas, for them, *Alētheia* was absolutely opposed to *Lēthē* and *Apatē*, in Parmenides' system this choice is no longer exclusive but may be modified according to the needs of the discussion. The radical opposition is now between Being and Non-Being, not between *Alētheia* and *Apatē*.[128]

Parmenides' *Alētheia* provides the best expression of the ambiguity of first philosophy, which offers the public a knowledge simultaneously declared to be inaccessible to most.[129] Parmenides' *Alētheia*, truth pronounced by a type of man connected in some way to the lineage of the masters of truth, is also the first kind of truth in ancient Greece that is open to rational challenge. It is the first version of objective truth, a truth established in and through dialogue.[130]

CHAPTER SEVEN

Ambiguity and Contradiction

Alētheia is a crucial player in the transition from mythical thought to rational thought. As both a religious power and a philosophical concept, *Alētheia* not only introduces a radical break between religious thought and philosophical thought but also establishes certain affinities between the two. The affinities are found in two domains: where particular types of men are involved and where frameworks of thought are concerned. From the king of justice to the most abstract philosophers, truth remained the prerogative of particular types of men. In archaic Greece, it was an attribute of certain special functions, just as flippers or wings are attributes of particular natural species.[1] Inspired poets, diviners, and kings of justice were automatically masters of truth. As soon as the philosopher entered the scene, he took over from such figures. Like them, in the wake of the magi and ecstatic individuals, the philosopher claimed the ability to attain and reveal a truth that was at once the "homologue and the antithesis" of religious truth.[2]

Furthermore, while in many respects philosophy was directly opposed to traditional religious ideas, it could also be seen from the perspective of the problems it tackled as the heir to religious thought. Jean-Pierre Vernant has observed that "the physical thought of the Milesians evolved within the framework of the major oppositions established by the religious thought of the Greeks between a whole series of antinomic terms: the gods–men, the invisible–the visible, immortals–mortals, the permanent–the changing, the powerful–the impotent, the pure–the mixed, the assured–the uncertain."[3] We have detected a necessary connection between, on the one hand, the religious powers *Alētheia* and *Peithō* and, on the other, the double and parallel problems of the efficacy of speech on others and the relationship between speech and reality. Here, too, rational inquiry, whether as pursued by philosophy or sophistry, developed within a framework defined by religious thought.

In certain aspects, *Alētheia* is positioned at the very heart of rational thought, where it constitutes one of the terms most clearly affirming a line of continuity between religion and philosophy. But in other respects, it simultaneously constitutes one of the clearest indications of the fundamental break between rational and religious thought. Along with other powers *Alētheia* maintains certain necessary relations that determine the nature of its own meanings. The most fundamental of these is the solidarity between *Alētheia* and *Lēthē*, for they form a pair of contraries that are both antithetical and complementary. All these levels of thought are characterized by ambiguity, the interplay between truthfulness and falsehood. Truth is tinged with deception; what is true never fully negates what is false. In contrast, it is contradiction that structures the thought of the philosophicoreligious sects: in the dichotomic world of the magi, "truthfulness" rules out deceit. With Parmenides, *Alētheia* merges even with the imperious demand for noncontradiction. It is thus through *Alētheia* that we can best gauge the gap between two systems of thought, one of which obeys a logic of ambiguity, the other a logic of contradiction.

In a history of clashes, subject at times to the continuous, at other times to the discontinuous, change never occurs through the dynamism of the system itself. For the religious *Alētheia* to become a rational concept, a phenomenon of major importance had to take place. This was the secularization of speech, which was undeniably affected in turn by the evolution of new social relations and unprecedented political structures. For the insistence on noncontradiction to make itself felt and be formulated, the weight of another major social development was no doubt necessary: the establishment, in legal and political practice, of the presentation of two contrary theses, two possibilities between which it was necessary to choose.[4]

Notes

Please note that the following translations of classical texts have been used: Aeschylus, *Agamemnon*, trans. Richmond Lattimore (Chicago: University of Chicago Press, 1953); *Eumenides*, trans. Richmond Lattimore (Chicago: University of Chicago Press, 1953); *The Suppliant Maidens*, trans. Seth Benardete (Chicago: University of Chicago Press, 1953); Apollonius of Rhodes, *Voyage of the Argo*, trans. E.V. Rieu (Harmondsworth, UK: Penguin, 1959); Aristotle, *The Basic Works of Aristotle* (New York: Random House, 1941), *Topics*, trans. E.S. Forster (London and Cambridge, MA: Loeb Classical Library, 1965); Euripides, *The Suppliant Women*, trans. Frank William Jones (Chicago: University of Chicago Press, 1958); Herodotus, *The Persian Wars*, trans. George Rawlinson (New York: Modern Library, 1942); Hesiod, *Homeric Hymn to Hermes*, trans. Hugh G. Evelyn-White (London and Cambridge, MA: Loeb Classical Library, 1967), *Works and Days, Theogony, Shield of Herakles*, trans. Richmond Lattimore (Ann Arbor: University of Michigan Press, 1959); Homer, *Iliad*, trans. Richmond Lattimore (Chicago: University of Chicago Press, 1951), *Odyssey*, trans. Richmond Lattimore (New York: Harper & Row, 1965); Pindar, *Victory Songs*, trans. Frank Nisetich (Baltimore, Johns Hopkins University Press, 1980); Plato, *The Collected Dialogues of Plato*, E. Hamilton and H. Caims, eds. (Princeton, NJ: Princeton University Press, 1961); Plutarch, *Moralia*, trans. Frank Cole Babbit (London and Cambridge, MA: Loeb Classical Library, 1969); Sophocles, *Oedipus the King*, trans. David Grene (Chicago: University of Chicago Press, 1954); Theocritus, *Idylls*, trans. A.S.F. Gow (Cambridge, UK: Cambridge University Press, 1950); Xenophon, *Anabasis*, trans. Carleton L. Brownson (London and Cambridge, MA: Loeb Classical Library, 1968).

FOREWORD

1. I use the expression *classical city* for the sake of convenience. However, the earliest testimonials to the change Detienne analyzes by far predate Periclean classicism.

2. Jean-Pierre Vernant (ed.), *Problèmes de la guerre en Grèce ancienne*, Bibliothèque de l'Ecole Pratique des Hautes Etudes (VIth Section) (The Hague: Mouton, 1968).

PREFACE TO THE AMERICAN EDITION

1. In chronological order, "Homère, Hésiode et Pythagore: Poésie et philosophie dans le pythagorisme ancien," *Collection Latomus*, vol. 57 (Brussels, 1962); "De la pensée religieuse à la pensée philosophique: La notion de *Daimôn* dans le pythagorisme ancien," *Bibliothèque de la Faculté de Philosophie et Lettres de l'Université de Liège*, vol. 165 (Paris, 1963); "Crise agraire et attitude religieuse chez Hésiode," *Collection Latomus*, vol. 68 (Brussels, 1963).

2. "La Notion mythique d'*Alètheia*," *Revue des études grecques* 73 (1960).

3. Michel Foucault, *The Discourse on Language*, in *The Archaeology of Knowledge* (New York: Pantheon, 1972), p. 218.

4. Hesiod, *Theogony* 27-28, trans. Richmond Lattimore (Ann Arbor: University of Michigan Press, 1959).

5. Louis Gernet, "Les Origines de la philosophie," *Bulletin de l'enseignement public du Maroc* 183 (1945).

6. These "founding heroes" were Ignace Meyerson, with his "historical and comparative" psychology (the only truly Marxist psychology, as he and his most loyal disciples claimed), Louis Gernet, and Jean-Pierre Vernant (possibly somewhat despite Gernet). I will consider elsewhere the "service" performed at that time by Riccardo Di Donato and its reception.

7. Marcel Detienne, Louis Gernet, Jean-Pierre Vernant (eds.), *The Anthropology of Ancient Greece*, trans. John Hamilton and Blaise Nagy (Baltimore: Johns Hopkins University Press, 1981), p. 353.

8. See in particular ch. 11, "The Structural Study of Myth," *Structural Anthropology* (New York: Basic Books, 1963).

9. This work is currently in progress as part of the program of the research group "Histoire et Anthropologie: approches comparatives" at Ecole Pratique des Hautes Etudes/Centre National de la Recherche Scientifique, Université de Paris, and Johns Hopkins University.

10. For an analysis of the current state of studies on this subject, see *Annuaire de l'Ecole Pratique des Hautes Etudes* 99 (1990-91), pp. 243-46.

11. Foucault, *The Discourse on Language*, pp. 218-20.

12. Hesiod, *Theogony* 27-28 (*ethelein*); *Homeric Hymn to Hermes* 558-63

(*ethelein*).

13. The formula used by the herald is found in Euripides, *The Suppliant Women* 438–39 (*thelein*), trans. Frank William Jones (Chicago: University of Chicago Press, 1958); concerning the formula inscribed on stones designed to be legible and visible (*boulesthai*), see Marcel Detienne, "L'Ecriture et ses nouveaux objets intellectuels en Grèce," in Marcel Detienne (ed.), *Les Savoirs de l'écriture en Grèce ancienne*, 2nd ed. (Lille: Presses Universitaires de Lille, 1992 [1988]), p. 41.

14. Marcel Detienne, "La Phalange: problèmes et controverses," in Jean-Pierre Vernant (ed.), *Problèmes de la guerre en Grèce ancienne*, 2nd ed. (Paris: Editions de l'Ecole des Hautes Etudes en Sciences Sociales, 1958).

15. See the historian of France in the role of "priest of the nation," as he appears in Pierre Nora's part-historical, part-narcissistic work, *Les Lieux de mémoire*, 7 vols. (Paris: Gallimard, 1984–92). See, in particular, *Débat* 78 (1994) in which a comparison with other European nations prompts Nora to suggest that France possesses a historical predisposition to memory. In France, a nation given to commemoration, any comparative approach that would first insist on a critical analysis of the "categories" involved is derailed. The most pertinent remarks about this "very French" enterprise have come from outside, either from the United States or from a sociological perspective: Jean-Paul Willaime, "'Lieux de Mémoire' et imaginaire national," *Archives des sciences sociales des religions* 66.1 (1988); Steven Englund, "De l'Usage du mot 'nation' par les historiens et réciproquement," *Le Monde diplomatique* (March 1988), pp. 28–29.

16. Among other programmatical and polemical writings, I would single out Jean Bollack, "Réflexions sur la pratique philologique," *Informations sur les sciences sociales* 66.3–4 (1976).

17. I have in mind Pierre Judet de la Combe, who welcomed the collective work *Les Savoirs de l'écriture en Grèce ancienne*, which I edited. I am even more grateful to him because, at about the same time – between 1984 and 1988 – I presented my ideas on "The Gods of Writing" at the Townsend Lectures (February–April 1987) at Cornell University, to an audience convinced, apparently on the basis of strong arguments, that the only "god of writing" was Jacques Derrida, a fact that rendered null and void the ideas of Palamedes, the Egyptian accounts of Toth, and the Orphics' pronouncements on letters, the *grammata*. In a book I intend to write one day, I will also try to understand why the stories of "Mr. Palamedes" seemed so ridiculous to an audience that had been treated to revelations from the High Priest of Writing. I have presented an initial sketch of the mythical and intellectual representations of inventive writing in two chapters of *L'Ecriture d'Orphée* (Paris: Gallimard, 1989), pp. 101–30.

18. "Rencontre internationale Hésiode: Philologie, Anthropologie, Philo-

sophie" (October 12-14, 1989). (To be published as *Hésiode* [Paris: Editions du Cerf, 1995], including essays by Fabienne Blaise, Pierre Judet de la Combe, and Philippe Rousseau.)

19. This range is detectable in Bollack, "Réflexions," pp. 379-80, which refers to the explanations of "essayists of the structuralist schools" that appeal to "the system of representation and mental and psychological structures." He criticizes them for not being interested in the "unique meaning" of a work and for throwing light on works "by means of borrowing directly from social reality." A vague reference to "the influence of ethnology and anthropology" rules out any reflection on procedures for analyzing the narratives of "mythology" within the field of a *Greek* ethnographical context (cf. Marcel Detienne, Afterword, "Revisiting the Gardens of Adonis," *The Gardens of Adonis*, trans. Janet Lloyd [Princeton, NJ: Princeton University Press, 1994]).

20. Three mimeographed texts mark the development of Heinz Wismann's approach (Bollack's seminar of Jean Bollack [1976]; document for the Hesiod colloquium [1989]; "Propositions pour une lecture d'Hésiode" [1993]). I henceforth refer to them by their years.

21. Wismann, 1993, p. 3.

22. André Laks and Ada Neschke (eds.), *La Naissance du paradigme herméneutique (Schleiermacher, Humboldt, Boeckh, Droysen)* (Lille: Presses Universitaires de Lille, 1991).

23. *Ibid.*, p. 379.

24. Andrew Ford, *The Poetry of the Past* (Ithaca, NY: Cornell University Press, 1992), draws attention to the complexity of epic poetics.

25. Wismann, 1989, p. 5.

26. Wismann, 1976, p. 5, used the expression "immediate transparency of the meaning." He also defined the *alēthea* as "the level of true comprehension" (1989, p. 6) or as "the symbolism of the structure" (1989, p. 7), "the structures that the narrative's self-consciousness makes it possible to grasp" (structural muses?). In the 1993 version, p. 7, the only thing remaining is the work (*Theogony*), deploying "true meanings that philosophy will continue to work upon in order to derive its systems from it."

27. *Homeric Hymn to Hermes* 558-63, trans. Hugh G. Evelyn-White (Cambridge, MA: Loeb Classical Library, 1967).

28. A philologist can be recognized from afar by his stretched-out neck, slightly twisted as a result of his looking back, upstream, toward the works of the past or earlier authors; with the past before him, he walks backward.

29. *Iliad* 1.70.

30. Between 1976 and 1993, the horizon of thought involving "Truth-Memory-Oblivion" that emerged from my 1965 studies received no attention,

whereas flat, basic philology (e.g., Hans Joachim Mette and Tilman Krischer) was deemed worthy of discussion. Such tactics are not unconnected with the strategy of "the philologist's profession."

31. Wismann, 1989, p. 6. In 1993, p. 6, he was content simply to allude "to the regulating principle of memory," *Mnēmosynē*, which is thus taken simply as the antonym of *Lēthē*, from which *Alētheia* is derived with a privative α. In his "Autorité et auteur dans la *Théogonie* hésiodique" (*Hésiode*, n.18 above), Gregory Nagy produced a critique of the interpretation suggested by Thomas Cole, "Archaic Truth," *Quaderni urbinati di cultura classica* 13 (1983). While emphasizing again the essential relations between "memory" and "truth" in poetic thought (p. 35), Nagy tries to show that Hesiod's expression *alēthea gērusasthai* is meant to refer to a whole corpus of panhellenic myths felt to be radically different from the local versions that are invariably at odds with one another.

32. Wismann, 1989, p. 10.

33. Hesiod, *Theogony* 4, 31, followed at 1.32 by "the power" – for Hesiod, inspired by them – "to sing the story of things of the future, and things past," i.e., in the same fashion as the diviner, with mantic speech (at 31 *thespis* is found alongside *aoidē*), trans. Richmond Lattimore (Ann Arbor: University of Michigan Press, 1959).

34. These powers include the power of the Muses, the power of speech. As early as 1965, Greek scholars such as Nagy and Segal recognized that, as powers of sung speech, the Muses, whose remarkable names constitute a theology of articulated song, represent an essential aspect of self-conscious reflection on speech and language. Hermeneutics – at least in the case of Wismann, 1989, p. 8 – seems to discover this unaffected by any evidence other than that found in the literal meaning.

35. Hesiod, *Theogony* 211–32; *Thanatos* and *Hypnos* at 212; *Mōmos*, blame, at 215; *Apatē*, deception, at 224; *Pseudeis Logoi*, words of deception, at 229. As I have pointed out, Hermes reigns over *Pseudea* as well as *haimulioi logoi*, which directly affects both Pandora and the fact that speech is shared by men and the gods.

36. Hesiod, *Theogony* 233–36.

37. See Gregory Nagy, *The Best of the Achaeans* (Baltimore: Johns Hopkins University Press, 1979), and *Pindar's Homer: The Lyric Possession of an Epic Past* (Baltimore: Johns Hopkins University Press, 1990).

38. The Derveni Papyrus was discovered in 1962, announced by Styliano G. Kapsomenos in 1964, and "edited" by M.L. West (*Zeitschrift für Papyrologie und Epigraphik* 47 [1982]) in anticipation of the delayed publication by the discoverers themselves. It was the subject of a 1993 colloquium at Princeton University (the proceedings of which are forthcoming).

39. G. Pugliese-Carratelli, *La Parola del passato* 29 (1974); Kyriekos Tsantsonoglou and George Michael Parassoglou, "Two Gold Lamellae from Thessaly," *Hellenika* 38 (1987).

40. See F. Graf, "Textes orphiques et rituel bacchique: propos des lamelles de Pélinna," in Phillipe Borgeaud (ed.), *Orphisme et Orphée* (Geneva: Droz, 1991). On the specificity of the choice of writing and books in the Orphic movement, see Marcel Detienne, *L'Ecriture d'Orphée* (Paris: Gallimard, 1989), pp. 101-32.

41. M.L. West, "The Orphics of Olbia," *Zeitschrift für Papyrologie und Epigraphik* 45 (1982).

42. A good guide to the paths taken by *Alētheia*, as seen by Heidegger, is Marlène Zarader, *Heidegger et les paroles de l'origine*, 2nd ed. (Paris: Vrin, 1990), pp. 49-82.

43. See André Doz, "Heidegger, Aristote et le thème de la vérité," *Revue de philosophie ancienne* 1 (1990), in particular p. 96.

44. See *ibid.*, p. 76.

45. See Martin Heidegger, *Introduction to Metaphysics*, trans. Ralph Manheim (New Haven, CT: Yale University Press, 1959); see also Heidegger, *Gesamtausgabe*, vol. 53 (1984), p. 100; cf. pp. 98-99. Heidegger's interpreters tell us that it is not just a matter of the way a word is put together or linguistic motivations. Heidegger attempted to illuminate what the Greeks themselves did not understand: e.g., "concealment totally rules the essence of being"; *Alētheia* is an "enigma," where the veiling and unveiling of Being meet. An unveiling of veiling? Why not? Clarifying and flushing out? But all this is a matter for Heidegger and his *own* poetic and philosophic reflection on being. The Greeks are simply used as hostages. However, if one believes that Heidegger tries to clarify "the basis for what they said and thought," as Zarader, p. 82, does, this interpretation, like all others, ought to come to terms with objections, recognize its mistakes, and discuss arguments coming from other horizons. There can be no masters of truth where there is no demonstration in the "geometric" manner.

46. Heidegger goes even further, claiming that neither Plato nor Aristotle thought out the essence of the *polis* (*Gesamtausgabe* 53 [1984], p. 99). Who is correct? His followers are on the run and still running.

47. An open discussion supported by textual evidence may be found in Dominique Janicaud, *L'Ombre de cette pensée: Heidegger et la question politique* (Grenoble: Millon, 1990). I have reviewed it in both France and Italy; see Marcel Detienne, "Pour une anthropologie avec les Grecs," in André Bonnard (ed.), *Civilisation grecque*, vol. 1, 2nd ed. (Brussels: Editions Complexe, 1991). All these publications have been greeted with impenetrable silence. I am returning to this and will continue to do so in connection with the project sketched out in "Pour une anthropologie."

48. I refer to Janicaud, *L'Ombre de cette pensée*.

49. Arnaldo Momigliano, *Rivista storica italiana* 94 (1982) (= *Ottavo contributo alla storia degli studi classici e del mondo antico* [Rome, 1987]).

50. Marcel Detienne, *The Creation of Mythology*, trans. Margaret Cook (Chicago: University of Chicago Press, 1986). Momigliano was not alone in misunderstanding this.

51. See Detienne, *Gardens of Adonis*.

52. "La Mythologie grecque change de sens," an interview with Jean-Pierre Vernant by Henri de Saint Blanquat, *Sciences et avenir* (January 1982), pp. 105–10.

53. This had not been exactly the case when, in 1974–75, at the ex-sixth section, I embarked on a historiographical and critical analysis of ancient and contemporary representations of "myth" and "mythology."

54. Louis Gernet, *The Anthropology of Ancient Greece* (Baltimore: Johns Hopkins University Press, 1981), pp. 96, 102, 104, 150; Ernst Cassirer, *Philosophy of Symbolic Form*. Vol. 2: *Mythological Thought* (New Haven, CT: Yale University Press, 1953).

55. See Jean-Pierre Vernant, *Myth and Thought among the Greeks* (London: Methuen, 1983), in particular the chapter "From Myth to Reason."

56. The comparison emerged from Lévi-Strauss's 1970 seminar and was published as "La Cuisine de Pythagore," *Archives de sociologie des religions* 29 (1970). I used these methods for more than three years (Ecole Pratique des Hautes Etudes, sixth section, 1969–72) in connection with bees, honey, Orion, and Orpheus, although I have not yet published any of this work except "Orphée au miel," in Jacques Le Goff and Pierre Nora (eds.), *Faire de l'histoire*, vol. 3 (Paris, 1974). I have sketched this "new meaning" in the afterword to *The Gardens of Adonis*, and "Mito" (in *Enciclopedia delle scienze sociali* [Rome: Istituto della Enciclopedia, 1995]).

57. See the seminars on *Thémis* summarized in the *Annuaire de l'Ecole Pratique des Hautes Etudes: Sciences religieuses* 49 (1990–91).

58. On the "psychological function," see Ignace Meyerson, *Journal de psychologie normale et pathologique* 66 (1969).

59. For two approaches to Parmenides, fr. 7.5–6, see David Furley, "Truth as What Survives the *Elenchos*: An Idea of Parmenides," in Pamela Huby and Gordon Neal (eds.), *The Criterion of Truth* (Liverpool: Liverpool University Press, 1989); Nestor Luis Cordero, "La Déesse de la raison en Grèce," in Jean-François Mattéi (ed.), *La Naissance de la raison en Grèce* (Paris: Presses Universitaires de France, 1990), pp. 207–14.

60. See Marcel Detienne (ed.), *Transcrire les mythologies* (Paris: Albin Michel, 1994), in particular "Ouverture" and "Manières grecques de commencer."

61. Maurice Caveing, "La Laïcisation de la parole et l'exigence rationnelle,"

Raison présente (January 1969), pp. 85–98.

62. I am thinking here of pp. 100–101 in *ibid.*, at the end of the chapter "Le Procès de laïcisation."

63. In my inquiry into writing and its new intellectual subjects, I stressed this point: even if writing down laws shaped the public space and the field of politics, it was the intellectuals – philosophers, doctors, and geometrical astronomers – who used writing to invent unprecedented subjects that opened up the intellect to new paths of exploration; see Marcel Detienne, "L'Ecriture et ses nouveaux objets intellectuels en Grèce," in Marcel Detienne (ed.), *Les Savoirs de l'écriture en Grèce ancienne*, 3rd edition (Lille: Presses Universitaires de Lille, 1994). I return briefly to this point in "Ouverture," in Marcel Detienne (ed.), *Transcrire les mythologies: Tradition, écriture, historicité* (Paris: Albin Michel, 1994).

64. Geoffrey Lloyd, *Demystifying Mentalities* (Cambridge: Cambridge University Press, 1990), is an original and rich comparison of different models of reasoning, taking as its starting point an important inquiry into types of proof, verification, and argumentation between rival types of knowledge.

CHAPTER ONE: TRUTH AND SOCIETY

1. See Henri van Lier, *Le Nouvel âge* (Paris: Casterman, 1962).

2. See Victor Brochard, *De l'Erreur*, 3rd ed. (Paris: Alcan, 1926). Here I am simply dealing with the commonsensical notion of truth. Clearly, such a representation does not coincide with the many other kinds of modern "truths" (those of physicists, mathematicians, economists, historians, etc.).

3. "Implicitly or explicitly, it is accepted that categories of the mind as presented by common sense or as elaborated by philosophers and psychologists have always existed, are in some way consubstantial with man, and have undergone no change, whereas material life, social life, knowledge, and intellectual life in general have been constantly changing." Ignace Meyerson, *Les Fonctions psychologiques et les oeuvres* (Paris: Vrin, 1948), p. 120.

4. See the analysis by Jacques Duchesne-Guillemin, *Zoroastre: Etude critique* (Paris: G.P. Maisonneuve, 1948), pp. 58–68, and *La Religion de l'Iran ancien* (Paris: Presses Universaires de France, 1962), pp. 193–96. On the concept of truth in India as an appropriate formula and a means of acting on things, see Paul Masson-Oursel, *L'Inde et la civilisation indienne* (Paris: La Renaissance du Livre, 1933), pp. 144–47; and the remarks on *satya* made by Jean Varenne, in his edition of the *Mahā Nārāyana Upanishad*, vol. 2 (Paris: Editions de Boccard, 1960), pp. 30–31. Georges Dumézil, *Servius et la fortune* (Paris: Gallimard, 1943), p. 241, points out that qualitative appreciation and truth are linked in India. The problem of truth in the Indo-European world has been the subject of a number of studies; see, e.g., V. Pisani, "Parole indo-europe pro 'vero' e 'falso,' "

Rivista Indo-Greca-Italica di filologia (1936), following Hjalmar Frisk, "'Warheit' and 'Lüge' in den indogermanischen Sprachen. Einige morphologische Beobachtungen," *Högskolas Årsskrift 41* (1935). On *ṛta* and its relations with words stemming from the same Indo-European root (*ōrdō, ritus,* ἀριθμός, ἀρμονία, ἀρετή, etc., in which the notion of *adjustment* predominates) as well as with related Indian concepts (*dhāman-, dharman-, Varta-*), see the remarks of Huguette Fugier, *Recherches sur l'expression du sacré dans la langue latine* (Paris: Editions les Belles Lettres, 1963).

5. On this thought, see, e.g., Jean André Wahl, *La Pensée de l'existence* (Paris: Flammarion, 1951), pp. 239–88; Alphonse de Waelhens, *Phénoménologie et Vérité: Essai sur l'évolution de l'idée de Vérité chez Husserl et Heidegger* (Paris: Beatrice-Nauwelaerts, 1953).

6. A few words are necessary here concerning Wilhelm Luther's *"Wahrheit" und "Lüge" im ältesten Griechentum* (Leipzig: Noske, 1935). The conclusions of this work are repeated in his *Weltansicht und Geistesleben* (Göttingen: Vandenhoeck & Ruprecht, 1954), and, with a few modifications, in "Der frühgriechische Wahrheitsgedanke im Lichte der Sprachen," *Gymnasium* 65 (1958). Luther's study claims to be simply an objective chronology. He apparently assumes that all he should do is give the meanings of words, which he takes to be whatever is most conscious for his subjects and most superficial for the observer. This entire early study is deeply ambiguous. Even if the most obvious result of Luther's work is to show that Greek "truth" is not the same as ours, he persists throughout in belaboring one particular, trivial, and rhetorical concept of truth, using it as the starting point for determining which Greek expressions and words refer to truth. But rather than begin from what is *signified*, collecting words that seem to convey the same meaning, he should have instead started from the signifier, i.e., ἀλήθεια, to see how the "semantic field" of the word was organized from one specific period to another (see Arnaldo Momigliano's review of Luther's book in *Rivista di filologia e d'istruzione classica* 15 [1937]).

For my present study, a particular course seemed appropriate: determining the main lines of the lexical system and distinguishing relationships of opposition and association – in short, applying the methods of structural lexicology and testing the possibilities of the theory of a "semantic field" in archaic Greece (see Georges Matoré, *La Méthode en lexicologie: Domaine français* [Paris: M. Didier, 1973]; and the remarkable thesis by Jean Dubois, *Le Vocabulaire politique et social en France de 1869 à 1871: A Travers les oeuvres des écrivains, les revues et les journaux* [Paris: Librarie Larousse, 1962]. On structural semantics, see the work and remarks of Stephen Ullmann, *The Principles of Semantics: A Linguistic Approach to Meaning* [Oxford: Basil Blackwell, 1959]; and Walther von Wartburg, *Problèmes et méthodes de la linguistique*, trans. Pierre Maïllard [Paris: Presses

Universitaires de France, 1963], ch. 3). However, there were serious difficulties with this method. A study of structural lexicology must be exhaustive to be useful, i.e., it must be based on a lexical system in its totality. Furthermore, the inquiry should focus on a *very short* time span, since the associations and oppositions between the various elements are constantly changing (in *Le Vocabulaire politique*, Jean Dubois limits his inquiry to a period of three years). However, as is well known, our knowledge of the Greek archaic period, which covers at least two centuries, is as full of gaps as a papyrus eaten away by time.

7. See p. 123 above.

8. My present study is clearly defined and delimited (see n.6 above). However, it represents only one historical line of inquiry and certainly does not exhaust the entire subject of Greek "truth." I have deliberately not included a whole series of aspects and levels of *Alētheia* and refer the reader to Luther, *Wahrheit und Lüge*; Heribert Boeder, "Der frühgriechische Wortgebrauch von Logos und Aletheia," *Archiv für Begriffsgeschichte* 6 (1959); and Ernst Heitsch, "Die nichtphilosophische ἀλήθεια," *Hermes* 90 (1962), and "Wahrheit als Erinnerung," *Hermes* 91 (1963).

9. I will speak not of truth in general, but of the notion described by *Alētheia*. Truth is clearly not a simple idea. Gaston Bachelard, *The New Scientific Spirit*, trans. Arthur Guldhammer (Boston: Beacon, 1984), has correctly observed: "And there is no such thing as a simple idea, for...no idea can be understood, until it has been incorporated into a complex system of thoughts and experiences," (p. 148).

The expression *mythical thought* needs a word of explanation. Compared with the archaic civilizations studied by Americanists or Africanists, Greece is poor in "mythical thought." Apart from Hesiod, Greek civilization presents us only with bursts of myth, preserved in *scholia* of late date or antiquarian accounts and reused by students of myth in scholarly reconstructions. But what about Hesiod himself? Can it really be claimed that the *Theogony* is the product of mythopoetic creation analogous to that of the Bambara and the Bororo? As has been frequently pointed out, Hesiodic thought represents, rather, *one level* of mythical thought, between religion and philosophy. (There is no such thing as a *single* kind of mythical thought, as has been pointed out on several occasions; see Luc de Heusch, "Situation et position de l'anthropologie structurale," in *L'Arc* 26 [1965], p. 12). Mythical thought is always specific, and addressed to its own particular problems (see the comments of Jean-Pierre Vernant in his review of Clemence Ramnoux's *La Nuit et les enfants de la nuit*, published in *Journal de psychologie normale et pathologique* [1960]). Under these circumstances, to speak of "mythical thought" runs the risk of extrapolating. These reservations notwithstanding, however, Hesiod remains the principal source of evidence for certain modes of organization and a particular type of logic characteristic of religious thought, differentiated from the new forms of thought appearing during the sixth century B.C.

10. On this crucial problem of change, see Meyerson, *Les Fonctions psychologiques*, and his important articles, particularly "Discontinuités et cheminements autonomes dans l'histoire de l'esprit," *Journal de psychologie normale et pathologique* (1948), "Thèmes nouveaux de psychologie objective: l'histoire, la construction, la structure," *Journal de psychologie normale et pathologique* (1954), and "Problèmes d'histoire psychologique des oeuvres: spécificité, variation, expérience," in *Mélanges Lucien Febvre* (Paris: A. Colin, 1953). On problems of change and structure, see the remarks of Claude Lévi-Strauss, "Les Limites de la notion de structure en ethnologie," in *Sens et usages du terme structure* (The Hague: Mouton, 1962); and the reflections of Jean Piaget, "Genèse et structure en psychologie de l'intelligence," in *Entretiens sur les notions de "genèse" et de "structure"* (The Hague: Mouton, 1964).

11. I would like to express my admiration for the exemplary work of Louis Gernet and to note the importance of his splendid studies, e.g., "Droit et prédroit en Grèce ancienne," *L'Année sociale*, 3rd series (1948-49) (1951). In homage to the memory of this great scholar, I would also add that, in 1960, Gernet recognized what was interesting in the notion of *Alētheia*, when I myself was only beginning to glimpse it (see my brief article "La Notion mythique d'Ἀλήθεια," *Revue des études grecques* 73 [1960]). My greatest debt of gratitude, however, is to Jean-Pierre Vernant. Over three years of "conversation," he has helped me so much and so generously that I fear that I have taken too much from him and am no longer able to disentangle his ideas from my own. I would like to offer him my warmest thanks. Pierre Vidal-Naquet has been a severe but friendly critic. His comments and suggestions have been of great value to me. With very few exceptions, the references to modern publications stop at January 1965. Cf., however (p. 215), an additional, updated bibliography. M. Papathomopoulos (C.N.R.S.) helped me to reread the proofs of this book and through his meticulous care considerably improved the presentation of these pages for the French edition (Paris, 1965).

CHAPTER TWO: THE MEMORY OF THE POET

1. Much has been written on the Muses, their religious significance, and their place in poetic thought. M. Mayer, *s.v. Musai, R.-E.* (1933), c. 680-757, has collected and organized a rich fund of evidence. Karoly Marót, *Die Anfänge der griechischen Literatur, Ungarische Akademie der Wissenschaften* (1960), is also an important study. Other contributions worth mentioning include William W. Minton, "Homer's Invocations of the Muses: Traditional Patterns," *Transactions*

of the Proceedings of the American Philological Association 91 (1962); and Silvio Accame, "L'Invocazione alla Musa e la 'Verità' in Omera e in Esiodo," *Rivista di filologica e di istruzione classica* 91 (1963).

These "past events" certainly do not refer to a "historical past." Homer's heroes are situated in a time of their own, poetic time; see the remarks of Pierre Vidal-Naquet, "Homère et le monde mycénien. A propos d'un livre récent et d'une polémique ancienne," *Annales: Economies, sociétés, civilisations* (1963), esp. pp. 716–17. It should be added, however, that this poetic time is not entirely devoid of "historical" perspective: Max Treu, *Von Homer zur Lyrik* (Munich: Beck, 1955), pp. 33ff., 126ff., has emphasized the importance of ἄνδρες πρότεροι as *models* of the Homeric heroes. See also Moses I. Finley, "Myth, Memory and History: History and Theory," *Studies in the Philosophy of History*, vol. 6 (New York: Harper & Row, 1965), pp. 281 – 302, and "The Trojan War," *Journal of Hellenic Studies* 84 (1964).

2. *Iliad* 2.484ff., trans. Richmond Lattimore (Chicago: University of Chicago Press, 1951). Greek does not distinguish, as we do, between "to recall" and "to mention." Μιμνήσκω always means both (as pointed out by Emile Benveniste, "Formes et sens de μνάομαι," *Sprachgestichte un Wortebdeutung: Festschrift A. Debrunner* [Berne: Francke, 1954]). However, the genealogical – i.e., structural – relationship between the Muse and memory makes it legitimate to stress the sense of "recall" in μνησαίαθ'.

3. In the following pages I aim essentially to define the system of poetic representations (see the excellent collection by Giuliana Lanata, "Poetica pre-platonica: Testimonianze e Frammenti," *Bibliotèca di studi superiori*, vol. 43 [Florence: La Nuova Italia, 1963]), but this can be only an indirect contribution to the sociology of ancient poetry. On this subject, its means, and its limits, see the essay by François Lasserre, "La Condition du poète dans la Grèce antique," *Etudes de lettres* 5 (1962). Bruno Snell, *Poetry and Society: The Role of Poetry in Ancient Greece* (Bloomington: Indiana University Press, 1961), despite its title, is only minimally sociological.

4. See Jean-Pierre Vernant, "Aspects mythiques de la mémoire en Grèce," *Journal de psychologie normale et pathologique* (1959), pp. 1ff., which cites the example of Erōs, Aidōs, Phobos, Pistis, Atē, Lyssa, etc. (reprinted in his *Myth and Thought among the Greeks* [London: Routledge & Kegan Paul, 1983], hereafter *M.T.*).

5. *Homeric Hymn to Hermes* 477: song that relieves unavoidable cares (μοῦσα ἀμηχανέων μελεδώνων); Aeschylus, *Eumenides* 308: a song of horror (μοῦσαν στυγεράν); *The Suppliant Maidens* 695: the pious tones of bards (εὔφημον… μοῦσαν); Pindar, *Nemean* 3.28: to sing for Ajax (μοῖσαν φέρειν), which could equally well be read as Μοῖσαν φέρειν, since the two meanings frequently coex-

ist; Euripides, *Phoenician Women* 50: songs of the Sphinx (μούσας Σφιγγός); *Phoenician Women* 788: to sing an air (μέλπῃ μοῦσαν); Sophocles, *Trachiniae* 643: divine songs of the flute; Plato, *Laws* 829D: nonapproved poetic composition (ἀδόκιμον μοῦσαν) (see also *Republic* 411C, 548B); Euripides, *Alcestis* 962: to cross the field of sung words (διὰ μούσας); Pindar, *Pythian* 5.65: to bestow sung speech or the Muse (δίδωσι μοῖσαν or Μοῖσαν); Euripides, *Ion* 757: modulated speech (μοῦσα); Aristophanes, *Clouds* 313 (μοῦσα αὐλῶν); Euripides, *Antiope*, frag. 184N²; Sophocles, frag. 162N²; Agathon, frag. 2N²; Euripides, *Palamedes*, frag. 588N²; *Palatine Anthology* 5.139, 5.5; Plutarch, *Eroticos*, 759B; *Banquet of the Seven Wise Men* 156D (Muse and *Logos*). On the Laconian Μῶά, a kind of singing mixed with words, see K.M.T. Chrimes, *Ancient Sparta* (Westport, CT: Greenwood Press, 1971). The "atomist" etymology of Μοῦσα has given rise to a number of interpretations, briefly summarized in Alessandro Setti, "La Memoria e il canto: Saggio di poetica arcaïca greca," *Studi italiani di filologia classica* 30 (1958), pp. 129–30 n.1, and in a discussion in Marót, *Die Anfänge der griechischen Literatur.*

6. Philo, *De Plantatione* 30.126, in Paul Wendland (ed.), vol. 2, p. 158. The English here is based on the French translation by Franz Cumont, "Un Mythe pythagoricien chez Posidonius et Philon," *Revue de philologie* 43 (1919), p. 79. See also Pierre Boyancé, "Les Muses et l'harmonie des sphères," *Mélanges dédiés à la mémoire de Félix Grat*, vol. 1 (Paris: En dépot chez Mme Pecqueur-Grat, 1946).

7. As has been noted by, e.g., Bruno Snell, *Die Entdeckung des Geistes: Studien zur entstehung des europaischen Denkens bei den Grieschen* (Hamburg: Classem, 1955), and *Die Welt der Götter bei Hesiod, La notion du divin depuis Homère jusqu'à Platon* (Geneva: Vandoeuvres, 1952).

8. Pausanias, 9.29.2–3. On this tradition, see the study by Bernard Abraham van Groningen, "Les Trois Muses de l'Hélicon," *L'Antiquité classique* (1948), which gives reasons for believing that the tradition of Pausanias predates Aristotle.

9. On the meanings of *Meletē* and the fortunes of this idea in philosophico-religious circles, see Vernant, *M.T.*, pp. 75–106.

10. "In principle, this can only mean rhapsodic performances (for which ἀείδειν is the technical term par excellence) or, in a pinch, monodic song, that is, heroic or didactic epic or lyric in the manner of Anacreon or Sappho" (van Groningen, "Les Trois Muses," p. 290). It is worth noting (as Jules Labarbe points out) that these three types of ancient invocation more or less cover the three aspects of the poetic function – organization, preservation, and creation – in the theory put forward by Sophia-Jacomina Suys-Reitsma, *Het homerische Epos als orale Schepping van een dichterhetairie* (Amsterdam: H.J., 1955). See Jules Labarbe and Albert Severyns, "La Poésie homérique," *La Table ronde* (December 1958).

11. Cicero, *De natura deorum* 3.54, in Pease (ed.), vol. 2 (Cambridge, MA:

Harvard University Press, 1958), pp. 1100–101.

12. See Vernant, *M.T.*, pp. 72–106.

13. See, e.g., Setti, "La Memoria e il canto."

14. The Muses must have been the subject of a cult from very early times in bardic circles, even though both epigraphical evidence (Wilhelm Dittenberger, *Sylloge Inscriptionum Graecarum* [Hildesheim: Olms, 1960] 457.1117) and archaeological evidence (cf. G. Roux, "Le Val des muses et les musées chez les auteurs anciens," *Bulletin de correspondance hellénique* 78 [1954]) is mostly of later date. See the remarks of Fiehn, *s.v. Musai, R.-E.* (1933), c. 696f. On the "cult of the Muses among the Greek philosophers," see the studies of Pierre Boyancé, *Le Culte de muses chez les philosophes grecs* (Paris: Editions de Boccard, 1937).

15. See Hesiod, *Theogony* 54ff., 135, 915ff.; and the texts cited by Samson Eitrem, *s.v. Mnemosyne, R.-E.* (1932), c. 2265ff. Bruno Snell, "Mnemosyne in der frühgriechischen Dichtung," *Archiv für Begriffsgeschichte* 9 (1964), is too concise.

16. Plutarch, *Quaestiones convivales* 9.14.743D. See Ulrich von Wilamowitz, *Der Glaube der Hellenen*, vol. 1 (Berlin: Weidmannsche, 1931), p. 251. On μνεία-μνήμη, see Sophocles, frag. 96N². See *Iliad* 2.492; Pindar, *Nemean* 1.12: Μοῖσα μεμνᾶσθαι φιλεῖ. However, we should also note that the Muses can "make one forget," i.e., deprive the poet of the memory he has acquired, if he proves unworthy (see *Iliad* 2.599–600), just as they can dispense oblivion through their songs (see p. 83).

17. Mnēmosynē is the "queen of the slopes of Eleuthera" (Hesiod, *Theogony* 54; see also the Preface to the Paul Mazon edition [Paris: Editions les Belles Lettres, 1951]). On aspects of its cult, see Eitrem, *s.v. Mnemosyne, R.-E.* (1932), c. 2267–69.

18. Plutarch, *De Pythiane oraculis* 407ff. See *Orphicorum fragmenta* frag. 297c (Otto Kern, ed.) (on the preserving role of memory in the history of civilization) and the texts cited by Francis Vian, *Les Origines de Thèbes: Cadmos et les Spartes* (Paris: Klincksieck, 1963), p. 106. Georges Dumézil, *Mythes et dieux des Germains* (Paris: Editions Leroux, 1939), pp. 5–6, stressed the importance in Indo-European society of priestly bodies responsible for preserving the memory of "an ideal corpus of myths, rituals, and sacred words and expressions."

19. On the problems of the oral tradition, see Jan Vansina, *Oral Tradition: A Study in Historical Methodology* (Chicago: Aldine, 1965); Henri Moniot, "Les Voies de l'histoire de l'Afrique: la tradition orale," *Annales: Economies, sociétés, civilisations* (1964).

20. See James A. Notopoulos, "Mnemosyne in Oral Literature," *Transactions of the American Philological Association* 69 (1938).

21. On formulary problems, see the general remarks on fundamental questions in Jules Labarbe, *L'Homère de Platon* (Liège: Editions les Belles Lettres, 1949);

Hermann Fränkel, *Dichtung und Philosophie des frühen Griechentums* (Munich: Beck, 1962). On the literary problems of oral composition, see the account in Geoffrey Stephen Kirk, *The Songs of Homer* (Cambridge: Cambridge University Press, 1962), who pays particular attention to the theses of Albert Bates Lord, *The Singer of Tales* (Cambridge: Cambridge University Press, 1960).

22. Labarbe, *L'Homère*, p. 16.

23. See Vernant, *M.T.*, pp. 73ff.

24. *Ibid.* I cannot concur with Setti, "La Memoria e il canto," when he speaks of "historical" memory, any more than I can accept the remarks of Accame, "L'Invocazione alla Musa," on what he claims to be the "historical truth" transmitted by poetry. Nor can I agree with the central thesis of those two articles. On a number of mythical aspects of memory in India, see the brief remarks of Mircea Eliade, *Mythologies of Memory and Forgetting: History of Religions* 2 (Chicago: University of Chicago Press, 1963), p. 329.

25. *Iliad* 1.70; Hesiod, *Theogony* 32, 38. On this type of seer-poet, see the classic work of F.M. Cornford, *Principium Sapientiae: The Origins of Greek Philosophical Thought* (Cambridge: Cambridge University Press, 1952).

26. See ch. 4 above on the essential features of this type of speech, shared by poets, diviners, and kings of justice.

27. Theocritus, *Idylls* 16.2, trans. A.S.F. Gow (Cambridge: Cambridge University Press, 1950). This is the double register of poets of the Hesiodic type: Hesiod, *Theogony* 100–101.

28. *Homeric Hymn to Hermes* 425ff., trans. Hugh G. Evelyn-White (London and Cambridge, MA: Loeb Classical Library, 1967). On the meanings of κραίνειν, see ch. 4 above.

29. According to the interpretation produced as early as 1955 by Leonard Robert Palmer, *Achaeans and Indo-Europeans* (Oxford: Oxford University Press, 1955), although it has been criticized by Denys Lionel Page, *History and the Homeric Iliad* (Berkeley: University of California Press, 1963). See Kirk, *The Songs of Homer*; Atsuhiko Yoshida, "Survivances de la tripartition fonctionelle en Grèce," *Revue de l'histoire des religions* (1964).

30. In his contribution to the collective volume Jean-Pierre Vernant (ed.), *Problèmes de la guerre en Grèce ancienne* (The Hague: Mouton, 1968), Michel Lejeune emphasized the exceptional importance of the Sc series of tablets from Knossos, in which about 140 "knights" were supplied with armor, chariots, and horses by the palace administration.

31. On military institutions in the Homeric world, Henri Jeanmaire, *Couroi et courètes: Essai sur l'éducation spartiate et cur les rites d'adolescence dans l'antiquité hellénique* (Lille: Bibliothèque Universitaire, 1939), remains essential reading.

32. An assessment of this problem can be found in Hans Schwabl, *s.v. Welt-*

schöpfung, R.-E. (1962), *Suppl. Band.*, 9, c. 1433f.

33. See Cornford, *Principium Sapientiae.*

34. Jean-Pierre Vernant, *The Origins of Greek Thought* (Ithaca, NY: Cornell University Press, 1982), pp. 108ff.

35. These hypothetical remarks stem from works that, like T.B.L. Webster's, have sought to demonstrate, *on the poetic level*, certain lines of continuity between Mycenae and Homer. Nevertheless, on the whole, M.I. Finley's conclusions on the economic and political break between Mycenae and Homer (*Historia* [1957], pp. 133–59) seem to me mostly well founded.

36. This function disappeared along with the role of sovereignty, one already forgotten by Hesiod. When Pindar, *Pythian* 2.13–14, wrote that poets praise kings for their virtues, this was no more than a variation on the theme of "ἐσθλὸν αἰνεῖν." On the poet as an "official of sovereignty," see the classic remarks of Georges Dumézil, *Servius et la fortune* (Paris: Gallimard, 1943).

37. For many years scholars, such as T.B.L. Webster (*From Mycenae to Homer* [London: Methuen, 1958]) have been hypothesizing the existence of Minoan poetry. A.J. Evans, "The Minoan and Mycenaean Element to Hellenic Life," *Journal of Hellenic Studies* (1912), p. 277, did not hesitate to speak of a Mycenaean poetic tradition. Furthermore, what some scholars have postulated for epic poetry (i.e., for Homer) could just as well be postulated for theogonic poetry (i.e., for Hesiod). We thus cannot totally rule out the possibility of tracing back to the Mycenaean civilization the traditional characteristics of religious poetry and, in particular, the type of magicoreligious speech based on memory. The use of writing in Mycenaean society does not rule out a privileged status for memory. Writing in this society seems to have been the privilege of a class of scribes, probably of Cretan origin, and reserved for administrative purposes. Given its imperfect system of notation, it could not have catered to the demands of publicity or founded a civilization based on writing (see Claire Préaux, "Du Linéaire B créto-mycénien aux ostraca grecs d'Egypte," *Chronique d'Egypte* 34 [1959]).

38. Hesiod, *Theogony* 28.

39. *Ibid.* 32, 38, trans. Richmond Lattimore (Ann Arbor: University of Michigan Press, 1959).

40. Plutarch, *Lycurgus* 8.3–4; 26.6. The poems recited in Sparta were usually devoted to "praise for those who died for Sparta, whose good fortune was proclaimed, and to the criticism of cowards, whose wretched and unhappy lives were described" (Plutarch, *Lycurgus* 21.2: ἔπαινοι and ψόγοι). Praise and blame played an important part in the *Preambles to the Laws* of Charondas and Zaleucos (see Armand Delatte, *Essai sur la politique pythagoricienne* [Liège/Paris: Vaillant-Carmanne/ E. Champion, 1922]), and in Plato's *Laws* (829C–E; 855A; 870A, etc.); in other words, they were important in works favoring archaic and "Doric" influences.

41. The tyranny of visibility in an egalitarian society such as Sparta was much more oppressive than the censure coming from the "mouth of the town" in a number of Oriental monarchies (see J.-R. Kupper, "L'Opinion publique de Mari," *Revue d'assyrologie et d'archeologie orientale* 58 [1964]).

42. Plutarch, *Lycurgus* 14.5.

43. *Ibid.* 25.3 (ἐπαινεῖν and ψέγειν).

44. On the *homoioi*, see the evidence collected by Schulthess, *s.v. Homoioi*, *R.-E.* (1913), c. 2252f.

45. Palusanias, 3.17.5. On marching music, see Plutarch, *Lycurgus* 21.4.

46. Plutarch, *Lycurgus* 21.7; *Apophthegmata laconica* 221A; *De cohibenda ira* 458E.

47. Plutarch, *Instituta laconica* 238C.

48. See Max Greindl, "ΚΛΕΟΣ, ΚΥΔΟΣ, ΕΥΧΟΣ, ΤΙΜΗ, ΦΑΤΙΣ, ΔΟΞΑ." Eine Bedeutungsgeschichtliche Untersuchung des epischen und lyrischen Sprachgebrauchs," Ph.D. thesis, (Lengerichiwa: Lengericher Handelsdruckerei, 1938), and the analyses in Wilhelm Luther, *Weltansicht und Geistesleben* (Göttingen: Vandenhoeck & Ruprecht, 1954).

49. On κῦδος, see Fränkel, *Dichtung und Philosophie*, p. 88 and n. 14.

50. Two examples help to assess the importance of "reputation" in the warrior and aristocratic world. First, in *Iliad* 20.203ff., Aeneas tells Achilles: "You and I know each other's birth, we both know our parents, since we have heard the lines of their fame from mortal men (πρόκλυτ' ἀκούοντες ἔπεα)." Second, in the episode in the *Little Iliad* (Albert Severyns, *Le Cycle épique dans l'école d'Aristarque* [Paris: Editions Champion, 1928], p. 330ff., on frag. 2 Allen), the clash between Odysseus and Ajax over possession of Achilles' arms is decided by the paeon of *praise* produced by the young Trojan women in favor of Odysseus.

51. It is worth remembering the words of Tyrtaeus, frag. 9.1D³: οὔτ' ἂν μνησαίμην οὔτ' ἐν λόγῳ ἄνδρα τιθείην κτλ. With no "memory," there is no *logos*.

52. The warrior strives his entire life for this song of glory, a good memory: "Let me at least not die without a struggle, inglorious, but do some big thing first, that men to come shall know of it" (*Iliad* 22.304–305). Hector's declaration has an exemplary force; see Pindar, *Pythian* 4.185ff. A warrior goes off to war "for fear that the *dēmos* should pour scorn upon his reputation" (Apollonius of Rhodes 1.141, 447). The fear that haunts the Argonauts is that they might die "νώνυμνοι καὶ ἄφαντοι'" (Apollonius Rhodes 4.1306; see 2.892–93).

53. Pindar, *Pythian* 9.95ff.; *Nemean* 9.6–7, trans. Frank J. Nisetich (Baltimore: Johns Hopkins University Press, 1980).

54. Pindar, *Nemean* 1.5–6; 4.93; 5.19; 11.17ff.; *Pythian* 1.43; 2.66–67; *Isthmian* 3.7–8; 5.59; 1.43ff.; etc.

55. Pindar, *Pythian* 3.112–15.

56. Pindar, *Nemean* 4.83–84.

57. Pindar, *Nemean* 7.63; *Pythian* 1.68. On this aspect of speech, see ch. 4 above.

58. See Dumézil, *Servius et la fortune*, pp. 76–77.

59. Pindar, including frag. 59 (Puech, ed.): μῶμον ἔπαινος κίρναται.

60. Pindar, *Pythian* 2.53. The data are collected by Tümpel, *s.v. Mōmos, Roscher's Lexicon*, 2.2 (1894–97), c. 3117. See also Wilhelm Kroll, *s.v. Mōmos, R.-E.* (1933), c. 42.

61. Pindar, *Nemean* 7.61–63.

62. *Mōmos* is called Σκοτεινός according to Pindar, *Nemean* 7.61 (σκοτεινὸς ψόγος is opposed to κλέος ἐτήτυμον αἰνεῖν). Hesiod, *Theogony* 214.

63. Blame and oblivion are linked: Pindar, *Olympian* 2.105ff. However, sometimes silence has extremely positive connotations, as, e.g., in the Bambara culture (cf. Dominique Zahan, *La Dialectique du verbe chez les Bambara* [Paris: Mouton, 1963], pp. 149–66), which simultaneously recognizes its negative aspect. It is worth pointing out that Zahan draws attention in his conclusion to certain similarities between the Bambara culture and "what we know of third century B.C. Greece, particularly in relation to Stoic philosophy." The creative values of silence in the Indo-European world, in particular in India and Rome, have been illuminated by the analyses of Georges Dumézil, "Déesses latines et mythes védiques," *Collection Latomus*, vol. 25 (1956). Claude Lévi-Strauss, *The Raw and the Cooked* (Chicago: University of Chicago Press, 1983), studies silence or mutism as a category of mythical thought paired with noise.

64. According to Plutarch, *De E apud Delphos* 394A, *Lēthē* and *Siōpē* stand in opposition to *Mnēmosynē* and the Muses in the same as is shining (Φοῖβος) stands to what is dark (Σκότιος). *Mnēmosynē* is opposed to *Lēthē* in the "Little Orphic Crater," frag. 297c. Kern. Sophocles, frag. 145N[2] sets the λάθα στυγερά of the Pieridae in opposition to μνᾶστις μελέων.

65. This pair reappears on a number of levels (see below).

66. Bacchylides, 3.13–14 Snell[6]. "Men have a certain saying: hide not in the ground, in silence (μὴ χαμαὶ σιγᾶ καλύψαι) a noble deed accomplished. [What it deserves is the acclaim of] a wonder of song" (Pindar, *Nemean* 9.6–7).

67. Pindar, *Isthmian* 2.43–44; 4.30ff.; 5.56–57; *Olympian* 7.92; *Nemean* 7.12–13 (opposition between Mnēmosynē and σκότος); *Nemean* 9.6–7.

68. Pindar, *Pythian* 6.14ff.; 9.89–90; *Paeans*, frag. 2.66ff. Puech.

69. Pindar, *Olympian* 1.83, 6.92; *Nemean* 7.12–14; 61; *Isthmian* 5.56. See Apollonius of Rhodes 2.892–93.

70. Pindar, *Isthmian* 7.16ff.

71. One is reminded of the power that the Greeks call Ὄσσα (from the root *wek-*, "divine voice"): this is the "noise that comes from Zeus" (*Odyssey* 1.282).

See Henri Fournier, *Les Verbes "dire" en grec ancien* (Paris: C. Klincksieck, 1946), pp. 227ff. On the voice and its meanings in epic, see Charles Mugler, *Les Origines de la science grecque chez Homère: L'homme et l'univers physique* (Paris: Klincksieck, 1963), pp. 82ff.

72. Theocritus, 6.42ff. (Legrand, ed.). On Sappho's μνημοσύνη (frag. 55 Lobel-Page), see Herwig Maehler, *Die Auffassung des Dichterberufs im frühen Griechentum bis zur Seit Pindars* (Göttingen: Vandenhoeck & Ruprecht, 1963), pp. 59-60.

73. Pindar, *Pythian* 5.49. It is the Muses that bestow "memory": Pindar, *Isthmian* 8.63; *Olympian* 6.92; *Nemean* 7.80ff. Of course, human memory also has a role to play, that of registering things and transmitting them.

74. See, e.g., Pindar, *Pythian* 5.46-49; *Isthmian* 8.62-63.

75. Bacchylides, 10.9 frag. Snell[6]. Following others, Franz Cumont, *Recherches sur le symbolisme funéraire des Romains* (Paris: Guenther, 1942), pp. 253ff., has devoted a long analysis to the relations between the Muses and certain forms of immortality.

76. Pindar, *Olympian* 10.3-4.

77. Bacchylides, frag. 57 Snell[6].

78. Bacchylides, 13.202-204 Snell[6]; 5.187 frag. Snell[6].

79. Bacchylides, 5.187 frag. Snell[6].

80. Bacchylides, *Hyporchema* frag. 14 Snell[6].

81. See Pindar, *Olympian* 10.1ff.; *Nemean* 5.17-18; Bacchylides, 5.187 frag. Snell[6].

82. Bacchylides, 8.4-5 Snell[6]. See Euripides, *Iphigeneia in Tauris* 1026: κλεπτῶν γὰρ ἡ νύς, τῆς δ'ἀληθείας τὸ φῶς. On *Alētheia* and light, see Werner Beierwaltes, *Lux intelligibilis: Untersuchung zur Lichtmetaphysik der Griechen* (Munich, 1957), pp. 75ff.

83. Bacchylides 5.188 Snell[6].

84. Pindar, *Olympian* 1.28, 2.101.

85. Pindar, *Nemean* 7.25. See *Nemean* 5.17; *Pythian* 3.103.

86. Hesiod, *Works and Days* 1ff., 661-62.

87. See *Iliad*; Hesiod, *Works and Days* 661-62, trans. Richmond Lattimore (Ann Arbor: University of Michigan, 1959).

88. Hesiod, *Works and Days* 10. On ἐτεός, ἔτυμος, and ἐτήτυμος, see the analysis by Wilhelm Luther, *"Wahrheit" und "Lüge" im ältesten Griechentum* (Leipzig: R. Noske, 1935), pp. 51-61.

89. Hesiod, *Works and Days* 397, 769. This is a more concise version of the analysis developed at greater length in my earlier work "Crise agraire et attitude religieuse chez Hésiode," *Collection Latomus*, vol. 68 (Brussels: Latomus, 1963), pp. 42ff.

90. Hesiod, *Works and Days* 765–68, 818, 824.

91. See the proofs provided in my "Crise agraire et attitude," pp. 44ff.

92. Louis Gernet's pages on the behavior patterns of the nobility are extremely helpful. See "Les Nobles dans la Grèce antique," *Annales d'histoire économique et sociale* (1938).

93. See ch. 5 above.

94. See the rather sketchy analyses of René Schaerer, "*Alētheia*: Héritage antique et vérité d'aujourd'hui," *Actes du XXᵉ Congrès des Sociétés de Philosophie de Langue Française* (1965), whose conclusions I cannot accept.

CHAPTER THREE: THE OLD MAN OF THE SEA

1. On the children of the Night, see Clemence Ramnoux, *La Nuit et les enfants de la nuit dans la tradition grecque* (Paris: Flammarion, 1959). In a paper delivered to the Association des Etudes Grecques, April 1963, Jean-Pierre Vernant suggested an interpretation of Nereus close to my own here, detecting an image of the good king and master of justice behind the Old Man of the Sea. This figure resorts to practices such as ordeals involving scales and lottery procedures based on trials by water (*Revue des études grecques* 76 [1963]). On Nereus, see Martin P. Nilsson, *Geschichte der griechische Religion*, vol. 1 (Munich: Beck, 1955), pp. 240–44; G. Herzog-Hauser, *s.v. Nereus, R.-E.* (1936), c. 24f.

2. Hesiod, *Theogony* 233–36, trans. Richmond Lattimore (Ann Arbor: University of Michigan Press, 1959). According to Reinhold Merkelbach, "Konjekturen zu Hesiod," *Studi italiani di filologia classica* (1956), pp. 289–90, the epithets for Nereus can be explained by an etymological play on words.

3. *Homeric Hymn to Hermes* 368–69.

4. Νημερτής is an epithet peculiar to the Old Man of the Sea (*Odyssey* 4.349, 384, 401; 17.140). It is the name of one of his daughters (*Iliad* 17.46; cf. the Νημερτής of Empedocles, frag. 122 ap. Diels, *Fragmenta Veterorum Stoicorum*[7], vol. 1, p. 361.6, and the remarks of G. Herzog-Hauser, *s.v. Nereiden, R.-E.* (1936), c. 18. Together with ἀψευδής (see n.5 below), ἀληθής, and ἀλήθεια (see below), νημέρτεια is a special term used to qualify an oracle or an infallible diviner (see Sophocles, *Trachiniae* 173); *Homeric Hymn to Apollo* 252–53; Apollonius of Rhodes, *Argonautica* 4.1565; *Odyssey* 9.137). The basic sense is an absence of errors (in this passage of the *Theogony*, it is worth noting the relationship between νημερτής and ἄμάρτη in 1.222), of ἁμάρτημα (see Wilhelm Luther, *"Wahrheit" und "Lüge" im ältesten Griechentum* [Leipzig, 1935], pp. 33ff.; Louis Gernet, *Recherches sur le développement de la pensée juridique et morale en Grèce* [Paris: Editions Leroux, 1917], pp. 305ff.). Errors would no doubt include the fault of "oblivion": "And yet, unlooked for, oblivion comes, a cloud stealing knowledge of the right way from their minds – and so it was with them: they went up but

left the seed of blazing fire behind" (Pindar, *Olympian* 7.45ff., trans. Frank J. Nisetich [Baltimore: Johns Hopkins University Press, 1980]). Compare forgetting a sacrifice (*Iliad* 9.537; Stesichorus, frag. 46/223 Page) and a man such as Epimetheus, who is ἁμαρτίνοος (Hesiod, *Theogony* 512).

There are three notable points about ψευδής in Greek archaic thought. First, the fundamental opposition is not between ψευδής and ἀληθής but between ψευδής and ἀψευδής. Second, ψευδής does not mean "lying." Our concept of lying does not adequately convey the diversity of the Greek vocabulary. Its meaning is closer to "trickery," which covers not only ψεῦδος but also δόλος, μῆτις, and ἀπάτη. Third, as used in archaic Greece, ψευδής conveys two inseparable meanings. Ψευδής means speech that aims to deceive, but since one characteristic of such speech (and generally all ἀπάτη) is that it presents the "appearances" of reality without, however, being reality, it can also mean speech without "fulfillment" devoid of efficacy, never to be realized. This meaning is particularly attested in the image of mantic speech. On the first point, the *Theogony* leaves no room for doubt: the ἀψευδέα of line 233 stands in opposition to the ψευδέας of line 229, just as the ἀληθέα also in line 233 corresponds to the λήθεται of line 236. The relations between ψεῦδος and ψευδής and forms of ἀπάτη appear clearly as early as in the *Theogony*: the Ψευδέας τε Λόγους (line 229) are among the children of Eris, the sister of Ἀπάτη (1.224-25) (Paul Maas, "Zum griechischen Wortschatz," *Mélanges Emile Boisacq*, vol. 2 [Brussels: Université Libre de Bruxelles, 1938], pp. 129-31, has suggested reading Ψεύδεά τε Λόγους ⟨τ᾽⟩ at line 229). Elsewhere, in *Works* 1.78, the ψεύδεα are linked with αἱμύλιοι λόγοι, "engaging words," in the representation of Pandora, who is Zeus's ἀπάτη. Other examples of affinities with the world of trickery are to be found in Theognis, 390 (ψεύδεά τ᾽ἐξαπάτας τ᾽ούλομένας τ᾽ἔριδας); Pindar, *Olympian* 1.28 (ποικίλα ψεύδεα); *Iliad* 21.276 (ψεύδεσσιν ἔθελγεν); *Odyssey* 14.387 (ψεύδεσσι χαρίζεο μήτε τι θέλγε); *Iliad* 2.80-81 (ὄνειρον... ψεῦδος... νοσφιζοίμεθα); Pindar, *Pythian* 2.37 (where the cloud created by Zeus, his δόλος, is a ψεῦδος γλυκύ); Pindar, *Pythian* 3.29-30 (ψευδέων δ᾽ούχ ἅπτεται κλέπτει τέ νιν οὐ θεός); Pindar, *Pythian* 9.43 (ψεῦδος associated with παρφάμεν...). Ἀπάτη is thus the essential phenomenon here, as forcefully demonstrated by what happened to Hector. In *Iliad* 22.226ff. (trans. Richmond Lattimore [Chicago: University of Chicago Press, 1951]), Athena "likened herself in form and weariless voice to Deïphobus" to "persuade" (cf. πεπιθήσω in 1.223) Hector to engage in single combat with Achilles, with Deïphobus's assistance. But when the duel took place and Hector, having lost his spear, called loudly for Deïphobus to come to his aid, "Deïphobus was not near him" and he realized "that it was Athene cheating me" (ἐξαπάτησεν in 1.299). Deïphobus is there but at the same time not there. It was only his εἴδωλον, just as in the case of the εἴδωλον of Patroclus (*Iliad* 23.65ff.). A whole series of closely associated Greek images converge in the notion of trickery: those of πάρφασις, λόγοι ποικίλοι, and λόγοι αἱμύλιοι, but also images reflecting the notion of "bent," "tortuous," or "oblique," e.g., μῦθοι σκολιοί (Hesiod, *Works* 193ff.; Pindar, frag. dub. 90 [Peuch, ed.] σκολιαῖς ἀπάταις; see Luther, *"Wahrheit" und "Lüge,"* pp. 144ff.). Thus, σκολιός is opposed to ἰθύς, εὐθύς, ὀρθός, all that is straight, without deviation, and σκολιός refers to the image of the sickle (ἅρπη) of Cronos, the mythical weapon of μῆτις (Hesiod, *Theogony* 161–62). The image of deviation reappears in expressions such as παρὲξ εἰπεῖν παρακλιδόν, παρατεκταίνεσθαι (Luther, *"Wahrheit" und "Lüge,"* pp. 110–11) and in a negative form in ἀτρεκέως καταλέγειν, ἀγορεύειν, to speak "without deviousness" (Luther, *"Wahrheit" und "Lüge,"* pp. 43–50). (On the relations between ἀπάτη and παρὲξ εἰπεῖν παρακλιδόν, cf. *Odyssesy* 4.348, 17.139.) The domain of error (Ἄτη) is also that of prayers that are limping, squinting in both eyes, "oblique women" (see Fernand Robert, *Homère* [Paris: Presses Universitaires de France, 1950], pp. 54ff.).

The epithet ἀψευδής qualifies speech, actions, or people lacking the intention to deceive. It is applied in particular to figures such as the Old Man of the Sea and diviners and to oracular speech. Oracles may always be ambiguous and the gods certainly seek to deceive (see pp. 84–85 below). Ἀψευδής is the name of a daughter of Nereus, associated with Νημερτής (*Iliad* 18.46). It is also the epithet applied to μαντοσύνη (Otto Kern, *Orphicorum fragmenta* [Berlin: Weidmann, 1963], frag. 103); cf. Euripides, *Iphigeneia in Tauris* 1254 (ἐν ἀψευδεῖ θρόνῳ μαντείας); Aeschylus, *The Seven Against Thebes* 26 (diviner: ἀψευδεῖ τέχνῃ); Aeschylus, *Eumenides* 615 (Apollo: μάντις ὢν δ'οὐ ψεύσομαι); Aeschylus, *Choephoroe* 559 (Apollo: μάντις ἀψευδής); Aeschylus, frag. 284A5 (H.-J. Mette, ed.) (τὸ φοίβου θεῖον ἀψευδὲς στόμα...); Herodotus, *The Persian Wars* 1.49, 2.152 (μαντήιον ἀψευδές); 2.174 (ἀψευδέα μαντήια); Pausanias, 9.23, 6 (μαντεῖον...ἀψευδές); Corinna, cited by Pierre Guillon, *Les Trépieds du Ptoion,* vol. 2 (Paris: Editions de Boccard, 1943), pp. 147–49, 144ff., and the metric dedication of Aristichus (l.5–6: ἀψευδῆ ...φήμην...τελέαν). See also Pindar, *Olympian* 4.17, 6.66–67; *Pythian* 9.42. The word ψευδήΩ refers to ambiguous speech that seems to be reality but is merely reality's illusory shadow. Thus ψευδής can frequently mean speech "unfulfilled, unrealized": *Iliad* 10.534 (ψεύσομαι, ἢ ἔτυμον ἐρέω); 19.107 (ψευστήσεις οὐδ' αὖτε τέλος μύθῳ ἐπιθήσεις); Euripides, *Orestes* 1666–67 (οὐ ψευδόμαντις ἦσθ' ἄρ', ἀλλ' ἐτήτυμος); Aeschylus, *Prometheus Bound* 1032ff. (ψευδηγορεῖν γὰρ οὐκ ἐπίσταται στόμα τὸ Δῖον, ἀλλὰ πᾶν ἔπος τελεῖ). Compare ἀψεύδεστατος reinforced by τέλος: ap. Archilochus, frag. 223 in *Archilogue, Fragments,* ed. François Lassere, trans. André Bonnard (Paris: Editions les Belles Lettres, 1958).

5. Nereus is εὔβουλος (Pindar, *Pythian* 3.93). In *Pythian* 9.94ff., Pindar reports a λόγος Νηρέως.

6. The two most famous consultations are those of Heracles (G. Herzog-

Hauser, *s.v. Nereus, R.-E.* [1936], c. 27) and Paris (*ibid.*).

7. Euripides, *Helena* 13ff.

8. Euripides, *Orestes* 362-65; cf. Weicker, *s.v. Glaukos, R.-E.* (1910), c. 1408-13.

9. On the affinities between these gods of the sea, see Albin Lesky, *Thalatta: Der Weg der Griechen zum Meer* (Vienna: Rohrer, 1947), pp. 111ff.

10. *Homeric Hymn to Hermes* 561. On the Bee-Women, see Charles Picard, "L'Ephésia, les amazones et les abeilles," *Revue des études anciennes* 42 (1940) (*Mélanges Radet*).

11. Pindar, *Pythian* 11.6.

12. Sophocles, *Oedipus the King* 299, 356, 369.

13. Euripides, *Iphigeneia in Tauris* 1256-67, 1276-79.

14. Aeschylus, *Agamemnon* 1241.

15. Cf. Aeschylus, *The Seven Against Thebes* 710; Lucion, *Vera historia* 2.33 ap. Diels, *Fragmenta Veterorum Stoicorum*[7], vol. 2, 337.10f.

16. Pindar, *Olympian* 8.1-3.

17. Plutarch, *Quaestiones convivales* 3.9.2.657E. Cf. also Plato, *Phaedrus* 275E ("true" stone or oak).

18. Clemence Ramnoux, *Mythologie ou la famille olympienne* (Paris: A. Colin, 1962), pp. 141ff., points out in connection with Poseidon, the horse-god, and his affinities with the Old Man of the Sea that in his appearances he often adopts the likeness and characteristics of a wise old man or a diviner (*Iliad* 22.48-80, 14.135-154). On the affinities between Glaucus "Halios-Geron" and Poseidon, see Edouard Will, *Korinthiaka* (Paris: Editions de Boccard, 1955), pp. 188-91.

19. Hesiod, *Theogony* 235-36.

20. Euripides, *Helena* 1002.

21. Diels, *Fragmenta Veterorum Stoicorum*[7], vol. 1, p. 32.19-21. See Paul Faure, *Fonctions des cavernes crétoises* (Paris: Editions de Boccard, 1964), pp. 96ff., on traditions relating to Mounts Ida and Dikte.

22. Hesychius, A2924 (K. Latte, ed.). Simonides of Ceos, frag. 137/642. Page describes δικαιοσύνη as ἀληθῆ τε λέγειν καὶ ἃ ἂν λάβηι τις ἀποδιδόναι; see also *Lex Gudianum*, pp. 86, 44 (A. Stefani, ed.), and *Etymologicum Magnum*, pp. 62, 51.

23. Plutarch, *Quaestiones romanae* 12.266ff.

24. Mimnermus, frag. 8 Bergk[4].

25. Solon, 3.15 Diehl[3]. Dike is πρόμαντις (Sophocles, *Electra* 476); cf. Euripides, frag. 555N[2]; *Electra* 771. On the affinities between *Dike* and *Alētheia* in Solon, see Erik Wolf, *Griechisches Rechtsdenken*, vol. 1 (Frankfurt: Klostermann, 1950), p. 193.

26. See Euripides, *Helena* 13ff.

27. Theognis, 543ff.

28. *Scholia Platonica ad Rempublicam* 10.611D (Greene, ed.); Euripides, *Orestes* 362–65. See Will, *Korinthiaka*, pp. 188–91.

29. Charles Picard, "Ordalies suméro-hittites et préhelléniques," *Revue hittite et asianique (Hommage à E. Cavaignac)* 18 (1960), fasc. 66–67, pp. 129–42, on the subject of remarks made by Georges Dossin, "Deux lettres de Mari relatives à l'Ordalie," *Comptes rendus des seances. Academie des Inscriptions et Belles Lettres*, 19 Dec. 1958 (1959), pp. 387–92.

30. See Georges Dossin, "Un Cas d'ordalie par le dieu-fleuve d'après des lettres de Mari," *Symbolae ad iura orientis antiqui pertinente Paulo Koschaker dedicatae* (Leiden: E.J. Brill, 1939), pp. 112–18. See also the remarks of P. Montet, "A Propos des ordalies suméro-hittites et préhelléniques," *Revue archéologique* (Paris: Ernest Leroux, 1961), pp. 1–4.

31. The significance of this type of ordeal is not the same everywhere. Whereas in Mari it was the innocent who escaped from the river god, as in India (according to Louis Renou in *Comptes rendus des seances. Academie des Inscriptions et Belles Lettres*, 1958 [1959], p. 393), in Africa and Indo-China the guilty were rejected by the waters (on Indo-China, see Georges Coedès, *Comptes rendus des seances. Academie des Inscriptions et Belles Lettres*, 1958 [1959], p. 393; on Africa, see Denise Paulme, "La 'Pierre du menteur' en Afrique occidentale," *L'Année sociologique*, 3rd series, 1951 [1953], pp. 344–51). See also Françoise Le Roux, *Les Druides* (Paris: Presses Universitaires de France, 1961), p. 89, on a similar type of Celtic ordeal. *Recueils de la Société Jean Bodin* 18 (3), devoted to "proof" (Brussels: De Boeck Université, 1963), contains several accounts of types of proof used in archaic societies.

32. See Picard, "Ordalies suméro-hittites," p. 133. Gustave Glotz, *Etudes sociales et juridiques sur l'antiquité grecque* (Paris: Hachette, 1906), p. 92, already noted, "King Minos and the dispenser of justice, Themison, applied proof in the manner of Hammurabi."

33. Picard, *ibid.*, pp. 133–34, according to Bacchylides, 17 Snell[6]. On this type of mythical image, see Louis Gernet, "La Notion mythique de la valeur en Grèce," *Journal de psychologie normale et pathologique* (1948).

34. See Glotz, *Etudes sociales et juridiques*, pp. 69–97. On the justice of the sea, see also Gustave Glotz, *L'Ordalie dans la Grèce primitive* (Paris: Faculté des Lettres de Paris, 1904), pp. 61ff.

35. Herodotus, *The Persian Wars* 4.154.

36. Solon, frag. 11 Diehl[2].

37. Antiphon, *Sur le meurtre d'Hérode* 81–84. See Glotz, *Etudes sociales et juridiques*, pp. 64ff.

38. In "Sur le Vieux de la Mer chez Hésiode" (*Theogony* 233–37), Vernant provides new information about the "clod of earth" and how it was used in "judi-

cial" procedures of lottery based on trials by water. In particular, he cites the instance of the clod offered to Euphemus by Triton and cast back into the sea (Pindar, *Pythian* 4.33ff.; Apollonius of Rhodes, *Argonautica* 4.1547ff.), evidence concerning a *traditio per glebam* (Plutarch, *Quaestiones graecae* 13, 22), the story of Perdiccas (Herodotus, *The Persian Wars* 8.137–38), the drawing of lots in Messenia (Pausanias, 4.3.4–7; Apollod., 2.8.4–5), and modalities of the lottery of ordeals by water (Plautus, *Casina* 4.177; 5.285).

39. Charles Picard, "Sur le travail poétique d'Homère," *Pagkarpeia: Mélanges Henri Grégoire*, vol. 1 (Brussels: Secretariat de l'Institut, 1949), pp. 493ff.

40. *Iliad* 18.497–508. An excellent commentary on this text may be found in Louis Gernet, "Droit et prédroit en Grèce ancienne," *L'Année sociologique*, 3rd series (1948–49) (Paris: Presses Universitaires de France, 1951), pp. 71–76.

41. Picard, "Sur le travail," p. 494, which refers the reader to Axel W. Persson, *Bulletin de correspondance hellénique* 70 (1946), pp. 444ff. On the ideogram of the scales and the problem of the Mycenaean talent, see Louis Deroy, *Initiation à l'épigraphie mycénienne* (Rome: Editions de l'Ateno, 1962), pp. 60–61.

42. *Homeric Hymn to Hermes* 324.

43. *Iliad* 19.223ff.; 8.69; 22.209.

44. On measuring practices, see John Chadwick, "Une bureaucratie préhistorique," *Diogène* 26 (1959). On the overseer in Mycenaean society, see Michel Lejeune, *Mémoires de philologie mycénienne*, vol. 1 (Paris: Centre National de la Recherche Scientifique, 1958), pp. 187–201.

45. On this tuberculate plant, see F. Chamoux, *Cyrène sous la monarchie des Battiades* (Paris: Centre National de la Recherche Scientifique, 1958), pp. 246–63. On the bowl of Arcesilas, see *ibid.*, pp. 258–61.

46. In general, see E. Michon, *Libra* in the *Daremberg-Saglio-Pottier*, vol. 3 (Paris: Hachette, 1904), pp. 1222ff.; Charles Picard, *Les Religions préhelléniques (Crète et Mycènes)* (Paris: Presses Universitaires de France, 1948), p. 290. Many extremely fragile, small, golden pairs of scales have been discovered in tombs at Mycenae, Knossos, Argos, etc. Their significance is uncertain, but it seems reasonable to suppose they were connected with religious representations of the scales of justice, either of Zeus or his overseer. See *Iliad* 16.658, which mentions the "sacred" scales of Zeus (cf. *Iliad* 22.219ff.; Theognis, 157ff.; Aeschylus, *The Suppliant Maidens* 402ff.; 821–22). Zeus is responsible for the scales of justice, the τάλαντα Δίκης (*Palatine Anthology* 6.267; Bacchylides, 17.25), which, when one side rises, conveys an irrevocable decision. On a possible representation of Zeus as an overseer equipped with scales, from a Cypro-Mycenaean pot, see Nilsson, *Geschichte der griecheschen Religion* (Munich: Beck, 1955–61), vol. 1, p. 367 n.1; Picard, *Les Religions préhelléniques*, p. 290; T.B.L. Webster, *From Mycenae to Homer* (London: Methuen, 1964).

47. Herodas, *Mimes* 2.90. On the relations between τρυτάνη and τάλαντον, see Eust., pp. 196, 36ff.

48. [Plato], *Axiochos* 371B. The divine king, judge, and legislator, sits on the throne of Ἀλήθεια, according to the *Coré Cosmou* (Festugière, ed.) (*Hermès Trismég.* 4 frag. 23.38). The texts on judgments in Hades are collected in L. Ruhl, *De mortuorum judicio, RGVV* 2.2 (1903), pp. 33–105. On traditions relating to Minos, see R.F. Willetts, *Cretan Cults and Festivals* (London: Routledge & Kegan Paul, 1962). See pp. 119–27 above.

49. *Scholia in Euripides Hipp.* 1200; Apollodorus 3.15.8.3 (cf. other references provided by James Frazer in his edition, vol. 2 [1921], p. 117 n.3).

50. Other evidence also points to the link between the scales and truth. In *Iliad* 12.433ff., where the poet describes the struggle between the Trojans and the Achaeans, in which neither side can gain the upper hand, he introduces the following comparison: the battle "held evenly as the scales which a careful (ἀληθής) widow holds, taking it by the balance beam, and weighs her wool evenly at either end, working to win a pitiful wage for her children." As has been pointed out elsewhere, the comparison likens the woman holding the scales to Zeus doing the same, as he so often does when presiding over an argument between two parties. But the epithet ἀληθής, which Paul Mazon curiously translates into French (and Lattimore into English) as *soigneuse*, "careful" (see also Hilda Lorimer, *Homer and the Monuments* [London: Macmillan, 1950], p. 490 n.2), has seemed strange to some scholars. Luther, *"Wahrheit" und "Lüge,"* pp. 24ff., proposed emending ἀληθής to ἀλῆτις, suggesting a wandering working woman belonging to some kind of "itinerant proletariat." However, Rudolf Hirzel, *Themis, Dike und Verwandtes* (Leipzig: Hirzel, 1907), p. 111 n.1, had already correctly underlined the relation between the epithet ἀληθής and the participle ἰσάζουσα, pointing out that this woman was acting like a judge (cf. ἰσάζειν in a text of a juridical nature, ap. Aristotle, *Nicomachean Ethics* 5.7.1132A7, A10). If this working woman is described as ἀληθής, it is probably because she is holding a pair of scales, the symbol and instrument of justice. This is just one additional piece of evidence testifying to the strict and fundamental complementarity linking the scales and truth.

51. On the association of names, see Bruno Snell, "Die Welt der Götter bei Hesiod," in *Notion du divin depuis Homère jusqu'à Platon* (Geneva: Vandoeuvres, 1952), pp. 100–105. On the political virtues, see Paul Mazon's edition of the *Theogony* (Paris: Collection des Universités de France [repr. 1951], pp. 40–41 n.3); Hesiod, *Theogony* 257–61.

52. Hesiod, *Theogony* 234. On the "political" role of the γέρων, see Henri Jeanmaire, *Couroi et courètes* (Lille: Bibliothèque Universitaire, 1939), pp. 14ff.; and, above all, Pierre Roussel, "Etude sur le principe d'ancienneté dans le monde

hellénique," *Mémoires de l'Académie des Inscriptions et Belles-Lettres* 43.2 (1951).

53. Hesiod, *Theogony* 235.

54. See M. Lacroix, "Ἤπιος-Νήπιος," *Mélanges offerts à A.M. Desrousseaux par ses amis et ses élèves, en honneur de la cinquantieme année* (Paris: Hachette, 1937), pp. 266ff. "Father" is qualified by ἤπιος in *Iliad* 24.770; *Odyssey* 2.47; 2.234; 5.8-12; 15.152. It is also an epithet used for Zeus in his relations with Athena: *Iliad* 22.184. On νηπιέη see Eduard Buchholz, *Die homerischen Realien*, vol. 3.2 (Leipzig: Engelmann, 1885), pp. 152-61.

55. An epithet for a herald: ἠπύτα κῆρυξ (*Iliad* 7.384). Ἠπυτίδης is the name of a herald (*Iliad* 17.324-325).

56. See *Odyssey* 2.47; 2.234; 5.8-12; 14.139.

57. See Lacroix, "Ἤπιος-Νήπιος," p. 270.

58. Vernant, in *Sur le vieux*, has shown that the justice of Nereus is "gentle and persuasive,...ensuring revenge for the injured party...without violence and without the risk of indefinitely reawakening the spirit of strife in an ever-renewed cycle of murder and retaliatory countermurder." This notion of justice contrasts with that placed under the sign of Eris, Nēmēsis, and Horkos, which is an "inexpiable justice, founded on vengeance, which demands that every wrong be paid for with its *poinē* according to the law of retaliation" (*Revues des étudiants grecques* 76 [1963], p. 17).

59. On Nereus as a figure of royalty, see Wolf, *Griechisches Rechtsdenken*, vol. 1, p. 123; Peter Walcot, "Hesiod and the Law," *Symbolae Osloenses* (Oslo: Inaedibus some et sociorum, 1963), pp. 15-16.

60. These rich mythical traditions have not yet (so far as I know) been systematically studied, but Louis Gernet recognized their importance, particularly in "La Notion mythique de la valeur," *Journal de psychologie normale et pathologique* (1948), pp. 451-60, and "Droit et prédroit," *L'Année sociologique*, 3rd series (1948-49) (1951). See also Vernant, *M.T.*, pp. 3-33.

61. On the king's wealth, with its two aspects of riches to be collected and those to be circulated, see Jean-Pierre Vernant, "Hestia-Hermes: The Religious Expression of Space and Movement in Ancient Greece," in *M.T.*, pp. 127-30.

62. See Plutarch, *Quaestiones graecae* 12, pp. 295ff.; the Delphic *Charila*; and Louis Gernet, "Frairies antiques," *Revue des études grecques* (1928), pp. 356-57.

63. See Jean-Pierre Vernant, *The Origins of Greek Thought* (Ithaca, NY: Cornell University Press, 1982), pp. 52-54. Eaquus is a king of this type; he is linked with the "raining Zeus" of Aegina (Isocrates, *Evagoras* 14; Pausanias, 3.29.6-9).

64. Such a schema is also attested in Hesiod's *Theogony*, although here the ritual fault has become a moral fault. In *Odyssey* 19.109-125, the just king is associated with images of trees laden with fruit, fecund flocks, prolific peoples,

etc. On the meanings of λοιμός in *Oedipus the King* (l.25–30), see Marie Delcourt, *Stérilités mystérieuses et naissances maléfiques dans l'antiquité classique* (Liège-Paris: Bibliothèque de la Faculté de Philosophie et Lettres de l'Université de Liège, 1938), pp. 16ff. On a ritual of royal justice, see the famous passage in Plato, *Critias* 119D–120C: this is a nocturnal judgment, involving the ritual swearing of an oath on the blood of a bull captured without any weapon of iron; thanks to this oath, each of the ten kings becomes identified with Poseidon and can thus deliver perfect justice. See, e.g., A. Vincent, "Essai sur le sacrifice de communion des rois d'Atlantide," *Mémorial Lagrange* (Paris: J. Gabalda, 1940) (R. Dussaud, *Revue de l'histoire des religions* [Paris: Presses Universitaires de France, 1941], pp. 89–90); Gernet, "Droit et prédroit," pp. 59ff.

65. See Gernet, "La Notion mythique," p. 451.

66. See *ibid.*, pp. 451–52, "Droit et prédroit," pp. 99ff.; *pace* Victor Ehrenberg, *Die Rechtsidee im frühen Griechentum* (Leipzig, 1921), pp. 22ff.; *contra* H. Vos, ΘΕΜΙΣ (Assen, 1956), p. 29 n.3. On θέμιστες oracles, see, e.g., Pindar, *Pythian* 4.54; *Paeans* 9.41; frag. 70 (Puech, ed.); Wolf, *Griechisches Rechtsdenken*, vol. 1, pp. 73ff.

67. On the oracular aspects of *Thēmis*, see Vos, ΘΕΜΙΣ, pp. 56ff. I should also mention the reflections on *Thēmis* (published after the first edition of the present book went to press) by H. van Effenterre and H. Trocmé, "Autorité, justice et liberté aux origines de la cité antique," *Revue de philosophie* (Paris: P. Tequi, 1964), pp. 405–34.

68. See Willetts, *Cretan Cults and Festivals*.

69. Erwin Rohde, *Psyche* (Freeport, NY: Books for Libraries, 1972). The author notes in particular an analogy between the period spent in the "cave of Zeus" and that spent in the cavern of Trophonius (see pp. 63, 84 above).

70. See Chester G. Starr, "The Decline of the Early Greek Kings," *Historia* 10 (1961), pp. 129–38. A different perspective has been defended, somewhat polemically, by Pavel Oliva, "ΠΑΤΡΙΚΗ ΒΑΣΙΛΕΙΑ," in *Geras: Studies Presented to George Thomson on the Occasion of His Sixtieth Birthday* (Prague: Charles University, 1963), pp. 171–81.

71. Pausanias, 2.31.3–4. See R. Hanslik, *s.v. Pittheus, R.-E.* (1950), c. 1873f.

72. *Scholia in Euripides Hippol.*, 11; cf. Euripides, *Medea* 685–86. Plutarch, *Theseus* 3.5.

73. Pausanias, 2.31.5. See Vos, ΘΕΜΙΣ, pp. 75–76.

74. On Thebes, see Pausanias, 9.23.3. On the "oracles of Laius" (Herodotus, 5.43), see Marie Delcourt, *Oedipe ou la légende du conquérant* (Paris: Editions Droz, 1944), pp. 97ff. On Sparta, see Herodotus, 6.57.

75. Erechtheus was raised by Athena and then installed in her sanctuary (*Iliad* 2.547–49). Cadmus and Demeter also live together, according to Pausanias,

9.16.5 (see Francis Vian, *Les Origines de Thèbes: Cadmos et les Spartes* [Paris: Klincksieck, 1963], pp. 136ff.). See Charles Picard, "Le 'Présage' de Cléomène (507 av. J.C.) et la divination sur l'acropole d'Athènes," *Revues des études grecques* 43 (1930), pp. 262–78, esp. p. 273. See Roland Crahay, *La Littérature oraculaire chez Hérodote* (Paris: Editions les Belles Lettres, 1956), pp. 168–69.

76. Herodotus, *The Persian Wars* 5.72; cf. Picard, "Le 'Présage,'" pp. 265ff.

77. Herodotus, *The Persian Wars* 5.90; cf. Picard, "Le 'Présage,'" p. 269.

78. See Emile Bourguet, "Sur une inscription d'Argos," *Revue des études grecques* 43 (1930).

79. According to *IG* 5.1.1317, cited in *ibid.*; cf. K. Scherling, *s.v. Pasiphae*, *R.-E.* (1949), c. 2070f.

80. Plutarch, *Banquet of the Seven Wise Men* 159A.

81. Pausanias, 9.39.5ff. See Vernant, *M.T.*, pp. 75–106; W.K.C. Guthrie, *The Greeks and Their Gods* (London: Methuen, 1950); Kurt Latte, *s.v. Orakel*, *R.-E.* (1939), c. 833–35.

82. A.B. Cook, *Zeus*, vol. 2, Appendix K, pp. 1073ff.

83. Curiously enough, Martin P. Nilsson, "Die Quellen der Lethe une der Mnemosyne," *Eranos* 41 (1943), pp. 1ff. (cf. *Geschichte der griechischen Religion*, vol. 2 [Munich: Beck, 1962], pp. 226ff.), has defended the Hellenistic origin of this pair of powers; cf. the criticisms by Walter Burkert, *Love and Science in Ancient Pythagoreanism* (Cambridge, MA: Harvard University Press, 1972); Karl Kérényi, *Die Geburt der Helena* (Zurich: Rhein-Verlag, 1945), pp. 94ff. Nilsson's thesis seems to me to be undermined by the role played in philosophicoreligious thought by the memory-oblivion pair (cf. pp. 119–27 above).

84. The "throne of memory" is opposed to the "throne of oblivion," on which Theseus and Pirithous are seated in Hades. There one becomes like a stone, i.e., like one who is dead (cf. Marie Delcourt, *Hephaistos* [Paris: Editions les Belles Lettres, 1957], p. 98). The meaning of the throne of oblivion is reinforced by the seated position itself, which symbolizes the death and annihilation of those who are guilty (cf. Louis Gernet, "Quelques rapports entre la pénalité et la religion dans la Grèce ancienne," *L'Antiquité classique* 5 [1936]).

85. Pausanias, 9.39.13. See *Scholia in Aristophanes Clouds* 508; and the adventure of Parmeniscos, recounted by Athen., 14.614A (Diels, *Fragmenta Veterorum Stoicorum*[7], vol. 1, pp. 112.34ff.). On this and similar adventures, see Kurt von Fritz, *s.v. Parmeniskos*, *R.-E.* (1949), c. 1569; Walter Burkert, *Weisheit und Wissenschaft. Studien zu Pythagoras, Philolaos und Platon* (Nuremberg: H. Carl, 1962), p. 132 n.229.

86. See Cratinos, frag. 221 Kock and Philostrates, *Vitca Apollonii* 2.37; Ludwig Deubner, *De Incubatione: Capita quattuor* (Leipzig: B.G. Tuebner, 1900), p. 16.

87. Theognis, 705, 1216; Aristophanes, *Frogs* 186; Lucian, *De luctu* 5; Oppian, *Cynegetica* 2.417; Babrius, *Fab.* 75 Crus.; Plutarch, *De sera numinis vindicta* c. 2141-44; Rohde, *Psyche*. On a number of mythical and philosophical meanings of *Lēthē* in the utopias of Theopompus, see Louis Gernet, "La Cité future et le pays des morts," *Revue des études grecques* 46 (1933), pp. 297ff.

88. See Vernant, *M.T.*, pp. 106ff. Vernant stresses the resemblance between the person consulting Trophonius and a figure such as Ethalides, who always retains the memory of what he has seen, even when he crosses the Acheron, as do diviners such as Tiresias and Amphiaraus (*Odyssey* 10.493-95; Sophocles, *Electra* 841). In the world of oblivion (see *Iliad* 22.387), they alone never forget and always retain the strength to "remember."

89. *Iliad* 1.70; Hesiod, *Theogony* 32, 38.

90. Euripides, *Iphigeneia in Tauris* 1261ff.

91. Euripides, *Helena* 13ff.

92. Diels, *Fragmenta Veterorum Stoicorum*[7], vol. 1, pp. 32.19-21.

93. Philostratus, *Imagines* 1.17.3, p. 332, 30K.

94. Lucian, *Vera historia* 2.33 ap. Diels, *Fragmenta Veterorum Stoicorum*[7], vol. 2, pp. 337.10ff. On the relations between *Apatē* and *Lēthē*, see p. 77 above.

95. Hesiod, *Theogony* 235-36. Hesychius A2921 (Kurt Latte, ed.). It is worth noting that passages such as this (see the list in Ernst Heitsch, "Die nicht-philosophische Ἀλήθεια," *Hermes* 90 [1962], pp. 24-33) do not prove that the "fundamental meaning" of Ἀλήθεια is really *das Unverborgenheit*. They simply testify to *one particular meaning* of Ἀλήθεια in Greek. As pointed out by Joseph Vendryes, *Bulletin de la Société Linguistique* (1953), every word may have a double etymology. The first is traditional: atomist and diachronic; the second, by contrast, is a synthetic and synchronic "static etymology." While the aim of the first is to attain the *Ur-Bedeutung*, the second, which is less hypothetical, attempts to pinpoint the meaning of a word within a language at a particular point in time. According to the program set out by Vendryes, this involves defining the place each word holds in the mind and establishing its meaning and use. By locating and examining every context in which the word appears, one may hope to gain an approximative idea of it. Heitsch's article contributes to that kind of etymology, as do the analyses (cited above) of Heribert Boeder. See H.D. Rankin, "A-ΛΗΘEIA in Plato," *Glotta* 61 (1963), pp. 51-54 (cf. in the Platonic tradition, the etymology of Plutarch, *De anima* 7 ([Bernardakis, ed.] vol. 7, pp. 29, 19).

96. Hesiod, *Theogony*, 227: *Lēthē*; 233: ἀληθέα; 235-36: ουδὲ...λήθεται.

97. On ancient mechanisms of proof, see Louis Gernet, "Le Temps dans les formes archaïques du droit," *Journal de psychologie normale et pathologique* (1956), pp. 385ff.; and, above all, G. Sautel, "Les Preuves dans le droit grec

archaïque," *Recueils de la Société Jean Bodin* 16.1 (1965).

98. In this chapter, I have considered the function of the diviner only from the perspective of its relations with the function of sovereignty, leaving aside a whole series of other aspects. But it should at least be noted that a diviner's relationship to the king could take a number of forms. Broadly speaking, the diviner may be a servant of the king (see the "palace diviner," Aeschylus, *Agamemnon* 408–410) or even identified with the king, who is himself a diviner; alternatively, the diviner may be opposed to the king, in open conflict with the sovereign power. The king-diviner is a well-known figure, including Nereus, Pittheus, and Tenerus (cf. *Scholia Lycophroris*, 1211). The diviner-king is equally common, e.g., Melampous (Herodotus, 9.34), and Polyidos (Cicero, *De divination*, trans. William Armistead Falconer [London: W. Heinemann, 1946], 1.40ff.; *Scholia in Il.* 5.48). Tiresias (Sophocles, *Oedipus the King*) is an example of the type of diviner who stands in opposition to the royal figure, but this kind of clash stemmed from the more general problem of the rivalry between the king or military leader and the "priest" (see Ernst Wüst, "Hektor and Polydamas: Von Klerus und Staat in Griechenland," *Rheinisches Museum für philologie* 98 [1955]; Vian, *Les Origines de Thèbes*, pp. 238ff.).

99. On forms of *logos* in archaic Greece, see Heribert Boeder, "Der frühgriechische Wortgebrauch von Logos und Aletheia," *Archiv für Begriffsgeschichte* 6 (1959).

CHAPTER FOUR: THE AMBIGUITY OF SPEECH

1. Excellent examples are to be found in Louis Gernet, "Droit et prédroit en Grèce ancienne," *L'Année sociologique*, 3rd series (1948–49) (1951). Maurice Leenhardt, *Do Kamo: La personne et le mythe dans le monde mélanésien* (Paris: Gallimard, 1947), pp. 164–97, provides an anthropological analysis of Melanesian "speech." See also his remarks on "the powers of speech in the Ṛgveda," in Louis Renou (ed.), *Etudes védiques et paninéennes*, vol. 1 (Paris: Editions de Broccard, 1955). See also Dominique Zahan, *La Dialectique du verbe chez les Bambara* (Paris: Mouton, 1963).

2. *Iliad* 1.234ff. See Gernet, "Droit et prédroit," p. 69 n.1. "Ὅρκος is, strictly speaking, whatever it is that one makes contact with when swearing an oath." See also Emile Benveniste, "L'Expression du serment dans la Grèce ancienne," *Revue de l'histoire des religions* 134 (1948); Jean Bollack, "Styx et serments," *Revue des études grecques* 71 (1958), pp. 1–35.

3. *Iliad* 9.565–72, trans. Richmond Lattimore (Chicago: University of Chicago Press, 1951); see Gernet, "Droit et prédroit," pp. 92–94.

4. Gernet, "Droit et prédroit," pp. 84–88. In an earlier study, "Quelques rapports entre la pénalité et la religion dans la Grèce ancienne," *L'Antiquité*

classique 5 (1936), pp. 332–37, Gernet showed how the seated posture symbolized annihilation and death.

5. Gernet, "Droit et prédroit," pp. 104–105.

6. *Ibid.*, pp. 81ff. Henri Fournier, *Les Verbes "Dire" en grec ancien* (Paris: C. Klincksieck, 1946), pp. 1–12, collected data on the religious aspects of speech, aspects conveyed by the etymology of the roots **wek^w* (divine voice), **wer-* (a sacred or legal formula), and **bha-* (a sacred declaration or an oracle). On these types of magicoreligious speech in Eastern religions (e.g., Egyptian, Sumero-Accadian, and Phoenician of Ras-Shamra), see Helmer Ringgren, *Word and Wisdom: Studies in the Hypostatization of Divine Qualities and Functions in the Ancient Near East*, pt. 1 (Lund: H. Ohlssons boktr., 1947); Ernst Cassin in *L'Année sociologique*, 3rd series (1948–49) (1951), pp. 328–31.

7. On this word, see Eduard Fraenkel, *Aeschylus, Agamemnon*, vol. 2, *Commentary on 1-1055* (Oxford: Clarendon Press, 1950), p. 193; Wilhelm Luther, *"Wahrheit" und "Lüge" im ältesten Griechentum* (Leipzig: R. Noske, 1935), p. 53 n.3, and *Weltansicht und Geistesleben* (Göttingen: Vandenhoeck & Ruprecht, 1954), pp. 33–34.

8. Aeschylus, *Agamemnon* 1488; cf. Aeschylus, *The Seven Against Thebes* 426; *Iliad* 1.41; 1.504. On this point, it is impossible to separate the uses of κραίνω from those of τελεῖν, τελήεις, τέλειος, etc. (see *L.S.J.*, *s.V.*), or from those of ἐτεός, ἔτυμος, ἐτήτυμος (see Luther, *"Wahrheit" und "Lüge,"* pp. 51–61; Kurt Latte, "Hesiod's Dichterweihe," *Antike und Abendland* 2 [Hamburg: M. von Schroeder, 1946]; André Rivier, "Sur les fragments 34 et 35 de Xénophane," *Revue de philologie* 30 [1956], p. 45). On the meanings of τέλος, see D. Holwerda, ΤΕΛΟΣ, *Mnemosyne*, 1963, pp. 337–63.

9. *Odyssey* 5.170, trans. Richmond Lattimore (New York: Harper & Row, 1965).

10. Euripides, *The Suppliant Women* 139, trans. Frank William Jones (Chicago: University of Chicago Press, 1958).

11. Aeschylus, *Agamemnon* 369; *Eumenides* 759; Euripides, *Electra* 1248. The opinion of Zeus "is irrevocable, does not deceive, and is not vain" (οὐ παλινάγρετον οὐδ' ἀπατηλὸν οὐδ' ἀτελεύτητον), according to *Iliad* 1.526.

12. Pindar, *Pythian* 9.67ff., trans. Frank J. Nisetich (Baltimore: Johns Hopkins University Press, 1980): Ὠκεῖα δ'ἐπειγομένων ἤδη θεῶν πρᾶξις ὁδοί τε βραχεῖαι. See also Aeschylus, *The Suppliant Maidens*, 93ff. On the god who "accomplishes" everything, see Xenophanes, ap. Diels, *Fragmenta Veterorum Stoicorum*[7], vol. 1, p. 135.9 (together with the correction defended by Guido Calogero, in *Studi di filosofia greca in onore di Rodolfo Mondolfo* [Bari, 1950]).

13. See Sophocles, *Oedipus at Colonus* 1451: "I do not know of any divine decision that has been in vain."

14. *Homeric Hymn to Hermes* 427. The same verb designates the efficacy of the wand of opulence and wealth (531: ἐπικραίνουσα). In their commentary, Thomas Allen, William Halliday, and Edward Sikes (*The Homeric Hymns*, 2nd ed. [Oxford: Oxford University Press, 1963], p. 333) have in mind a rare sense of κραίνειν that is supposed to mean γεραίρειν.

15. See Pindar, *Pythian* 4.174–76 (ἐκράνθη). The praise of the poet is ἐτήτυμον (*Nemean* 7.63).

16. *Mahābhārata* 5.9.8ff. On this point I follow Georges Dumézil, *Servius et la fortune* (Paris: Gallimard, 1943), p. 65.

17. Pindar, *Pythian* 4.3; Pindar, *Isthmian* 6.11–12. The notion of "natural growth" is already found in *Odyssey* 22.347–48.

18. Pindar, *Nemean* 8.40ff.

19. Bacchylides, 13.58ff.; Bacchylides, frag. 56 Snell[6]; Pindar, *Pythian* 8.92; Pindar, *Isthmian* 6.13ff.; Pindar, *Pythian* 1.66ff.; Pindar, *Nemean* 2.14–15; Pindar, *Pythian* 4.279ff.; Pindar, *Isthmian* 7.29; Pindar, *Pythian* 4.69; Pindar, *Nemean* 7.32ff. On this last testimony and the affinities between this concept of speech and the *logos* of the soul in Heraclitus, see Clemence Ramnoux, *Héraclite ou l'Homme entre les choses et les mots* (Paris: Editions les Belles Lettres, 1959), pp. 116ff.

20. Aeschylus, *Eumenides* 368–70, trans. Richmond Lattimore (Chicago: University of Chicago Press, 1953); see Ramnoux, *Héraclite*, pp. 116ff.

21. See Pausanias, 8.34.1ff.; Jean-Pierre Vernant, "Hesiod's Myth of the Races: An Essay in Structural Analysis," in *M.T.*, p. 28 n.36. See also J. Harrison, "Delphika," *Journal of Hellenic Studies* 29 (1899), pp. 209ff.; Ernst Wüst, *s.v. Erinys*, *R.-E. Suppl.-B*, VIII (1956), c. 87.

22. On the Charites associated with the Muses, see Jacqueline Duchemin, *Pindare poète et prophète* (Paris: Editions les Belles Lettres, 1955), pp. 54ff. In Bambara society, the griot is the master of *pasaw*, "tonic" words. He is the creator of literature "based, according to Bambara thought, on the reality of a latent force that lies in everything that is, a force that certain words have the power to draw forth from slumber and exalt. This force is *nyama*, probably comparable to a vibratory movement that is the common principle of all beings": Zahan, *La Dialectique du verbe*, p. 133.

23. Euripides, *The Suppliant Women* 139; *Ion* 464. See Aeschylus, *Prometheus Bound* 211. Pierre-Maxime Schuhl, *Essai sur la formation de la pensée grecque* (Paris: Presses Universitaires de France, 1949 [1934]), p. 45, writes: "an omen seems... often to be a cause as well as a sign," and "an oracle – which in this respect is akin to a curse – owes part of its power to the very act of proferring it." Data on divination are collected by Martin P. Nilsson, *Geschichte der griechischen Religion*, vol. 1 (Munich: Beck, 1955), pp. 164ff. However, it must be recognized that the classificatory categories inherited from the worthy "Bouché-

Leclercq" do not help much in truly understanding the mechanisms of divination. No one has written in a more illuminating fashion on these problems than Jacques Vernant, "La Divination: Contexte et sens psychologique des rites et des doctrines," *Journal de psychologie normale et pathologique* (1948), pp. 299-325.

24. The diviner had by now changed considerably from the figure described in the late fifth century. He had become no more than an intelligence man analogous to a statesman. He understood the future in a way similar to Themistocles (see the definition given by Euripides, frag. 973N[2]; Antiphon, ap. Diels, *Fragmenta Veterorum Stoicorum*[7], vol. 2, p. 337.18-20. On the first of these texts, see André Rivier, *Un Emploi archaïque de l'analogie chez Héraclite et Thucydide* [Lausanne: F. Rouge, 1952], p. 48).

25. Aeschylus, *Agamemnon* 1255.

26. *Odyssey* 19.565-67.

27. *Homeric Hymn to Hermes* 559, trans. Hugh G. Evelyn-White (London and Cambridge, MA: Loeb Classical Library, 1967).

28. *Ibid.* 560-61.

29. See p. 61 above.

30. Aeschylus, *The Suppliant Maidens* 375, trans. Seth Benardete (Chicago: University of Chicago Press, 1956); see also the uses of κραίνειν in lines 608, 943. On the special meaning of the royal hearth and on its relations to "the public hearth," see Louis Gernet, "Sur le symbolisme politique en Grèce ancienne: le foyer commun," *Cahiers internatinaux de sociologie* 11 (1951), pp. 26ff.

31. *Homeric Hymn to Hermes* 529-33. See J. Orgogozo, "L'Hermès des Achéens," *Revue histoire des religions* 136 (1949), p. 145; Louis Gernet, "La Notion mythique de la valeur," *Journal de psychologie normale et pathologique* (1948), pp. 451-53.

32. Louis Gernet, *Droit et société dans la Grèce ancienne* (Paris: Sirey, 1955), pp. 69ff.

33. For example, the art of Calchas is not vain (οὐκ ἄκραντοι); ap. Aeschylus, *Agamemnon* 249. In Aeschylus, *Choephori* 844ff., ἀληθῆ is opposed to μάτην. See Pindar, *Olympian* 1.86; *Iliad* 2.137-38; *Homeric Hymn to Hermes* 549. On ἅλιος, "vain, useless," see Bruno Snell, *Lexikon des frühgriechischen Epos* (Göttingen: Vandenhoeck & Ruprecht, 1955), *s.v.* ἅλιος, II, c. 487-88.

34. Pindar, *Olympian* 2.86-87.

35. *Odyssey* 19.565; see Aeschylus, *Choephori* 534. A good example is provided by the "great eagle with crooked beak" (*Odyssey* 19.525-38) that Penelope sees in a dream and that, later on (at first it is αἰετὸς ὄρνις), tells her: "This is no dream, but a blessing real as day. You will see it done (ὅ τοι τετελεσμένον ἔσται)" (547). There are many different degrees of efficacy, as Jean Bayet has shown (see Bayet, "Présages figuratifs déterminants dans l'antiquité gréco-latine," in

Mélanges Franz Cumont, vol. 1 [Brussels: Secretariat de l'Institut, 1936], and "La Croyance romaine aux présages déterminants: aspects littéraires et chronologie," in *Mélanges Bidez* [Brussels: Secretariat de l'Institut, 1934]). He later studied the Roman mechanisms that made it possible to change the meaning of a divinatory sign and to convert an unfavorable omen to a favorable one (see Bayet, "L'Etrange 'omen' de Sentinum et le celtisme en Italie," in *Hommages à Albert Grenier*, vol. 1 [Brussels: Latomus, 1962]).

36. Aeschylus, *Agamemnon* 249.

37. See Apollonius of Rhodes, *Argonautica* 4.387. In contrast, the will of Zeus is "so certain it falls without slips, by sign of Zeus fulfilled" (Aeschylus, *The Suppliant Maidens* 90ff.).

38. *Odyssey* 2.202. Halitherses is a diviner of the "Cassandra type"; lacking *peitho*, he is condemned to unreality (see p. 57 below). G. Méautis, "Halimède et le devin du fronton Est d'Olympie," *Revue archeologique* (1954), interprets the name "Halimedes" to be that of a diviner "with vain and useless thoughts," who deplores what he knows of the future but has no power to change it. He is not so much a "useless" diviner but an "unfortunate" one.

39. See Jean-Pierre Vernant in *L'Année sociologique* (1953), p. 348, on the category of action in religious thought.

40. Aeschylus, *Agamemnon* 581-82. See *The Suppliant Maidens* 598-99: "His deeds are quick as words. He hastens what counsel decrees."

41. Aeschylus, *Persians* 739: Χρησμῶν πρᾶξις, which is the equivalent of τελευτὴν θεσφάτων (740).

42. Aeschylus, *The Seven Against Thebes* 840: ἐξέπραξεν. On *Praxidikē* and the *Praxidikai*, see Marie C. Van der Kolf. *s.v. Praxidikē, R.-E.* (1954), c. 1751-61.

43. Jean-Pierre Vernant, "Work and Nature in Ancient Greece," in *M.T.* On πρᾶξις and πράσσειν, see also Otfrid Becker, "Das Bild des Weges und verwandte Vorstellungen in frühgriechischen Denken," in *Hermes, Einzelschriften, Heft*, vol. 4 (Berlin: Weidmann, 1937), pp. 52ff.

44. See Gernet, "Droit et prédroit," p. 94, and "Le temps dans les formes archaïques du droit," *Journal de psychologie normale et pathologique* (1956), pp. 385-86.

45. See Sophocles, *Oedipus the King* 870: "Laws begotten in the clear air of heaven, whose only father is Olympus; no mortal nature brought them to birth, no forgetfulness shall lull them to sleep; for God is great in them and grows not old."

46. Aeschylus, *Prometheus* 516; *Eumenides* 383; Sophocles, *Ajax* 1390. Μῆνις is also μνάμων, according to Aeschylus, *Agamemnon* 155. (On μῆνις, see Louis Gernet, *Recherches sur le développement de la pensée juridique et morale en Grèce* [Paris: E. Leroux, 1917], p. 147.) We should bear in mind the relations between

ἀλάστωρ, ἀλαστεῖν, and memory of vengeance, as set out by Gernet, *Recherches sur le développement*, pp. 324–25. They are convincingly confirmed in Plutarch, *Quaestiones grecquae*, p. 297A: "ἀλάστωρ" μὲν κέκληπται ὁ ἄληστα καὶ πολὺν χρόνον μνημονευθησόμενα δεδρακώς κτλ. Kurt Latte, *Heiliges Recht* (Tubingen: J.C.B. Mohr, 1920) has defended the hypothesis of a connection with μνήμων (see E. Weiss, *s.v., Mnemones, R.-E.* [1932], c. 2261f.). This hypothesis is well received by Fraenkel, *Aeschylus, Agamemnon*, vol. 2 *Commentary on l-1055*, p. 94.

47. Aeschylus, *The Seven Against Thebes* 720ff.; 886; 946. In addition to these three passages of Aeschylus, *Agamemnon* 743–49; and *The Seven Against Thebes* 655; 766ff.; 790ff.; etc. also testify to the importance of the notion of efficacy in the representation of the Erinyes and the Curses.

48. It is impossible not to compare the μνήμονες Erinyes and the ἀληθεῖς Erinyes, which provides an extra reason for emphasizing the privative ἀ in Ἀλήθεια.

49. Bacchylides, 13.44. See Aeschylus, *Choephori* 462.

50. See p. 31 above.

51. Pindar, *Nemean* 3.29; Pindar, *Olympian* 6.12–13.

52. Pindar, *Nemean* 3.29; Pindar, *Pythian* 9.95–96; Pindar, *Olympian* 2.105–106: when jealousy threatens praise, it is "contrary to justice." *Alethēia-Dikē* is opposed to *oblivion-injustice*; see Pindar, frag. inc. 90 (Puech, ed.), where ἀπάτη is opposed to δίκη.

54. Bacchylides, 8.202.

55. Pindar, *Nemean* 8.40ff.

56. Pindar, *Pythian* 8.70–71.

57. Gernet, *Droit et société*, p. 68, points out that "in the most ancient texts, the very word *dikē* cannot fail to imply the idea of a normal order of humanity that judgments respect and sanction."

58. Bacchylides, 13.221; Pindar, *Pythian* 4.233; Herodotus, 1.66; 1.73; 2.141; 5.92; Sophocles, *Trachiniae* 77.

59. On the concept of Pistis as linked with promises, see Pindar, *Olympian* 11.5–6. On the parallel with Roman *Fides*, see Eduard Fraenkel, "Zur Geschichte des Wortes 'Fides,'" *Rheinisches Museum für philologie* (Bonn: E. Weber, 1916), pp. 187ff.; Antoine Meillet, "Lat. Credo et Fides," *Mémoires Société de Linguistique de Paris* 22 (1922), pp. 215ff.; Georges Dumézil, *Mitra-Varuna* (New York: Zone Books, 1988); "Latin CREDO, Armenian ARIT^c: Mots et légendes," *Revue Philologie* 64 (1938); Gernet, "Droit et prédroit," p. 117 n.1.

60. Sophocles, *Oedipus at Colonus* 1593–95; Pausanias, 1.30.4. See Rudolf Hirzel, *Der Eid ein Beitrag zu seiner Geschichte von Rudolf Hirzel* (Leipzig: S. Hirzel, 1902), p. 125 n.5.

61. On Pistis, the link of royalty between Homeric heroes, see Henri Jeanmaire, *Couroi et courètes* (Lille: Bibliothèque Universitaire, 1939), pp. 101–103.

62. In Greece, Pistis is a very ancient concept, as the Homeric texts testify. It is an aristocratic power in Theognis, 1135ff., where it associated with Sōphrosynē and the Charites. It watches over the ὅρκοι... πιστοὶ ἐν ἀνθρώποισι δίκαιοι. There is no reason for believing that it only became a deity at a late date in Greece, as has sometimes been suggested. See Pierre Boyancé, "Fides et le serment," *Hommages à Albert Grenier*, vol. 1, pp. 329–41, together with the remarks of Charles Picard, "De la πίστις hellénique à la 'fides romana,'" *Revue archéologique* (1962), pp. 226–28.

63. Aeschylus, *Agamemnon* 1241.

64. *Ibid.* 1195.

65. *Ibid.* 1208; 1212; Servius, *In Virgilium Commentarius* 2.247. See Juliette Davreux, *La Légende de la prophétesse Cassandre* (Paris: Editions Droz, 1942), pp. 3ff., 22ff., 49ff., 67ff.

66. According to the unknown tragic poet cited by Plutarch, *Praecepta gerendae rei publicae* 28.5, p. 821B (= *Tragic fragmentae adespotes* 414N^2), Cassandra is condemned to ἄκραντα, but according to [Orpheus], *Lithika* 765 (Abel, ed.), although she pronounces ἐτήτυμα, her words are ἄπιστα (according to the emendation by Merrick, rather than ἄπαντα).

67. Aeschylus, frag. 279A (H.J. Mette, ed.). On Peithō, see Voigt, *s.v. Peitho, R.-E.* (1937), c. 194–217; Mario Untersteiner, *The Sophists* (Oxford: Blackwell, 1954), pp. 107–108. In addition to the figurative evidence to which Voigt draws attention, see the remarks of Adolf Greifenhagen, *Griechische Eroten* (Berlin: De Gruyter, 1957), pp. 77ff. On the epigraphic evidence, see the observations of Franciszek Sokolowski, *Lois sacrées des cités grecques: Supplément* (Paris: Editions de Boccard, 1962), p. 134, on a ruling in Thasos relating to the cult of Peithō.

68. Aeschylus, *Prometheus Bound* 172. On honeyed words, see Wilhelm Heinrich Roscher, *Nektar und Ambrosia* (Leipzig: Teubner, 1883), pp. 69–72.

69. Eupolis, *ap. Scholia in Aristophanes, Acharniensem* 530; Quintilian, *Institutione Orat.* 10.1.82; Nonnus of Panopolis, *Dionysiaka* 41.250ff. (Rudolf, ed.); Keydell Cicero, *Orat.* 15.

70. *Odyssey* 1.337; Plutarch, *Eroticos* 759B; Pindar, *Nemean* 4.2ff.; see Alessandro Setti, "La Memoria e il canto," *Studi italiani filologia classica* 30, n.s. (Florence; F. le Monnie, 1958), pp. 161ff.; Giuliana Lanata, *Poetica pre-platonica* (Florence: La Nuova Italia, 1963), p. 16.

71. Muse, *Thelxinoē*, according to Aratus, cited by Johannes Tzetzes, *In Hesiodi Opera et dies*, p. 23 Gaisford (= *Anecdota oxoniensia* 4, pp. 424–25, (Cramer, ed.). See Cicero, *De natura deorum* 2 (Pease, ed., 1958, pp. 1100–101). Siren, *Thelxinoe, ap. Scholia in Apollonium Rhodium* 4.892; Eustathius, p. 1709.45. On the kinship of the Muses and the Sirens, see Apollonius of Rhodes, *Argonautica* 4.892–96.

72. See *Odyssey* 12.39–46; 184–93. On the Sirens, see Karoly Marót, *Die Anfänge der griechische Literatur: Ungarische Akademie der Wissenschaften* (Budapest: Verlag der Ungarschen Akademie der Wissenschaften, 1960), pp. 106–211.

73. See the portrait of the Good Sovereign in Hesiod, *Theogony* 80ff.: "sweetness upon his speech," "blandishing words from his mouth," leading hearts "with gentle arguments" (μαλακοῖσι παραιφάμενοι ἐπέεσσιν on πάρφασις, see p. 80 below) (trans. Richmond Lattimore [Ann Arbor: University of Michigan Press, 1959]). Cornutus, *Theologia graeca* 14, correctly declares that Hesiod's Calliope is rhetoric with a beautiful voice, "thanks to which one can guide the city and address the people, leading it by persuasion rather than force toward whatever one has chosen." It is to the good *Peithō* that Athena appeals in Orestes' trial: "But if you hold Persuasion has her sacred place of worship, in the sweet beguilement of my voice, then you might stay with us" (Aeschylus, *Eumenides* 885). See also Pausanias, 1.22.3; Plutarch, *Quaestiones convivales* 9.14.7–10, p. 746F. Aeschylus, *Agamemnon* 385; 386; Aeschylus, *Persians* 97ff.; *Atē* is the δολόμητις ἀπάτα (93).

74. On "caressing words," see Theognis, 704 (πείσας ... αἱμυλίοισι λόγοις). In the expressions ψευδεῖς λόγοι and αἱμύλιοι λόγοι, it is important to stress the aspect of plurality that Heribert Boeder (*Der frühgriechische Wortgebrauch von Logos und Aletheia: Archiv für Begriffsgeschichte*, vol. 4 [Bonn, 1959], p. 90) rightly sets in opposition to an essential aspect of *Alētheia*, but one that rational thought – and only rational thought – was to define as ἁπλοῦς, as opposed to διπλοῦς (see p. 130 above).

On *Apatē*, see Hesiod, *Theogony* 889–90: Zeus tricks (ἐξαπατήσας) Mētis with affectionate words (αἱμυλίοισι λόγοισιν). Sisyphus is a master of αἱμύλιοι λόγοι (Theognis, 704), as is Odysseus (Sophocles, *Ajax* 389). Calypso resorts to μαλακοῖσι καὶ αἱμυλίοισι λόγοιΩ to make Odysseus forget his native Ithaca (*Odyssey* 1.565). But αἱμύλιοι λόγοι (along with ψεύδεα and ἐπίκλοπον) are more particularly placed under the patronage of Hermes, the nocturnal and cunning one (Hesiod, *Works* 78), who lodges them in the breast of Pandora, Zeus's ἀπάτη (see also *Works* 373–74: μηδὲ γυνὴ ἐξαπατάτω αἱμύλα κωτίλλουσα). On the relations between αἱμυλία and χάρις, see Plutarch, *Numa* 8.19 (on the subject of a king) and Philodemus, *Volumina rhetorica* (Sigfried Sudhaus, ed.), vol. 2 (Amsterdam: A.M. Hakkert, 1964), p. 77 (an allusion to Odysseus).

75. See Hesiod, *Theogony* 224; 227: Ἀπάτη and Λήθη are both children of Night. On *Lēthē*, see Wilhelm Kroll, *s.v.* Lethe, *R.-E.* (1925), c. 2141–44.

76. Aeschylus, *The Suppliant Maidens* 1040–41.

77. *Ibid.* 1037. Right from birth, Aphrodite was assigned Ἔρως and Ἵμερος as companions: she presides in particular over the whisperings of maidens (παρθενίους τ᾽ ὀάρους) and smiles (μειδήματα) and deceits (ἐξαπάτας) with sweet delight (τέρψιν τε γλυκερήν) and love (φιλότητα) and graciousness (μειλιχίην) (Hesiod, *Theogony*

201-206). The function of Aphrodite is to πεπιθεῖν φρένας and ἀπατῆσαι (*Homeric Hymn to Aphrodite* 33); all the gods fear her ὀάρους καὶ μήτιας (*Homeric Hymn to Aphrodite* 249). Nonnus of Panopolis, *Dionysiaka* 33.111ff. (Keydell, ed.), gives her *Charis, Peithō,* and *Pothos* as companions and mentions her λάθρια... ἔργα (34.268). Plutarch, *Eroticos* (Flacelière, ed.) (Paris: Edition les Belles Lettres, 1953), p. 758C associates her with the Muses, the Charites, and Eros.

78. *Iliad* 14.160ff.

79. *Ibid.* 14.198.

80. *Ibid.* 14.208: ἐπέεσσι παραιπεπιθοῦσα φίλον κῆρ. In such mythical thought, rhetoric and erotic seduction are not differentiated. The same *Peithō* operates on both levels.

81. *Ibid.* 14.211 (φιλομμειδής) and 14.216. Nonnus of Panopolis, *Dionysiaka* 31.26ff. (Keydell, ed.), dealt with the theme of the "trickery of Hera," but with a very assured sense of the mythical associations and affinities in the vocabulary. See also Nonnus of Panopolis, *Dionysiaka* 8.113, which is equally rich.

82. Hesiod, *Theogony* 205, 206.

83. *Ibid.* 224, 227, 229.

84. *Ibid.* 77-78: ψεύδεά θ'αἰμυλίους τε λόγους καὶ ἐπίκλοπον ἦθος. See *Theogony* 229; *Works* 789 (ψεύδεά θ'αἰμυλίους τε λόγους κρυφίους τ'οὑρισμούς); Aesop, *Fables* 111, 112.

Aeschylus, *Choephorai* 726-28: Πειθὼ δολία and Ἑρμῆς Χθόνιος Νύχιος. See Ramnoux, *La Nuit*, pp. 162f. At l.815-16, Hermes pronounces the invisible word (ἄσκοπον ἔπος) "which spreads over eyes the shadows of Night." The ποικιλόμητις Odysseus uses it similarly: ἀλλά μοι ἄσκοπα κρυπτά τ'ἔπη δολερᾶς ὑπέδυ φρενός (Sophocles, *Philoct.* 1111-12). On the relations between Hermes and night, the *Homeric Hymn to Hermes* is perfectly explicit: the night is Hermes' domain, the domain of his works and his kind of intelligence. Further evidence that Hermes is truly the "black one" is provided by the fact that, according to the *Paroemiasraphi graeci* 2, p. 184, the expression "a white Hermes" (λευκός) was applied to those who were incapable of concealing their bad behavior.

Hermes is frequently associated with the cult of Aphrodite (Plutarch, *Conjugalia praecepta* 138C): in Cyllene (Pausanias, 4.26.5), in Argos (Pausanias, 2.19.6), in Megapolis (with a Μαχανῖτις Aphrodite, "a weaver of cunning tricks," a description that Pausanias, 8.31.6, explains by the cunning that the goddess uses in both words and actions), and in Athens (with a ψίθυρος Aphrodite and a ψίθυρος Eros, according to Harpocration, *s.v.* ψιθυριστής). According to Aristophanes, *Peace* 456, he is associated with Aphrodite, *Peitho, the Charites and the Hours* (cf. Samson Eitrem, *s.v. Hermes, R.-E.* [1912], c. 760-61). Nonnus of Panopolis, *Dionysiaka* 8.221, presents *Peitho* as Hermes' wife. We must leave aside the problem of the negative aspects of Aphrodite and the positive aspects of Hermes.

85. Hermes has close links with *logos*, as Plato describes in the *Cratylus* 407E–408A (cf. Plutarch, *De audiendis poetis*, 44E, where Hermes' association with the Charites is justified by the κεχαρισμένον and προσφιλές nature of *logos*), and those links seem to determine the definition of *logos* in the rhetoric of "Gorgias" as well as certain aspects such as *psychagogia* and the image of the spur of *Peithō*.

86. Hesiod, *Works and Days* 77–78, trans. Richmond Lattimore (Ann Arbor: University of Michigan Press, 1959). Pandora is Zeus's "trick": a product of his *mētis*, a "sheer, impossible deception" (83). All the *mētis* of the gods combines to make her the most complete form of *mētis*: Hephaestus gives her "the likeness of a decorous young girl"; Athena teaches her the skills of the loom and "intricate weaving," which is an instrument of fascination; Aphrodite endows her with *Charis* and *Pothos*. The *Charites*, the Hours, and *Peithō* complete this work of art (60–82).

86. Pindar, *Nemean* 8.15ff.

87. Dionysius of Halicarnassus, *On the style of Demosthenes* 8, pp. 974–75 (Reiske, ed.); see Maximillian Egger, *Denys d'Halicarnasse: Essai sur la critique littéraire et la rhétorique chez les grecs du siècle d'Auguste* (Paris: A. Picard et fils, 1902), pp. 239–40.

88. Proteus is a god of *mētis*, as are Mētis, Nereus, Nēmēsis, Thētis, etc.

89. Plutarch, *Eroticos* 769C, which clearly underlines the ambiguity of these charms: while nature thus provides ample means for the dissolute woman to seduce her lovers and lead them into lasciviousness (πρὸς ἡδονὴν καὶ ἀπάτην), it also provides means for the good woman to win the friendship and affection of her husband.

90. *Iliad* 14.216. Odysseus, richly endowed with *mētis*, also knows how, at the instigation of the most cunning of goddesses, τὸ μαλακοῖσ' ἐπέεσσι παρφάσθαι (*Odyssey* 16.286–87 [19.5.6]). On Ὀαριστύς and Aphrodite, see pp. 78 and 99–100 above.

91. Hesiod, *Theogony* 90: μαλακοῖσι παραιφάμενοι ἐπέεσσιν. *Parphasis* also has a role to play in military circles; *Iliad* 11.793 mentions a "good" παραίφασις, which comes from the ἑταῖρος. Eustathius, p. 979, 34 describes it as a πειθὼ τὴν ἐξ ὁμιλίας.

92. Pindar, *Nemean* 8.32ff. Ajax was overcome by *Lēthē* (24) when he deserved the greatest praise. See the uses of παρφάμεν in *Olympian* 7.65; *Pythian* 9.42–43. Παράφημι contains an image of the crooked, sinuous progress of speech, as does the expression παρὲξ εἰπεῖν (see p. 159 n.4 above).

93. Pindar, *Nemean* 7.20–21. Old Nestor, λιγὺς ἀγορητής, is also called ἡδυεπής (*Iliad* 1.248). On poetry as shimmering, many-colored, malleable speech, see Herwig Maehler, *Die Auffassung des Dichterberufs im frühen Griechentum bis zur Zeit Pindars* (Göttingen: Vandenhoeck & Ruprecht, 1963), pp. 70, 90ff.

94. In Bambara society, the master of speech, the griot, produces tonic words (*pasaw*), which arouse "a latent force that lies in all that is," but those words (whether *burudyuw* or *balemaniw*) are embellishment and exaggeration. The griot is regarded as a "liar" whose "existence is indispensable to create ardour, courage and valour, all qualities founded upon the illusion that one is more than one really is." This kind of griot seems to be distinct from another kind, who plays an important role in initiatory societies and speaks only the truth (see Zahan, *La Dialectique du verb*, pp. 125–46).

95. Pindar, *Olympian* 1.28–34; φάτις ὑπὲρ τὸν ἀλαθῆ λόγον· δεδαιδαλμένοι ψεύδεσι ποικίλοις ἐξαπατῶντι μῦθοι. Χάρις δ', ἅπερ ἅπαντα τεύχει τὰ μείλιχα θνατοῖς, ἐπιφέροισα τιμὰν καὶ ἅπιστον ἐμήσατο πιστὸν ἔμμεναι τὸ πολλάκις.

Poets have *mētis* (Pindar, *Olympian* 1.9; *Nemean* 3.9). On the *poikilos* nature of language, see *Iliad* 2.248; Plutarch, *Eroticos* 759B, compares poetic fictions (ποιητικαὶ φαντασίαι) to daydreams: they possess the same force.

96. On Ἀπάτη, see Untersteiner, *The Sophists*, pp. 108ff., 116ff., 126–27, 150–52, 185ff., 248–49; Pierre-Maxime Schuhl, *Platon et l'art de son temps* (Paris: Presses Universitaires de France, 1952), pp. 31–35, 82–85; Louis Robert, *Hellenica*, vols. 11–12 (Paris: A. Maisonneuve, 1960), pp. 5–15; Thomas G. Rosenmeyer, "Gorgias, Aeschylus and 'Apate,'" *American Journal of Philology* 76 (1955), pp. 225–60; Luther, *"Wahrheit" und "Lüge,"* pp. 97–105; Wernicke, *s.v.* Ἀπάτη, *R.-E.* (1894), c. 2670. The double nature of Ἀπάτη appears very clearly in Hesiod, *Theogony* 205 (Aphrodite's ἐξαπάται) and 224 (Ἀπάτη, the child of Night); it is also attested in Aeschylus, frag. 601, *Der Verlorene Aischylos* (Hans Joachim Mette, ed.) (Berlin: Akademie Verlag, 1963) (who refers to a "good" ἀπάτη). On the relations between πειθώ, ἀπάτη, γοητεία, and λήθη, see Plato, *Republic* 412E–13E.

97. Hesiod, *Theogony* 55ff. Elsewhere, the Muses, which endow the poet with memory, can also deprive him of it and consign him to oblivion (*Iliad* 2.594–600). In a more detailed and systematic study of Lēthē, it would be necessary to take account of Boeder's analyses, *Der frühgriechische Wortgebrauch*, vol. 4, pp. 82–112, as well as the subtle interplay of opening and closing developed in the complementarity between λήθη and ἀλήθεια; at the same time one must distinguish between the levels of thought of *Lēthē* the mythical power and the meanings of forgetfulness (or λανθάνω) in the context of λόγος.

98. Hesiod, *Theogony* 98–103. See Pindar, *Nemean* 10.24; *Pythian* 1.6ff.; *Nemean* 8.49–50; *Olympian* 8.72; Bacchylides, 5.7. *Iliad* 22.281–82: *Lēthē* provoked by a figure described as ἐπίκλοπος...μύθων.

99. *Odyssey* 12.39–54; 12.157–200. In the philosophicoreligious sects and the neo-Platonic tradition, the Sirens were to be the ἡδοναί, carnal pleasures and the image of oblivion, sleep, etc., but in a quite different context of thought

(see, e.g., Pierre Courcelle, "Quelques symboles funéraires du néo-platonisme latin," *Revue des études anciennes* 46 [1944]). On the Sirens, see Marót, "Die Anfäge der griechischen Literatur."

100. Dio Chrysostomus, *Orationes* 12.51-52. It also procures "sweet sleep."

101. *Odyssey* 4.220ff. Rhetoric is also a τέχνη ἀλυπίας ([Plutarch], *Vita X Orat.*, 1, p. 833C *ap.* Diels, *Fragmenta Veterorum Stoicorum*[7], vol. 2, p. 336.35ff.). On this evidence, see Carlo Diano, "Euripide, auteur de la catharsis tragique," *Numen* 8 (1961), pp. 117-41.

102. Hesiod, *Theogony* 758-66; Pausanias, 5.18.1, on the coffer presented by Cypselus, where he tells us that twins have twisted feet. *Hypnos* is a double, ambiguous god (Alexis, *Hypnos* 2.385 K. *ap.* Athenaeus, 449D). He plays a very important role in the ἀπάτη of Hera (*Iliad* 14.231ff.); he is in love with Πασιθέη, one of the Charites (269 and 276); see Marie C. Van der Kolf, *s.v. Pasithea, R.-E.* [1949], c. 2089-90. He is also associated with *Lēthē* and the Muses (Pausanias, 2.31.3).

103. *Homeric Hymn to Hermes* 447-49. The three pleasures are εὐφροσύνη, ἔρως, and ἥδυμος ὕπνος.

104. Pindar, *Pythian* 1.6ff.

105. *Ibid.* 10ff. Oblivion, sleep, and silence are inseparable (see *Odyssey* 13.92; *Iliad* 3.420; etc.). On wine and oblivion, see Alceus, frag. 346 Edgar Lobel and Denys Page. In contrast, Alceus (see 366 Lobel-Page) was later to say: Οἶνος, ὦφίλε παῖ, καὶ ἀλάθεα. Wine, like *Peithō* and *Apatē*, is ambiguous, both good and bad (Theognis, 873-76). One aspect of Dionysus is his ability to make sorrows be forgotten (Euripides, *Bacchae* 380ff.; 423). On the relation between Dionysus and *Lēthē*, see Yvonne Vernière, "Le 'Lēthē' de Plutarque," *Revue des études anciennes* 66 (1964), pp. 22-23; Wilfried Uerschels, "Der Dionysoshymnos des Ailios Aristeides," Ph.D. diss., Bonn, 1962, pp. 46ff.

106. On the Charites, see *Scholia Iliadum* 14.276; Eustathius, 982.47. The same ambiguity reappears in the representation of the Charites, who are sometimes white and sometimes black. Like all other deities, they can only be defined through their affinities and oppositions, such as their affinities with both Hermes and Aphrodite. See also James Henry Oliver, *Demokratia, the Gods and the Free World* (Baltimore: Johns Hopkins Press, 1960), pp. 91ff. Documentation is provided by Raul Miguel Rosado Fernandes, *O Tema das Graças na Poesia Clássica* (Paris: Editions les Belles Lettres, 1962).

Hermes' lyre is his consolation; when he sings, he evokes a surge of brilliant visions (Sophocles, *Ichneutae* 317-23).

On the γάνος, see Euripides, *Bacchae* 261; 383. Henri Jeanmaire, *Dionysos* (Paris: Payot, 1951), pp. 27ff., noted how the notion of γάνος associated "ideas of brilliance and shimmering, life-giving humidity, succulent food and joy" (see also Jeanmaire, *Couroi et courètes*, pp. 436–37). Compare the procedure of γάνωσις used by Greek sculptors to impart the brilliance and force of a live body (see Charles Picard, *Manuel d'archéologie grecque: Sculpture, I, période archaïque* [Paris: Picard, 1935], p. 210 n.2).

107. See Plutarch, *Eroticos* 750A; Sappho, *Sapphousmele*, frag. 16.11 (Edgar Lobel, ed.) (Oxford: Clarendon Press, 1925). In the same dialogue (*Eroticos* 764Bff.), Plutarch recounts "Egyptian" myths in which heavenly love is opposed to the Sun, another form of love. While the latter strikes the memory with paralysis and fascinates the spirit with pleasure, real love is a fount of memory. Such mythicophilosophical variations naturally become grafted on to certain beliefs in mythical thought. On the sleep "of love," see, e.g., *Odyssey* 11.245. On a different level of thought, Plotinus plays on a double meaning of forgetfulness: it is both inattention, sensible memory, and sleep, all of which detach one from the intelligible (3.6.5; 4.4.2–8), and true oblivion, which permits one to pass from the sensible to the intelligible (4.3.32; 4.4.1). On this last point, I am following René Schaerer, *Le Héros, le sage et l'événement* (Paris: Aubier, 1965), pp. 193–94. On the problems of Plotinian memory, see Edward Warren, "Memory in Plotinus," *Classical Quarterly* (1965).

108. Jean-Pierre Vernant, "Hestia-Hermes: The Religious Expression of Space and Movement in Ancient Greece," in *M.T.*, pp. 126–76, provides a lengthy analysis of this complementarity and points out that polarity "is so fundamental a feature of this thought that it is even to be found within the deity of the hearth, *as if one part of Hestia necessarily already belonged to Hermes*" (emphasis mine).

109. Pherecydes, *ap.* Jacoby, *Fragmente der Grieschen Historike* 3F16A.

110. Pausanias, 2.31.3–4; see Hermog., *ap. Rhetores graeci*, vol. 4, p. 43 Walz.

111. Hesiod, *Theogony* 80ff. Hesiod's king brings about "changes," μετάτροπα ἔργα (*Theogony* 89). When the poet sings of the exploits of men and gods, one effect is certainly forgetfulness, but another is παρατρέπειν (*Theogony* 103). The same image of change is to be found in the rhetoric of Gorgias: ἔπεισε καὶ μετέστησεν αὐτὴν γοητεία (Diels, *Fragmenta Veterorum Stoicorum*[7], vol. 2, p. 291.2) and γνώμης τάχος ὡς εὐμετάβολον ποιοῦν τὴν τῆς δόξης πίστιν (Diels, *Fragmenta Veterorum Stoicorum*[7], vol. 2, p. 292.11–12); and also in the "pronouncements" of Protagoras (*ap.* Plato, *Thaeatetus* 166D–167D). These "operations of reversal" are essential in rhetoric, as Plato (*Republic* 412E–413D) shows. Twice in this passage, three participles introduce the same fundamental idea of succumbing to *apatē*. At 412E6–7, we find γοητευόμενοι, βιαζόμενοι, ἐπιλανθανόμενοι; at 413B1, κλαπέντες, γοητευθέντες, βιασθέντες, three homologous terms. Κλέπτεσθαι belongs to the semantic field of Peithō and Apatē (see *Iliad* 14.217; Hesiod, *Theogony* 613; *Iliad* 1.32; Pindar, *Nemean* 7.23; 8.31–34; Hesiod, *Works* 789; Aristotle, *Rhetoric* 3.7.5). The image of theft refers to the mythical theme of Hermes the Thief, the master of ψευδεῖς

λόγοι, the Nocturnal One, who dispenses oblivion. As for the image of violence, this is closely associated with the notion of πειθώ (see p. 77 above). These three terms are reduced by Plato (*Republic* 413B–C) to a single common denominator: μεταδοξάζειν. To be robbed, fascinated, or violated essentially means to change one's mind or undergo a reversal of opinion. Furthermore, Georges Dumézil, "L'Idéologie tripartite des Indo-Européens," in *Collection Latomus*, vol. 31 (Brussels: Société d'Etudes Latins de Bruxelles, 1958), p. 21 (= *Latomus* 14 [1955]) detected in this Platonic passage a "triad of violations" of Indo-European origin. On the image of the Siren as applied to Pisistratus, see Cecil Maurice Bowra, *Greek Lyric Poetry*, 2nd ed. (Oxford: Clarendon Press, 1961), p. 322. Nestor, king of Pylos, the epitome of the wise king, is above all a king "with gentle speech" (ἡδυεπής: *Iliad* 1.248): "from [his] lips the streams of words ran sweeter than honey" (*Iliad* 1.249). See J. Schmidt, *s.v. Nestor, R.-E.* (1936), c. 120.

112. Philostratus, *Imagines* 1.17.3, p. 332.30K.

113. Plutarch, *De sera numinis vindicta* 22, p. 566D (on the oracle common to both Night and the Moon, which has no fixed seat but wanders everywhere among men, in dreams and apparitions). On a kind of dream that is δολοπλόκος and φάσματα ποικίλλουσα, see Nonnus of Panopolis, *Dionysiaka* 29.326 (Keydell, ed.). On the misleading dream that assails Xerxes, see Herodotus, 7.12ff. It is probably this dream, in the guise of Ἀπάτη represented on a red-figure vase, alongside Asia and facing Greece, surrounded by the gods (Baumeister, *Denkmäler* 1 (1885), pp. 408–12).

114. Lucian, *Vera historia* 2.33, *ap.* Diels, *Fragmenta Veterorum Stoicorum*[7], vol. 2, p. 337.10ff.

115. A line written by an anonymous poet, cited by Plutarch, *Eroticos* 764E.

116. *Odyssey* 19.562–67. There is clearly a play on the word κραίνειν in the image of the horn (κέρας); similarly, the image of ἐλέφας refers to the verb that a gloss of Hesychius (ἐλεφῆραι ᾽ἀπατῆσαι) interprets as "trickery." This verb is often rightly associated with ὀλοφώϊα, the tricks of the Old Man of the Sea (*Odyssey* 4.410) or the enchantress Circe (*Odyssey* 10.289; see also 17.248).

117. *Homeric Hymn to Hermes* 558. On the problem of the Σεμναί, see Kurt Latte, *s.v. Orakel, R.-E.* (1939), c. 832; Ulrich von Wilamowitz, *Der Glaube der Hellenen*, vol. 1, pp. 379ff. (Basel: B. Schwabe, 1956); Allen, Halliday, and Sikes, *The Homeric Hymns* (Oxford: Clarendon Press, 1936), pp. 346ff.; M. Feyel, *Revue archaeologique* (1946), pp. 9ff.; Pierre Amandry, *La Mantique apollinienne à Delphes* (Paris: Editions de Boccard, 1950), pp. 60–64; Jeanmaire, *Dionysos*, pp. 190–91.

118. In the invisible world in which the human mind is submerged in oblivion (see *Iliad* 22.387–90), some, such as Tiresias (*Odyssey* 10.493–95) and

Amphiaraus (Sophocles, *Electra* 841), are favored in that they remember everything. The case of Ethalides is another exceptional one (Apollonius of Rhodes, *Argonautica* 1.640ff.).

119. Plutarch, *De E apud Delphos*, p. 394A. Apollo is the *straight* one, but that does not prevent him from also being the *oblique* one.

120. This ambiguity of the Greek gods is analyzed at length by Clemence Ramnoux, *Mythologie ou la famille olympienne* (Paris: A. Colin, 1962). On the theological problem of deceptive gods, see K. Deichgräber, *Der Listensinnende Trug des Gottes* (Göttingen: Vandenhoeck & Ruprecht, 1952), pp. 108–41.

121. Aeschylus, *Agamemnon* 1178–79, trans. Richmond Lattimore (Chicago: University of Chicago Press, 1953). At the beginning of *Agamemnon* (1.36–39), the watchman says enigmatically: "I speak to those who understand, but if they fail, I *have forgotten everything* (λήθομαι)." On the ambiguity of oracles, see Roland Crahay, *La Littérature oraculaire chez Hérodote* (Paris: Editions les Belles Lettres, 1956), pp. 48–50, 153–54, 198, 244–55; William Bedell Stanford, *Ambiguity in Greek Literature: Studies in Theory and Practice* (Oxford: Blackwell, 1939), pp. 120ff.

122. See Sophocles, frag. 704N².

123. These are the Muses to whom Μνημοσύνη gives birth in order that they should be the λησμοσύνη of mortals.

124. Hesiod, *Theogony* 27–28. This text, which commentators usually interpret as referring to a clash between Hesiod and Homeric poetry, plays an important role in Accame, "L'Invocazione alla Musa," who detects in it the climax of a "crisis" in poetic intuition, of which the Greeks were well aware as early as at the time of the *Iliad*. However, he does not address the problem of the ambiguity of speech. For other references, see Lanata, *Poetica pre-platonica*, pp. 24–25.

125. See Jean-Pierre Vernant, "The Representation of the Invisible and the Psychological Category of the Double: The Colossos," in *M.P.*, pp. 305ff.

126. *Iliad* 23.65–107. See the definition of the φαντασίαι by Quint., *Instituto Oratoria* 6.2.29: Quas φαντασίας Graeci vocant (nos sane visiones appellemus) per quas imagines rerum *absentium* ita repraesentantur animo, ut eas cernere oculis ac *praesentes* habere videamur.

127. *Odyssey* 19.203: ἴσκε ψεύδεα πολλὰ λέγων ἐτύμοισιν ὁμοῖα. Theognis, 713: οὐδ' εἰ ψεύδεα μὲν ποιοῖς ἐτύμοισιν ὁμοῖα. This is the same formula used by Dionysius of Halicarnassus, 1, *Opusculorum* 30.13 (Hermann Usener and Ludwig Radermacher, eds.) (Stuttgart: Teubner, 1965) to describe the art of Lysias.

128. *Dissoi Logoi* 3.10, ap. Diels, *Fragmenta Veterorum Stoicorum*[7], vol. 2, pp. 410.29–411.2. On tragedy and ἀπάτη, see Thomas G. Rosenmeyer, "Gorgias, Aeschylus, and 'Apate,'" *American Journal of Philology* 76 (1955). For Plato, an

ambiguous reply is a "tragic" one (*Meno*, p.76E); the "tragic" belongs to the category of "trickery" (ψεῦδος) (*Cratylus*, p. 408C).

129. On this "sharing" see André Rivier, *Un Emploi archaïque de l'analogie chez Héraclite et Thucydide* (Lausanne: F. Rouge, 1952), esp. pp. 51ff. On *mimēsis*, see Hermann Koller, *Die Mimesis in der Antike* (Berne: A. Francke, 1954). On the difference between ὁμοῖα and ἐοικότα, see André Rivier, "Sur les fragments 34 et 35 de Xénophane," *Revue de philologie, de littérature, et d'histoire ancienne* 30 (1956), p. 51 n.7, who stresses (pp. 51–52) the distance between Xenophanes' expression (frag. 35) and that used by Hesiod (*Theogony* 27–28).

130. Good examples of mythic thought and ambiguity are provided in Louis Renou, "L'Ambiguité du vocabulaire du Ṛg-Veda," *Journal asiatique* 130 (1939).

131. See Vernant, "Representation of the Invisible."

132. Plato, *Cratylus* 408C.

133. Vernant, "Hestia-Hermes," shows how, in the Greek pantheon, complementarity between two deities "presupposes, in each of them, an internal opposition or tension that confers a fundamental ambiguity upon each as a deity." But on complementarity in religious thought generally, see the works of Georges Dumézil, particularly *Mitra-Varuna* (New York: Zone Books, 1988) and *Les Dieux des Indo-Européens* (Paris: Presses Universitaires de France, 1952).

The analysis of ambiguity needs to be extended in every direction, according to the method described by Claude Lévi-Strauss, "Structure and Form: Reflections on a Work by Vladimir Propp," in *Structural Anthropology*, vol. 2 (Chicago: University of Chicago Press, 1983), p. 135:

> But to understand the meaning of a term is always to change it in all its contexts. In the case of oral literature, these contexts are at first provided by the totality of the variants, that is, by the system of compatibilities and incompatibilities that characterize the permutable totality. That the eagle appears by day and that the owl appears by night in the same function already permits the definition of the former as a diurnal owl and of the latter as a nocturnal eagle, and this signifies that the pertinent opposition is that of day and night.
>
> If the oral literature considered is of an ethnographic type, other contexts exist, provided by the ritual, the religious beliefs, the superstitions, and also by factual knowledge. It is then to be noticed that the eagle and the owl together are put in opposition to the raven, as predators to scavenger, while they are opposed to each other at the level of day and night; and that the duck is in opposition to all three at the new level of the pairs sky-land and sky-water. Thus, a "universe of the tale" will be progressively defined, analyzable in pairs of oppositions, diversely combined within each charac-

ter who – far from constituting a single entity – is a bundle of differential elements, in the manner of the phoneme as conceived by Roman Jakobson.

Jacqueline Roumeguère-Eberhardt, *Pensée et société africaines: Essais sur une dialectique de complémentarité antagoniste chez les Bantu du Sud-Est* (The Hague: Mouton, 1963), provides a number of remarkable examples of "antagonistic complementarity."

134. On the necessary conditions for a history of philosophical thought, see Louis Althusser, "On the Young Marx," in *For Marx* (London: Verso, 1979).

CHAPTER FIVE: THE PROCESS OF SECULARIZATION

1. Obviously enough, I am not including profane uses of speech, although I certainly recognize their importance. However, of the types of speech that correspond to institutions, religious efficacious speech and profane dialogue-speech seem to constitute the two most important categories. At the level of profane speech, a whole history of "truth" must be considered, as the works of Wilhelm Luther, H. Boeder, et al. have shown.

2. See Henri Jeanmaire, *Couroi et courètes* (Lille: Bibliothèque Universitaire, 1939); Jean-Pierre Vernant, *Les Origines de la pensée grecque* (Paris: Presses Universitaires de France, 1962), pp. 9ff., and "Hesiod's Myth of the Races: An Essay in Structural Analysis," in *M.T.*, pp. 3–32; Francis Vian, *La Guerre des géants: Le Mythe avant l'époque hellénistique* (Paris: Klincksieck, 1952), and *Les Origines de Thèbes: Cadmos et les Spartes* (Paris: Klincksieck, 1963). See also Georges Dumézil, *Aspects de la fonction guerrière chez les Indo-Européens* (Paris: Presses Universitaires de France, 1956). On the problems of hoplite reform, see Martin P. Nilsson, "Die Hoplitentaktik und das Staatswesen," *Klio* (Berlin: Akademie-Verlag, 1928); Hilda Lorimer, "The Hoplite Phalanx with Special Reference to the Poems of Archilochus and Tyrtaeus," *Annual of British School at Athens* 42 (1947); A. Andrewes, *The Greek Tyrants* (London: Hutchinson's University Library, 1956), pp. 31–42; Paul Courbin, "Une Tombe géométrique d'Argos," *Bulletin de correspondance hellénique* (81), 1957; Anthony Snodgrass, "L'Introduzione degli opliti in Grecia e in Italia," *Rivista storica italiana* 77 (1965), "The Hoplite Reform and History," *Journal of Hellenic Studies* 85 (1965), and *Early Greek Armour and Weapons* (Edinburgh: University Press, 1964).

3. In the pages that follow, I draw freely on a number of points from "En Grèce archaïque: Géométrie, politique et société," *Annales: Economies, sociétés, civilisations* (1965).

4. On funerary games, see Ludolf Malten, "Leichenspiel und Totenkult," *Mitteilungen des deutsche archäologische Institut der Röme Abteilumgen* 38/39 (1923-24), pp. 300ff., and *s.v. Leichenagon, R.-E.* (1925), c. 1859-61. The jurid-

ical aspect of the games has been stressed by Louis Gernet, "Jeux et Droit (Remarques sur le XXIIIe chant de l'*Iliade*)," *Revue d'histoire du droit français et étranger* (1948), pp. 177ff.; repr. *Droit et société dans la Grèce ancienne* (Paris: Recueil Sirey, 1955).

5. In *ibid.*, Gernet writes: "The law that begins to appear on the scene does not seem to be a special professional technique. It simply emanated from the life of the games; there is certainly a continuity between the agonistic and the legal customs."

6. *Iliad* 23.256ff., trans. Richmond Lattimore (Chicago: University of Chicago Press, 1951). On the meaning of iron, see Louis Deroy, "Les Noms du fer en grec et en latin," *L'Antiquité classique* 31 (1962).

7. *Iliad* 23.704: γυναῖκ' ἐς μέσσον ἔθηκε. Other expressions, such as θῆκ' ἐς ἀγῶνα φέρων...(*Iliad* 23.799, 23.886), are also to be found. On the meanings of ἀγών in epic, see Roland Martin, *Recherches sur l'Agora grecque: Etudes d'histoire et d'architecture urbaines* (Paris: Editions de Boccard, 1951), pp. 19, 22, 48, 161, 169, 214. Most of the contents take place in the ἀγών, the middle of the assembly: *Iliad* 23.507; 23.685; 23.710; 23.814. Finally, it is worth noting that the verb τιθέναι is always used here, as also in the political vocabulary recorded by Herodotus (cf. p. 102 above). See *Iliad* 23.263; 23.631; 23.653; 23.656; 23.700; 23.740; 23.748; 23.750-51; 23.799; *Odyssey* 24.86; 24.91.

8. *Odyssey* 24.80-86.

9. [Hesiod], *Shield* 312; see *Iliad* 23.273.

10. Xenophon, *Anabasis* 3.1.21, trans. Carleton L. Brownson (London and Cambridge, MA: Loeb Classical Library, 1968) [translation adapted – TRANS].

11. Theognis, 994.

12. Demosthenes, *Philippicae* 1.4-1.5.

13. Booty belongs to the class of possessions the Greeks call κτήματα, as opposed to πατρῷα. See E.F. Brueck, "Totenteil und Seelgerät im griechischen Recht," *Münchener Beiträge zur Papyrusforschung und antiken Rechtsgeschichte*, vol. 9 (Munich: Beck, 1926), pp. 39ff. The author correctly points out that at this time there was no truly abstract concept of the right of property. "Individual property" is thus no more than a useful, if dangerous, abstraction used to cover various modes of possession. On booty in Homeric society, see Marie Delcourt, *Oedipe ou la légende du conquérant* (Paris: Editions Droz, 1944), pp. 239-44; Eduard Buchholz, *Die Homerische Realien*, vol. 2, pt. 1 (Leipzig: W. Engelmann, 1881), pp. 328ff. André Aymard, "Le Partage des profits de la guerre dans les traités d'alliance antiques," *Revue historique* (1958), pp. 233-49, does not consider the archaic data. Pierre Vidal-Naquet has drawn my attention to the passage in Thucydides, 7.85.3, in which the state's share of the booty (κοινόν) is opposed to individual shares. The idea of an agreement reached between the

fighting men plays an important role here. See also Alphonse Dain, "Le Partage du butin d'après les traités juridiques et militaires," *Actes du VIe congrès international des études byzantines*, vol. 1 (1950), who notes: "The division of the spoils was organized according to the degree of authority an individual held. The lots were distributed either among the fighting men themselves or among the various military units," but "the most distinguished soldiers were allowed the choicest pieces."

14. Theognis, 678ff.: δασμὸς δ'οὐκέτ' ἴσως γίνεται ἐς τὸ μέσον.

15. Sophocles, *Philoctetes* 609: Helenus is a "θήραν καλήν."

16. When Agamemnon asks Achilles for an extra honorific share to compensate for the one he has to reserve for Apollo, Achilles replies: "There is no great store of things lying about I know of. But what we took from the cities by storm has been distributed (δέδασται)" (*Iliad* 1.124–25). This text shows clearly that, before the δασμός, all the goods were ξυνήια.

17. See p. 97 above.

18. *Iliad* 328ff. See Gernet, *Droit et société*, p. 15.

19. See *ibid.*, p. 16.

20. The act of setting one's hand on something is often rendered by the verb ἀείρειν (ἀείρεσθαι, ἀναείρειν) which has "a concrete meaning" (*Iliad* 23.614; 23.778; 23.823; 23.856; 23.882), or by verbs such as λαμβάνειν, ἅπτεσθαι (23.273; 23.511; 23.666), or ἑλεῖν (23.613). Ajax's gesture is of this kind: "He takes the ploughing ox" (23.779–81). Gernet, *Droit et société*, p. 11, notes that Dares makes exactly the same gesture, in the games held in honor of Anchises (*Aeneid* 5.380ff.). The meaning of this gesture has been studied by Fernand de Visscher, *Etudes de droit romain* (Paris: Librairie du Recueil Sirey, 1931), pp. 353ff.

21. See *Iliad* 23.624; 23.537; 23.565. Gernet, *Droit et société*, p. 11, has emphasized the opposition between the gesture of presenting a gift and the gesture of setting one's hand on something.

22. Gernet, *Droit et société*, p. 13. Ernst Cassin, *L'Année sociologique* (1952), p. 119, believes that the prizes "are in reality dedicated by Achilles to the dead hero.... [T]hey are to be drawn from the Beyond by the valor, skill, or luck of the competitors." But nothing here suggests that the center has a religious significance. On the religious meanings of the center and how they relate to its other meanings, see Vernant in *M.T.*, pp. 176–90.

23. See *Iliad* 23.565.

24. On gifts, see Louis Gernet, "La Notion mythique de la valeur en Grèce," *Journal de psychologie normale et pathologique* (1948), pp. 430ff., and *Droit et prédroit en Grèce ancienne*, 3rd series, 1948–49 (1951), pp. 26ff.; Marcel Mauss, "Essai sur le don: Forme et raison de l'échange dans les sociétés archaïques," repr., *Sociologie et anthropologie* (Paris: Presses Universitaires de France, 1950),

pp. 145ff.; René Maunier, "Recherches sur les échanges rituels en Afrique du Nord," *L'Année sociologique*, n.s., vol. 2, 1924–25 (1927), pp. 11ff.; Moses I. Finley, "Marriage, Sale and Gift in the Homeric World," *Revue internationale des droits de l'Antiquité*, 3rd ser., vol. 2 (1955), pp. 167–94.

25. No doubt honorific shares were first allotted to various important figures. Lots would be drawn only for whatever remained. Although this procedure is not directly attested, it seems safe to assume it was common practice.

26. See *Iliad* 9.335.

27. *Ibid.* 19.173ff.

28. *Ibid.* 19.174.

29. *Ibid.* 19.242ff. This is more or less the same expression as that used in 23.704, when Achilles sets out the prizes for the games.

30. *Ibid.* 19.277ff.

31. *Ibid.* 1.126. In the *Odyssey*, the opposition between public and private is set out very clearly (2.32; 2.44; 3.82; 4.314; 20.264–65; all passages cited by Chester G. Starr, *The Origins of Greek Civilization* [New York: Knopf, 1961], p. 336).

32. Herodotus, *The Persian Wars* 7.152, trans. George Rawlinson (New York: Modern Library, 1942). The same story, but lacking any allusion to the μέσον, is to be found in the *Dissoi Logoi* 2.18 (Diels, *Fragmenta Veterorum Stoicorum*[7], vol. 2, pp. 409.2ff.). See Herodas, 2.90. During a trial in which he accuses a grain merchant of violating one of his "girls," Battaros declares that, if his adversary demands that the inquiry include interrogation under torture (since the victim is of servile origin) (see the introduction by John Arbuthnot Nairn and Louis Laloy, in *Collection des Universités de France* [Paris, 1928], pp. 47–48), he himself offers to take her place provided the award for damages is set down ἐν τῷ μέσῳ. See also Xenophon, *Economicus* 7.26.

33. Plutarch, *De amore fraterno* 483C-E: on the death of a father, Plutarch advises the sons to leave the use of his possessions to be shared in common (χρῆσιν δὲ καὶ κτῆσιν ἐν μέσῳ κεῖσθαι κοινὴν καὶ ἀνέμητον ἁπάντων). On this text, see Harry Louis Levy, "Property Distribution by Lot in Present-Day Greece," *Transactions of the Proceedings of the American Philological Association* 87 (1956), pp. 42–50. Lucian, *Cronosolon* 19, vol. 3, p. 312, Karl Jacobitz (ed.) (Leipzig: C.F. Koehler, 1936–41). Cf. Aristophanes, *Assembl.* 602. But the meaning of the expression may have been lost at an early date; e.g., in Euripides, *Ion* 1284, where κοινόν doubles up with ἐν μέσῳ.

34. *Iliad* 7.383–84.

35. *Ibid.* 7.417. The same procedure is followed in other military assemblies; see Xenophon, *Cyropaedia* 7.5.46. At 2.2.3 there is even a reference to ἐς μέσον in connection with the κύκλος κατακειμένων στρατιωτῶν.

36. *Odyssey* 2.37ff., trans. Richmond Lattimore (New York: Harper & Row, 1965).

37. *Iliad* 19.76-77.

38. See *Odyssey* 2.37ff.; Gernet's remarks on the meaning of the scepter in *Droit et prédroit*, p. 96.

39. *Odyssey* 2.28ff. On Aegyptius's declaration and the problem of the convocation of the assembly, see Martin, *Recherches sur l'Agora grecque*, pp. 31ff., who regards this as an example of what Albert Severyns (*Homère, le poète et son oeuvre* [Brussels: Office de Publicité, 1946], pp. 23-26) calls a "compound anachronism."

40. Ξυνόν is a political concept that played an important role in the seventh and sixth centuries. One of its most ancient uses appears in Tyrtaeus, 9.15ff., who develops the idea of a ξυνὸν ἐσθλόν for the *polis* and the *demos*. In Herodotus, *The Persian Wars* 7.53, common property is ξυνὸν ἀγαθόν, a synonym for κοινόν, used to refer to the state. The philosophers made great use of it: Democritus *ap*. Diels, *Fragmenta Veterorum Stoicorum*[7], vol. 2, pp. 195.15; 203.13; 205.10; Heraclitus, *ap*. Diels, *Fragmenta Veterorum Stoicorum*[7], vol. 1, pp. 151.2ff.; 169.4; 174.1; 176.4; etc. In a tendentious study entitled "Zur Sociologie des archaïschen Griechentums," *Gymnasium* 65 (1958), pp. 48-58, Bruno Snell suggested that the idea of a community, a ξυνωνίη (as opposed to the status of an individual, as it appears in, e.g., Archilochus of Paros, frag. 98.7 [François Lasserre and Bonnard, eds.] [Paris: Editions les Belles Lettres, 1958]), marked a decisive change from Homer. My own belief is that passages such as the one that I have studied here probably limit the force of Snell's conclusions, or at least point to the existence of links of continuity alongside any break that may have occurred. There is no break between the "common property" of the military group in epic and the ξυνόν of Tyrtaeus's *Homoioi*.

In a compound form, ἐπίξυνος, the same adjective is used to qualify a type of land that is unquestionably common property (*Iliad* 12.421ff.). See the remarks of Edouard Will, "Aux origines du régime foncier grec: Homère, Hésiode et l'arrière-plan mycénien," *Revue des études anciennes* 59 (1957), pp. 6ff.

41. Apollonius of Rhodes, *Argonautica* 3.173 (Hermann Fränkel, ed.) (Oxford: Clarendon Press, 1961).

42. Gernet, *Droit et société*, p. 16. When Achilles suggests awarding the second prize to Eumelos (*Iliad* 23.539ff.), the public approves (ἐπαινεῖν). All the suitors similarly approve Antinoos's speech (*Odyssey* 4.673).

43. *Iliad* 15.282-85. See Jeanmaire, *Couroi et courètes*, p. 42.

44. *Iliad* 9.443. See Pindar, *Nemean* 8.8; Bacchylides, 9.89-91 Snell[6].

45. However, in the Greek society of epic, the elders (γέροντες) are opposed to the young men (νέοι, κοῦροι). This opposition is reflected at the level of vocab-

ulary in the two terms *boulē* and *agora*: the *boulē* is the council, reserved for the elders and councillors (μήδοντες), while the *agora* is the plenary assembly of all men old enough to bear arms (see Jeanmaire, *Couroi et courètes*, pp. 14ff.).

46. André Aymard, "Sur l'Assemblée macédonienne," *Revue des études anciennes* 52 (1950), pp. 127ff. In the archaic Greek states, the army assembly was a permanent substitute for the citizens: Aristotle, *Politics* 4.10.10.1297B (cited by Aymard, p. 131). On the reciprocity between the citizens and the army, see Claude Mossé, *Revue des études anciennes* (1953), pp. 29–35 (1963); pp. 290–97.

47. Polybius, 5.27.1; 4; 6.

48. Ἰσηγορίη *ap.* Herodotus, 5.78 (see ἰσοκρατιά, 5.92): Ἰσαγόρης *ap.* Herodotus, 5.66; 5.70; 5.72; 5.74. See Emmanuel Laroche, *Histoire de la racine NEM- en grec ancien* (Paris: Klincksieck, 1949), p. 186.

49. Philodemos, Περὶ τοῦ καθ᾽"Ομηρον ἀγαθοῦ βασιλέως, frag. 19.14: Ἰσηγορίαν δ᾽ἔλοντες... [καὶ ἐν] ταῖς συνουσίαις καὶ τοῖς φ[ιδι]τίοις.

50. The *laos* have "meals of equal portions," in which no priorities prevail over the principle of equality. See *Iliad* 9.225, and the remarks of Athenaeus, p. 12C (A.M. Desrousseaux, ed.). On Homeric commensality, see Jeanmaire, *Couroi et courètes*, pp. 85ff., who compares these common meals to the Dorian *syssities*.

51. Schulthess collected many data in his article "*Homoioi*," *R.-E.*, 1913, c. 2252ff. but did not notice that Achilles calls himself the *homoios* of Agamemnon (*Iliad* 16.53ff.). It is possible to distinguish three kinds of *homoioi*: the professional warriors of epic; the *hippoboteis* or oligarchic *hippeis*; and sixth-century citizens (according to Maiandrios's declaration; see p. 100 above).

52. See *Odyssey* 2.30–32; 2.42–44.

53. See *Odyssey* 4.673; *Iliad* 23.539ff. Gernet, *Droit et société*, pp. 16ff., emphasized the importance of this quasi-juridical efficacy in the proclamation of the results of the games and the allotting of prizes to the winners.

54. In "Droit et prédroit," Gernet successfully showed how the efficacy of speech gave way to rational procedures. In law, its place was taken by the collective will and ratification by the social group; in philosophy, it was replaced by rationality and verifiable proofs.

55. See F. Solmsen, "The 'Gift' of Speech in Homer and Hesiod," *Transactions of the American Philological Association* 85 (1954), pp. 1–15. On the importance of πειθώ in epic, see Ebeling, *Lexicon homericum, s.v.*

56. *Iliad* 11.793; see Hesychius, *s.v.* παραίφασις ἀπολογία, παραλογισμός, παραμυθία, συμβουλία, παρηγορία, πειθώ, παραίνεσις ἤ ἀπάτη. Eustathius, 979.34: πειθὼ ἐξ ὁμιλίας. Tyrtaeus, frag. 9.19D[3] shows the importance of encouragement in military circles (θαρσύνηι δ᾽ἔπεσιν τὸν πλησίον ἄνδρα παρεστώς); see above, p. 84.

57. See *Iliad* 13.291 (ὀαριστὺς προμάχων); *Odyssey* 19.179; Hesiod, *Works* 789.

58. Paregoros is related to Πάρφασις and to Ὀαριστύς; she was present in one temple of Aphrodite, alongside Peithō, Erōs, Himēros, and Pothos (Pausanias, 1.43.6); and she is thought to be depicted on a red-figure Attic pot alongside Paris (*Archaeologische Zeitung* [1896], pp. 36ff.) (see G. Herzog-Hauser, *s.v. Paregoros, R.-E.* [1949], c. 1454). In the *Argonautica* (1.479ff.), Apollonius of Rhodes speaks of μῦθοι... παρήγοροι οἶσί περ ἀνὴρ θαρσύνοι ἕταρον (see 3.1347ff.).

59. On forms of prerhetoric in epic, see Eduard Buchholz, *Die Homerischen Realien*, vol. 3, pt. 2 (Leipzig: W. Engelmann, 1885), pp. 168ff.

60. Herodotus, *The Persian Wars* 3.142.

61. On the question of ὁμοῖος and its relations with ἴσος, see Rudolf Hirzel, *Themis, Dike und Verwandtes* (Leipzig: S. Hirzel, 1907), pp. 234ff.; Louis Gernet, *Recherches sur le développement de la pensée juridique et morale en Grèce* (Paris: Editions Leroux, 1917), pp. 457ff. The word and concept of ἰσονομία pose a number of problems. In the first place, from an etymological perspective, ἰσονομία could derive from νόμος and mean equality before the law, which is not the same as political equality. If it derives from νέμειν, as most commentators believe, it could mean an equal distribution of material shares or political rights (the sense favored by Emmanuel Laroche). If it is a matter of political equality, we should note (with Edouard Will, *Korinthiaka* [Paris: Editions de Boccard, 1955], p. 618, whose excellent account I am following here) that "the *iso-* element does not necessarily imply absolute equality." It could accommodate many different nuances of equality. However, instead of pursuing this somewhat sterile kind of inquiry into the atomist and diachronic etymology, one may prefer to investigate the kind of etymology that Vendryes, in *Bulletin Société de Linguistique de Paris* (1953), calls "static": an etymology at once synthetic and synchronic. In this method, one tries to determine the place of each word in the mind and to define its meaning and use. It is only by identifying and examining all the contexts in which the word is used that one can hope to form an approximative idea of it. At this point, we are faced by the problem of the nature of ἰσονομία in its various contexts. Following the studies of Victor Ehrenberg and others, Pierre Levêque and Pierre Vidal-Naquet have identified a number of aspects of ἰσονομία at the end of the sixth century: it can be negatively defined as the opposite to tyranny, and it appears to sometimes have an aristocratic sense. See Victor Ehrenberg, *Die Rechtsidee im frühen Griechentum* (Leipzig: S. Hirzel, 1921); *Isonomia, R.-E. Suppl.* VII, 1940 c. 293ff.; *Aspects of the Ancient World* (Oxford: B. Blackwell, 1946), ch. 4; "Origins of Democracy," *Historia* (1950), pp. 515ff.; "Das Harmodioslied," *Weiner Studien* (1956), pp. 57ff.; G. Vlastos, "Isonomia," *American Journal of Philology* (1953); J.A. Ottsen Larsen, "Cleisthenes and the Development of Democracy," *Mélanges Sabine* (Ithaca, NY: Cornell Univer-

sity Press, 1948); T.A. Sinclair, *A History of Greek Political Thought* (London: Routledge & Kegan Paul, 1951); Laroche, *Histoire de la racine NEM-*, pp. 186ff.; Will, *Korinthiaka*, pp. 618ff.; Charles Mugler, "L'Isonomie des atomistes," *Revue de philologie, de littérature et d'histoire ancienne*, 30 (1956), pp. 231ff.; Jean-Pierre Vernant, *The Origins of Greek Thought* (Ithaca, NY: Cornell University Press, 1982), pp. 24–32; Gregory Vlastos, in *Isonomia* (Berlin: Akademie Verlag, 1964), pp. 1–35.

62. According to the prudent formula of Levêque and Vidal-Naquet; see n.61.

63. See Edgar Lobel and Denys Lionel Page, *Poetarum Lesbiorum fragmenta* (Oxford: Clarendon Press, 1955), frag. 129, pp. 176–77.

64. Louis Robert, "Recherches épigraphiques, V, Inscriptions de Lesbos," *Revue des études anciennes* 62 (1960), pp. 300ff. There seems to be a necessary connection between the "political" expression ἐς μέσον and the name of a sanctuary in such a situation and with such functions. *Contra* Charles Picard, *Revue Archeologique* (1962), pp. 43–69.

65. Herodotus, *The Persian Wars* 1.170. See Vernant, *Origins of Greek Thought*, p. 127; and Pierre Levêque and Pierre Vidal-Naquet, *Clisthène l'Athénien* (Paris: Editions les Belles Lettres, 1964), pp. 66ff.

66. See Levêque and Vidal-Naquet, *Clisthène l'Athénien*, p. 66.

67. Herodotus, *The Persian Wars* 7.8; 1.207; 3.80. At 7.8, the expression τίθημι τὸ πρῆγμα ἐς μέσον is opposed to ἰδιοβουλέειν, "to take counsel from oneself alone." The expression is also sometimes used without any political implications (Herodotus, 6.129; 8.74). In this context, μέσον seems to have meanings that are close to κοινόν: Herodotus, 8.58, speaks of κοινὸν πρῆγμα. If an agreement is reached, the expression used is κοινῷ λόγῳ χρησάμενοι (1.166; 2.30). Τὸ κοινόν means not only the city, the state (1.67; 5.85; 6.14; 8.135; 9.117; 3.156; 5.109), but also the public treasury (6.58; 7.144; 9.85) or simply the general interest (3.82; 3.84). On κοινόν, see Georg Busolt, Heinrich Swoboda, and Franz Jandebeur, *Griechische Staatskunde*, vols. 1, 2 (Munich: Beck, 1920–26) (Index, vol. 2, *s.v.* κοινόν).

68. Herodotus, *The Persian Wars* 4.97; 3.83, respectively.

69. Herodotus, *The Persian Wars* 4.118; 8.21; 8.73; 3.83. To leave the μέσον is to condemn oneself to ἰδιοβουλέειν (7.8).

70. Euripides, *The Suppliant Women* 438–39, trans. Frank William Jones (Chicago: University of Chicago Press, 1958). After his famous speech praising equality, Theseus proudly tells the herald: "As for liberty, it lies in these words: whomsoever wishes...." The same expression reappears in *Orestes* 885, in a shorter form, which is also used by Demosthenes, *Pro corona* 170; Aristophanes, *Acharnian* 45; *Ecclesia.* 130; Aeschines, *Against Ctesiphon* 3. On this right of

ἰσηγορία, see, e.g., Busolt and Swoboda, *Griechische Staatskunde*, vol. 1, p. 453.

71. On "action-speech" in epic, see Buchholz, *Die Homerischen Realien*, vol. 3, pt. 2, pp. 120ff. Clemence Ramnoux, *Héraclite ou l'homme entre les choses et les mots* (Paris: Editions les Belles Lettres, 1959), pp. 51–57, 293–97, has explained its importance in the sixth century, when speech was being discovering in its opposition to action (see also Felix Heinimann, *Nomos und Physis* [Basel: F. Reinhardt, 1945], pp. 46ff.). The opposition between speech and action is a constant theme in Greek political thought; see, e.g., Protagoras, who boasts of his ability to teach everyone the talent of conducting city affairs perfectly both in actions and in words (Plato, *Protagoras* 318E–319A; see Thucydides, 1.139.4; Xenophon, *Anabasis* 3.1.45). The distinction between the two carries on the aristocratic theme of the man who excells in warfare as well as in the council (see Pindar, *Nemean* 8.8) and is "a speaker of words (μύθων τε ῥητῆρ) and one who accomplished in action (πρηκτῆρά τε ἔργων)" (see *Iliad* 9.443).

72. *Iliad* 13.128–29; 15.295–96 (ἄριστοι as distinct from πληθύς).

73. Jeanmaire, *Couroi et courètes*, p. 45.

74. See Gernet, *Droit et prédroit*, pp. 100–119; Clemence Ramnoux, *La Nuit et les enfants de la nuit* (Paris: Flammarion, 1959), pp. 145ff.

75. I am following Gernet's analysis, *Droit et prédroit*, pp. 98ff. More detailed analyses and references may be found in Louis Gernet, "Le temps dans les formes archaïques du droit," *Journal de psychologie normale et pathologique* (1956), pp. 387ff. See also Gerard Sautel, "Les Preuves dans le droit grec archaïque," *Recueils de la Société Jean Bodin* 16 (1965), pp. 128–30.

76. Aeschylus, *Eumenides* 432–33, trans. Richmond Lattimore (Chicago: University of Chicago Press, 1953).

77. From this perspective, two lines attributed to Hesiod are most interesting: μηδὲ δίκην δικάσῃς, πρὶν ἂν ἀμφοῖν μῦθον ἀκούσῃς (Hesiod, frag. 271 [*dubium*], ed. Rzach³). This saying, or variants of it, is frequently cited already by Euripides, *Heraclitus* 179–80; Aristophanes, *Wasps* 725, 919–20; *Knights* 1036; Euripides, frag. 362.9–10N². A number of authors (H.G. Evelyn-White, Schneidewin, etc.) have regarded it as a fragment of the Χείρωνος Ὑποθῆκαι, but Jacques Schwartz, *Pseudo-Hesiodeia* (Leiden: E.J. Brill, 1960), p. 77 n.3, 98, 239, 241), rejects that hypothesis. The fact remains that the recommendation "not to judge any cause before having heard both speeches" (see [Plato], *Demodocos* 382E–383A; Demosthenes, *De corona* 2; 6) conforms with the oath taken by heliasts, who undertook to listen to both the accuser and the accused with total impartiality (see Justus Hermann Lipsius, *Das attische Recht und Rechtsverfahren*, vol. 1 [Leipzig: O.R. Reisland, 1905], p. 151). It also constitutes the earliest evidence of a decisive change in judicial practice. On this level, it is also possible to detect one notion of truth: the *histōr* is a witness, one who *sees* and *hears*, and, as heir

to the *mnēmōn*, he is also a memorialist. His truth combines at least two components: nonforgetfulness and a complete and exhaustive account of what really happened. In this respect, *Iliad* 23.359–61 provides crucial evidence.

78. Aeschylus, *The Suppliant Maidens* 370ff., trans. Seth Benardete (Chicago: University of Chicago Press, 1956). On the special meaning of the royal hearth and its relation to the "public hearth," see Louis Gernet, "Sur le symbolisme politique en Grèce ancienne: le foyer commun," *Cahier international sociologie* 11 (1951), pp. 26ff.; Vernant, in *M.T.*, pp. 127ff.

79. Aeschlyus, *The Suppliant Maidens* 398–99.

80. *Ibid.* 604.

81. *Ibid.* 942–43: τοιάδε δημόπρακτος ἐκ πόλεως μία ψῆφος κέκρανται. Cf. 964–65: ὦνπερ ἥδε κραίνεται ψῆφος.

82. *Ibid.* 601: παντελῆ ψηφίσματα.

83. Vernant, *Origins of Greek Thought*, p. 49.

84. One entire section of the argument in Gorgias's *Encomium to Helen* is founded on the violence-persuasion relationship. According to Plato, *Philebus* p. 58A–B, reporting a remark made by Gorgias, the power of *logos* over the soul it is persuading is certainly that of a master over a slave; the only difference is that the soul is reduced to slavery by the mysterious constraint exercised through consent rather than force (see A. Diès, *Autour de Platon*, vol. 1 [Paris: Beauchesne, 1927], p. 120). On this point, the *Critias* (109B–C) is worth citing: after dividing up the earth by lot between all the gods, the gods "received each one his own and they settled in their countries; and when they had thus settled in them, they reared us up, even as herdsmen rear their flocks, to be their cattle and nurslings; only it was not our bodies that they constrained by bodily force, like shepherds guiding their flocks with stroke of staff, but they directed from the stern where the living creature is easiest to turn about, laying hold on the soul by persuasion, as by a rudder, according to their own disposition; and thus they drove and steered all the mortal kind." This is a remarkable text on two accounts: first on account of its pastoral images and images of navigation, the two types of metaphor dominating Greek political thought; second, its account of persuasion, which is at once similar to and different from violence. In this context the *Logos*-Hermes takes on his full significance. As an all-powerful lord, he guides his flock with the staff entrusted to him by Apollo.

85. From the vast relevant literature, see Ernst Hoffmann, *Die sprache und die archaïsche Logik* (Tübingen, 1925); Ramnoux, *Héraclite*.

86. See Vernant, *M.T.*, p. 50: "It was through its political function that *logos* first became aware of itself, its rules, and its efficacy."

87. See Eugène Dupréel, *Les Sophistes* (Neuchatel: Editions du Griffon,

1948); Mario Untersteiner, *The Sophists* (Oxford: Blackwell, 1954).

88. See the remarks of Ignace Meyerson, "Thèmes nouveaux de psychologie objective: l'histoire, la construction, la structure," *Journal de psychologie normale et pathologique* (1954), pp. 7ff.

CHAPTER SIX: A CHOICE BETWEEN ALĒTHEIA AND APATĒ

1. Ignace Meyerson, *Les Fonctions psychologiques et les oeuvres* (Paris: Vrin, 1948), p. 140.

2. This discussion of Simonides first appeared under the title "Simonides de Céos ou la sécularisation de la poésie," *Revues des études grecques* (1964).

3. In addition to Ulrich von Wilamowitz, *Sappho und Simonides* (Berlin: Weidmann, 1913), pp. 127–209, see also Wilhelm Schmid and Otto Stählin, *Geschichte der griechischen Literatur*, vol. 1, pt. 1 (Munich: Beck, 1929), pp. 505–23; Albert Severyns, *Bacchylide: Essai biographique* (Liège-Paris: Editions Droz, 1933); Georg Christ, "Simonidesstudien," Ph.D. diss. (Frieburg: Paulsdrackerei, 1941); Albin Lesky, *Geschichte der griechischen Literatur* (Berne, 1963), pp. 210ff.; Cecil Maurice Bowra, *Greek Lyric Poetry: From Alcman to Simonides* (Oxford: Clarendon Press, 1961), p. 308–72; Hermann Fränkel, *Dichtung und Philosophie des frühen Griechentums* (Munich: Beck, 1962), pp. 346–70. My remarks here owe much to Max Treu, *Von Homer zur Lyrik* (Munich: Beck, 1955), pp. 295–305. On Simonides' poetics, see also Guiliana Lanata, *Poetica pre-platonica* (Florence: La Nuova Italia, 1963), pp. 68ff.

4. See the texts cited in Schmid and Stählin, *Geschichte der griechischen Literatur*, p. 498 n.3; and those in Christ, "Simonidesstudien," pp. 61ff.; Wilhelm Nestle, *Vom Mythos zum Logos* (Stuttgart: A. Kroner, 1942), p. 153. Jean-Pierre Vernant, in *M.T.*, p. 104 n.99, has noted the importance of this change and comments on how it relates to other innovations attributed to Simonides.

5. Pindar, *Isthmian* 2.5ff. "Pindar himself, who lauds the old ways and deplores the new, in reality followed the latter" (Alfred Croiset, *Histoire de la littérature grecque*, vol. 2 [Paris: Fontemoing, 1914], p. 359). The matter was all the more scandalous in that Simonides included well-earned wealth (πλουτεῖν ἀδόλως) among man's three most estimable assets (Simonides, frag. 146/651 Page).

6. On the social and economic status of the artist, see Bernard Schweitzer, "Der bildende Künstler und der Begriff des Künstlerischen in der Antike," *Neue Heidelberger Jahrbücher, NF* (1925); Ranuccio Bianchi-Bandinelli, "L'Artista nell' Antichità classica," *Archeologica classica* 9 (1957); Margherita Guarducci, "Ancora sull'artista nell'Antiquità classica," *Archeologia classica* 10 (1958), pp. 138–50. See also François Lasserre, "La Condition du poète dans la Grèce antique," *Etudes de Lettres* 5 (Lausanne: Faculté des Lettres de l'Université de Lausanne, 1962); Bruno Gentili, "Aspetti del rapporto poeta, committente, uditorio nella lirica

corale greca," *Studi Urbinati* (Urbino: Università degli Studi di Urbino, 1965).

7. These criticisms were no doubt partly fueled by the repugnance Pierre-Maxime Schuhl, "Socrate et le travail rétribué," *Imaginer et réaliser* (Paris: Presses Universitaires de France, 1963), pp. 37–39, detects in Socrates, among others, at the idea of reducing an "intellectual activity" to the level of other techniques.

8. The data are cited in Schmid and Stählin, *Geschichte der griechischen Literatur*, p. 516 n.6. See Bowra, *Greek Lyric Poetry*, p. 363; Christ, "Simonides-studien," pp. 43ff.

9. Empedocles, frag. 23.2 *ap*. Diels, *Fragmenta Veterorum Stoicorum*[7], vol. 1, p. 321.10ff. See Pierre-Maxime Schuhl, *Platon et l'art de son temps*, 2nd ed. (Paris: Presses Universitaires de France, 1952), p. 90 n.4; on p. 90, Schuhl analyzes the passage in the *Timaeus* (68D) in which Plato declares that only gods are "sufficiently wise and powerful to blend the many into one and to dissolve again the one into many."

On *mētis* see Henri Jeanmaire, "La Naissance d'Athéna et la royauté magique de Zeus," *Revue archeologique* (1956), pp. 19ff.

10. Marcel Detienne and Jean-Pierre Vernant, "The Ploys of Cunning: Antilochus' Race," *Cunning Intelligence in Greek Culture and Society* (Hassocks, UK: Harvester Press, 1978).

11. See Δισσοὶ Λόγοι, 3.10 *ap*. Diels, *Fragmenta Veterorum Stoicorum*[7], vol. 2, p. 410.30ff.

12. The anecdote is reported by Plutarch, *De poetis audiendis* 15D. It has often been compared to Gorgias's theory of ἀπάτη (e.g., Schuhl, *Platon et l'art*, p. 84), a comparison used to justify even the attribution of the anecdote itself to Gorgias by, e.g., Wilamowitz, *Sappho und Simonides*, p. 143, followed by Mario Untersteiner, *Sofisti, Testimonianze e Frammenti*, vol. 2 (Florence: La Nuova Italia, 1949), pp. 142–43. However, as Thomas G. Rosenmeyer, "Gorgias, Aeschylus and Apate," *American Journal of Philology* 76.3 (1955), p. 233, correctly points out (and as I also hope to show), the anecdote only takes on its full meaning in light of frag. 55D. See also Abraham Bernard van Groningen, "Simonide et les Thessaliens," *Mnemosyne*, 4th ser., 1 (1948), pp. 1–7, in which the author seeks to prove that Simonides' Thessalian poems (see Severyns, *Bacchylides: Essai biographique*, pp. 30ff.) did not contain any myths or any "misleading elements." In van Groningen's view, the anecdote must obviously allude to the fact that the Thessalians did not appreciate poetry as such, since, for Simonides, all true poetry contained an element of ἀπάτη.

13. Treu, *Von Homer zur Lyrik*, pp. 298ff., has tried to define the role played by painting. In particular he stressed the importance of [Hesiod's] *Shield*, which marks a turning point with its technique of "illusion." In the description of Heracles' shield, images of resemblance recur repeatedly (191ff., 198, 206, 209,

210–11, 215, 228, 244) through adjectives such as ἵκελος and ἐοικώς (on which see also Carlo Ferdinando Russo, *Hesiodi Scutum* [Florence: La Nuova Italia, 1950], pp. 25ff.). However, to make more progress, it would be necessary to understand more about the delicate problems of εἰκός, the complexity of which has been demonstrated by André Rivier, *Un Emploi archaïque de l'analogie chez Héraclite et Thucydide* (Lausanne: F. Rouge, 1952). On the date of the *Shield*, see Pierre Guillon, *Etudes béotiennes: Le Bouclier d'Héraclès et l'histoire de la Grèce centrale dans la période de la première guerre sacrée* (Aix-en-Provence: Editions Ophrys, 1963).

14. Michel Psellos, Π. ἐνεργ. δαίμ., 821, Migne (*P.G.*, vol. 122). Bowra, *Greek Lyric Poetry*, emphasizes the importance of the word εἰκών.

15. On the image as "something distinct from the real thing" (Plato, *Sophistes*, 240A), see Pierre-Maxime Schuhl, *Etudes sur la fabulation platonicienne* (Paris: Presses Universitaires de France, 1947), p. 102, and *Platon et l'art*. On εἰκών, see the remarks of Karl Kérényi, ΑΓΑΛΜΑ, ΕΙΚΩΝ, ΕΙΔΩΛΟΝ, in "Demitizzazione e imagine," *Biblioteca dell' archivio di filosofia* (Padua: CEDAM, 1962), pp. 169ff.

16. Lillian Hamilton Jeffery, *The Local Scripts of Archaic Greece* (Oxford: Clarendon Press, 1961), pp. 62ff.

17. Simonides seems to mark the moment when the Greeks discovered the image and seems to have been the first to theorize it. Treu, of *Von Homer zur Lyrik*, p. 297, regards him as the first to subscribe to the doctrine of *mimēsis* (on which see Hermann Koller, *Die Mimesis in der Antike* [Berne: A. Francke, 1954]).

18. No matter how radical that break may have been, however, it did not imply a rejection pure and simple of all that one expected to find in the work of a poet. Simonides, of course, remained a poet who composed *epinicions* and invoked the Muses (see Simonides, frag. 73/578 Page). But his Muses are no longer those of Homer; see frag. 46 Theodor Bergk (often attributed to Stesichorus), with the commentaries by Treu, *Von Homer zur Lyrik*, p. 303; and Bowra, *Greek Lyric Poetry*, pp. 361–62. On this same fragment, see also Guiliana Lanata, "La Poetica dei Lirici Greci arcaici," in *Mélanges Ugo Enrico Paoli* (Genoa, 1956), p. 181; Herwig Maehler, *Die Auffassung des Dichterberufs im frühen Griechentum bis zur Zeit Pindars* (Göttingen: Vanderhoeck & Ruprecht, 1963), pp. 70ff.

19. Frag. 55 Diehl³ (see Bergk, *PLG⁴*, vol. 3, p. 420) (= *Poetae melici graeci* [Oxford: Clarendon Press, 1962], frag. 93/598 Denys Lionel Page). This is perhaps the place to make a few comments on the *P. Oxyr.* 2432 (Lobel, ed.) (= frag. 36/541 Page), which Lobel suggested should be attributed to Simonides. Line 5 reads: ἁ δ'ἀλάθε[ι]α παγκρατής κτλ. These lines have already prompted a number of long commentaries: M. Treu, "Neues zu Simonides" (*Oxyrhynchus Papyri* 2432), *Rheinisches Museum für Philologie* 103 (1960); Bruno Gentili, *Gnomon*

33 (1961), pp. 338ff.; Hugh Lloyd-Jones, *Classical Review* 11 (1961), p. 19; Fränkel, *Dichtung und Philosophie*, p. 357 n.22; Cecil Maurice Bowra, "Simonides or Bacchylides?" *Hermes* 91 (1963), pp. 257–67. The question of their attribution remains uncertain. Lloyd-Jones and Bowra favor Bacchylides, and Bowra's reasons for doing so are very persuasive. However, Gentili and Treu favor Simonides, and Treu's arguments are equally compelling. In his study, Treu recognizes that line 5 raises a problem and produces an excellent reason to believe it does not contradict what else we know of Simonides (pp. 325ff.). If this poem was the work of Simonides, it would in itself provide further arguments; indeed, the same ones Treu develops so as to point out the specific characteristics of Simonides. Gentili has on two occasions returned to the problem of the *Oxyrhynchus Papyri* 2432 (see Gennaro Perrotta and Bruno Gentili, *Polinnia: Poesia greca arcaïca* [Messina: G. d'Anna, 1965], pp. 313–20; Bruno Gentili, "Studi su Simonide, II. Simonide e Platone," *Maia* 16 [1964], pp. 278–306). His analyses, which argue convincingly for attributing the line to Simonides, furthermore allow an interpretation that agrees with my own interpretation here.

20. The references are cited by Schmid and Stählin, *Geschichte der griecheschen Literatur*, p. 521 n.12; Paul Maas, *s.v. Simonides, R.-E.* (1927), c. 192, 1f.; Christ, "Simonidesstudien," p. 75D. Schmid is careful to note the unmistakable affinities with the sophistic trend. F. Grégoire, "Mnemotechnie et mémoire," *Revue philosophique* (1956), pp. 494–528, is also useful reading.

21. See Schmid and Stählin, *Geschichte der griecheschen Literatur*, p. 522 n.1; Vernant, in *M.T.*, p. 108 n.99.

22. See François Lasserre, "La Condition du poète dans la Grèce antique," *Etudes de lettres* 5 (1962), pp. 11ff.

23. See Luc de Heusch, "Réflexions ethnologiques sur la technique," *Les Temps modernes* 211 (Dec. 1963). On the relation between writing and the administrative and economic needs of the Mesopotamian world, see M. Lambert, "La Naissance de la bureaucratie," *Revue historique* (1960). More generally, see Karl A. Wittfogel, *Oriental Despotism* (New York: Vintage, 1981), pp. 107–109; Claude Lévi-Strauss, *Tristes Tropiques* (New York: Atheneum, 1965), pp. 264–67, and "Entretiens," *Lettres nouvelles* 10 (1961).

24. Jean-Pierre Vernant, *The Origins of Greek Thought* (Ithaca, NY: Cornell University Press, 1982), pp. 52–54.

25. See Aristotle, *Physics* 4.13.222B.17 (= Diels, *Fragmenta Veterorum Stoicorum*[7], vol. 1, p. 217.10ff.); Vernant, in *M.T.*, pp. 75–106. The same passage from Aristotle, complemented by Simplicius's commentary, *ad loc.*, 754, 7 Diels, is reproduced in Page's *Poetae Melici graeci* (= Simonides, frag. 140/645).

This positivist concept of time existed alongside a different view of flowing, fleeting time, which was more germane to lyric poetry as a whole (see

Simonides, frag. 16/521 Page; frag. 22/527 Page; frag. 20/525, 21/526 on the θεός as πάμμητις).

26. This interpretation is supported by Christ, "Simonidesstudien," pp. 42ff.; Treu, *Von Homer zur Lyrik*, p. 298; Bowra, *Greek Lyric Poetry*, who points out the link between this fragment and Pindar, *Olympian* 1.30ff.; and *Nemean* 7.20ff., detecting in it an affirmation of the "deceiving influence of art."

27. Plato, *Republic* 365B–C (= Simonides, frag. 93/598 Page), trans. Paul Shorey, in *The Collected Dialogues of Plato* (Princeton, NJ: Princeton University Press, 1961).

28. See Pindar, *Isthmian* 4.46; the texts cited in Cecil Maurice Bowra, "The Fox and the Hedgehog," *Classical Quarterly* 34 (1940).

29. On the precise meaning of *skigraphie* in painting, see Schuhl, *Platon et l'art*, p. 9. These are "settings or paintings in which the interplay of shadows and colors reproduces appearances and, from a distance, creates an illusion of reality." But in Plato, this pictorial procedure means *trompe l'oeil* (*Phaedo* 69B) and is called ἀπατηλός (*Critias* 107D). On the relations between σκιαγραφία and θαυματοποιία, see Plato, *Republic* 602D. Here I follow Schuhl, *Platon et l'art*, pp. 10ff.; see also the suggestions of Ranuccio Bianchi-Bandinelli, "Osservazioni storico-artistiche a un passo del 'Sofista' Platonico," in *Studi in onore de Ugo Enrico Paoli* (Florence, 1955).

30. On the extremely close affinities between Ἀλήθεια and Δίκη, see p. 55 above.

31. Another argument may be drawn from βιᾶται. The image of "violence" is certainly characteristic of the world of *Peithō*: Pindar, *Nemean* 8.31-34. (*parphasis* exerts violence, βιᾶται, on dazzling merit); Aeschylus, *Agamemnon* 385 (βιᾶται δ'ἀ τάλαινα πειθώ); *Agamemnon* 182 (the χάρις βίαιος of the gods). According to Gorgias, cited by Plato, *Philebus* 58A–B, πειθώ is a kind of βία.

On δόξα in general, see Hjalmar Frisk, *Griechisches etymologisches Wörterbuch*, vol. 1 (Heidelberg: Universitatsverlag, 1960), pp. 409ff.; Johann Baptist Hofmann, *Etymologisches Wörterbuch des Griechischen* (Munich: R. Oldenbourg, 1949), pp. 54, 62; Manu Leumann, *Homerische Wörter* (Basel: F. Rheinhardt, 1950), pp. 173ff.; Bruno Snell, *Die Ausdrücke für den Begriff des Wissens in der vorplatonischen Philosphie* (Berlin: Weidmann, 1924), p. 53; Eino Mikkola, *Isokrates: Seine Anschauungen im Lichte seiner Schriften* (Helsinki: Svom a laisen Tiedeakatemia, 1954), pp. 98ff.; Jurgen Sprute, *Der Begriff der DOXA in der platonischen Philosophie* (Göttingen: Vanderhoeck & Ruprecht, 1962), pp. 33ff. See also Max Greindl, κλέος, κῦδος, Εὖχος, Τιμή, Φάτις, Δόξα: *Eine Bedeutungeschichtliche Untersuchung des epischen und lyrischen Sprachgebrauch* (Lengerich: Lengericher Handelsdruckerei, 1938), and "Zum Ruhmes und Ehrbegriff bei den Vorsokrarikern," *Rheinisches Museum für Philologie* 89 (1940), pp. 222ff.

32. See Diels, *Fragmenta Veterorum Stoicorum*[7], vol. 2, p. 291.10–12. Δόξα is ἀπιστότατον πρᾶγμα (vol. 2, p. 300.13); it is ruled by *peithō* (vol. 2, p. 292.6). On the δόξα of Gorgias, see Jurgen Sprute, *Der Begriff der DOXA*, p. 10; Mario Untersteiner, *The Sophists* (Oxford: Blackwell, 1954), pp. 116ff.; Nestle, *Vom Mythos zum Logos*, p. 316. See also the full commentary by Guiliana Lanata, *Poetica pre-platonica: Testimonianze e Frammenti* (Florence: La Nuova Italia, 1963), pp. 190ff.

33. See Dionysius of Halicarnassus, *De compositone verborum* p. 45.17 (Usener-Radermacher, ed.). This passage seems to be a quotation from Gorgias (see Pierre Aubenque, *La Prudence chez Aristote* [Paris: Presses Universitaires de France, 1963], pp. 99–100, 104).

34. Plato, *Meno* 97D, trans. W.K.C. Guthrie, in *The Collected Dialogues of Plato*. On Platonic δόξα, see Sprute, *Der Begriff der DOXA*.

35. Plato, *Republic* 479A–480A (see the scholia to this passage). In a long series of passages (*Lysis* 218C; *Charmides* 173A; *Symposium* 175E; *Republic* 414D; 443D; 476C–D; 510E; *Theaetetus* 201D; 202C; 208B; etc.) Plato assimilates δόξα to ὄναρ, the vision of a dream, which is opposed to ὕπαρ, a waking vision. But this sense seems to extend certain meanings of δόξα that Liddell Scott Jones, *s.v.* translates as "fancy," "vision": Pindar, *Olympian* 6.82; Aeschylus, *Agamemnon* 275; *Choephorai* 1051–53; Euripides, *Rhesus* 780; etc. In Aeschylus, *Agamemnon* 420, δόξαι are ὀνειρόφαντοι, πενθήμονες, φέρουσαι χάριν ματαίαν.

36. Plato, *Theaetetus* 194B, trans. F.M. Cornford, in *The Collected Dialogues of Plato*. See *Republic* 6.508D: "When [the soul] inclines to that region which is mingled with darkness, the world of becoming and passing away, it opines (δοξάζει) only and its edge is blunted, and it shifts its opinions hither and thither (ἄνω καὶ κάτω τὰς δόξας μεταβάλλον)." On ἄνω καὶ κάτε and its relations with κυλίνδεσθαι, see the note by Wilhelm Jacob Verdenius, *Mnemosyne* (1964), p. 387.

37. See *Homeric Hymn to Hermes* 409–11; Pindar, *Isthmian* 79–80; Pollux, 3.155; Aristophanes, *Acharniens* 385; *Clouds* 450; etc.

38. See Louis-Marie Régis, *L'Opinion selon Aristote* (Paris: Vrin, 1935), pp. 76ff. Indeed, this is probably a fundamental characteristic of δόξα, as Lyd., *De Mens.* 2.7 (*ap.* Diels, *Fragmenta Veterorum Stoicorum*[7], vol. 1, p. 51.11ff.), seems to suggest when he claims that οἱ περὶ φερεκύδην called the dyade δόξα, "ὅτι τὸ ἀληθὲς καὶ ψευδὲς ἐν δόξῃ ἐστι."

39. Pierre Aubenque, "Science, culture et dialectique chez Aristote," *Actes du Congrès de l'Association Guillaume Budé* (Paris, 1960), p. 145.

40. *Ibid.* Pierre Aubenque, *Le Problème de l'Etre chez Aristote: Essai sur le problèmatique aristotélicienne* (Paris: Presses Universitaires de France, 1963), pp. 256ff., notes that, according to *Topics* 1.1.100A.18, "dialectic" is defined in relation to ἔνδοξα. Dialectic is a method "by which we shall be able to reason on

all problems from generally accepted opinions" (ἐξ ἐνδόξων). And what are ἔνδοξα? They are "those theses that commend themselves to all (ἔνδοξα τὰ δοκοῦντα πᾶσιν) or to the majority or to the wise, that is, to all of the wise or to the majority or to the most famous and distinguished of them (τοῖς μαλιστα γνωρίμοις καὶ ἐνδόξοις)" (*Topics* 1.1.100B.21). As Aubenque writes (p. 259), "Aristotle defines a probable thesis (ἔνδοξος) as one that commends itself to the wise men who are *most approved of*." But the wise man here is no more than a guarantor of a universal consensus, the representative of human authority. The dialectician thus appears through a double mask: that of the universal man "in whom the universality of man is recognized" and that of "a vain speechifier who is content to argue *plausibly about everything*" (p. 260). Behind this dialectician, we should no doubt detect, *pace* Aubenque, an orator or a Sophist.

41. Georges Redard, "Du grec δέκομαι, 'je reçois' au sanskrit átka, 'manteau': Sens de la racine *dek-," *Sprachgeschichte und Wortebdeutung: Festschrift A. Debrunner* (Berne: A. Francke, 1954). A. Hus, *Docēre et les mots de la famille de docēre: Etude de sémantique latine* (Paris: Presses Universitaires de France, 1965), confirms Redard's conclusions.

42. In the *Meno* 97B–C, Plato declares that ὀρθὴ δόξα can lead to the same results as ἐπιστήμη: correct opinion is as good a guide as knowledge when it comes to the *accuracy of actions* (πρὸς ὀρθότητα πράξεως). The difference, however, is that whoever possesses ἐπιστήμη is always successful, whereas those who have only a δόξα are now successful, now unsuccessful.

43. The two points are made by Fränkel, *Dichtung und Philosophie*, pp. 346ff., 493–96. On the fragments of Simonides relating to these two great exploits, see Fränkel, *Dichtung und Philosophie*, pp. 362ff.; Bowra, *Greek Lyric Poetry*, pp. 344ff.

44. See Schmid and Stählin, *Geschichte der griecheschen Literatur*, pp. 508–509.

45. This critique reappears in the tradition reported in frag. 92R by Aristotle: Simonides is supposed to have defined "nobility" by wealth, but "old" wealth.

46. See Christ, "Simonidesstudien," pp. 24ff.; C.M. Bowra, "Simonides and Scopas," *Classical Philology* 29 (1934), pp. 230-39; L. Woodbury, "Simonides on Ἀρετή," *Transactions and Proceedings of the American Philological Association* 84 (1953), pp. 125-63; Bowra, *Greek Lyric Poetry*, pp. 326-36; Bruno Gentili, "Studi su Simonide, II," *Maia* 16 (1964), pp. 278-306. On the image of ὑγιὴς ἀνήρ, which became a commonplace in the second half of the fifth century, see Sophocles, *Philoctetes* 1006; Euripides, *Andromache* 448; *Bacchae* 948; frag. 496; 821; Herodotus, 1.8.3; 6.100.1; Thucydides, 4.22.2 (cited by Bowra, *Greek Lyric Poetry*, p. 335 n.2). The relation between Simonides and the democratic ideal is the subject of an excellent study in Perrotta and Gentili, *Polinnia*, pp. 307ff.

47. Frag. 53D. See G. Smith, "ΠΟΛΙΣ ΑΝΔΡΑ ΔΙΔΑΣΚΕΙ," *Classical Journal* 38 (1942–43).

48. For Aristotle, δόξα and βούλευσις are both concerned with contingency (see Aubenque, *La Prudence chez Aristote*, p. 113). The affinities between *doxa* and the political world have been stressed, in connection with Parmenides, by Edwin LeRoy Minar, "Parmenides and the Way of Seeming," *American Journal of Philology* 70 (1949).

49. It should certainly be recognized that a poet such as Archilochus of Paros prepared the way for Simonides, with his critique of the heroic ideal, his rejection of myth, and his willingness to be involved with politics. However, no poet marked such an abrupt turning point in the history of poetry as did Simonides of Ceos. (On Archilochus of Paros, see A. Bonnard's introduction to the edition of fragments of Archilochus published by Lasserre and Bonnard [Paris: Editions les Belles Lettres, 1958], pp. v–lvi. A synthesis on Archilochus may be found in *Entretiens sur l'Antiquité classique, Fondation Hardt*, vol. 10 [Geneva: Fondation Hardt, 1964]). In pointing to the relation between the use of *dokeīn* and a particular political context, I am simply pursuing on a different level Aubenque's analyses (*La Prudence chez Aristote*, pp. 111ff.) of the profound connection in Aristotelian thought between a theory of contingency and practice in the democratic system.

50. This is a point expounded at length by André Rivier, "Sur les fragments 34 et 35 de Xenophane," *Revue de philologie, de littérature et d'histoire anciennes* 30 (1956), pp. 39ff. But Felix Heinimann, *Nomos und Physis* (Bâle, 1945), pp. 43–58, esp. p. 57, had already pointed out that this type of opposition was not influenced by Parmenides (see also Hermann Langerbeck, *Gnomon* 21 [1949], p. 110), while Hermann Fränkel, was defending by 1925 the positive sense of δόκος, that of "valid opinion" (see Fränkel, *Wege und Formen frühgriechischen Denkens* [Munich, 1960], pp. 346–49). In his excellent study (see esp. p. 50), Rivier produces good reasons for believing that δόκος in Xenophanes "does not mean an intellectual act a priori devalued in relation to the truth." The two modes of knowledge recognized by Xenophanes are distinguished "by the particular kind of reality that each aims to apprehend: the visible or the invisible" (p. 44). Between these two, it is not a matter of "more or less objective value but rather of a greater or smaller degree of certainty for whoever employs them."

51. These affinities have often been noted: Croiset, *Histoire de la littérature grecque*, p. 358; Schmid and Stählin, *Geschichte der griechischen Literatur*, p. 518; Christ, "Simonidesstudien," pp. 41ff.; Treu, *Von Homer zur Lyrik*, pp. 299–300; Lesky, *Geschichte der griechische Literatur*, pp. 210ff. Bruno Snell, *Poetry and Society: The Role of Poetry in Ancient Greece* (Bloomington: Indiana University Press, 1961), pp. 50ff., sees Simonides instead as a precursor of philosophy.

52. Plutarch, *Themistocles* 2.6: "δεινότητα πολιτικὴν καὶ δραστήριον σύνεσιν." See G.-B. Kerferd, "The First Greek Sophists," *Classical Review* 64 (1950); Wilhelm Nestle, "Gab es eine ionische Sophistik?" *Philologus* 70 (1911), pp. 258ff.; J.-S. Morrison, "An Introductory Chapter in the History of Greek Education," *Durham University Journal* 11 (1949).

53. Herodotus, *The Persian Wars* 8.57–58. On the theme of the "wise adviser," see Richmond Lattimore, "The Wise Adviser in Herodotus," *Classical Philology* 34 (1939). Mnesiphilos seems to be a nonhistorical figure (see F. Geyer, *s.v. Mnesiphilos, R.-E.* [1932], c. 2280). See also Giovanni Ferrara, "Temistocle e Solone," *Maia* 16 (1964), pp. 55ff.; however, I disagree with many of his conclusions.

54. See Pierre-Maxime Schuhl, "De l'Instant propice," *Imaginer et réaliser* (Paris: Presses Universitaires de France, 1963). Themistocles is the kind of man who possesses *mētis*.

55. See Aubenque, *La Prudence chez Aristote*, esp. pp. 23–24.

56. Aristotle, *Nicomachean Ethics* 2.2.1104A.8–9, trans. W.D. Ross, in *The Basic Works of Aristotle* (New York: Random House, 1941); see Aubenque, *La Prudence chez Aristote*, p. 97.

57. See Dionysius of Halicarnassus, *De comptositione verborum* 45.17 Usener-Radermacher. Aubenque, *La Prudence chez Aristote*, p. 100, thinks this passage is inspired by Gorgias.

58. On the relations between *Kairos* and ambiguity, see Aubenque, *La Prudence chez Aristote*, pp. 97ff.

59. See D.A.G. Hinks, "Tisias and Corax and the Invention of Rhetoric," *Classical Quarterly* 24 (1940); Wilhelm Kroll, *s.v. Rhetorik, R.-E., Suppl.* VII (1940), c. 1039f.

60. Plato, *Gorgias* 463A, trans. W.D. Woodhead, in *The Collected Dialogues of Plato*; see Aubenque, *La Prudence chez Aristote*, pp. 99–100.

61. See Diogenes Laertius, 9.51; Euripides, *Antiope*, frag. 189N², etc. See Nestle, *Vom Mythos zum Logos*, pp. 289ff.; J. de Romilly, *Histoire et raison chez Thucydide* (Paris, 1956), pp. 180ff. On the logical relations between the two speeches, see Eugène Dupréel, *Les Sophistes* (Neuchâtel: Editions du Griffon, 1948), pp. 38ff.

62. This is a level of thought that comprehends contradiction, even though the principle of contradiction was not actually formulated until Aristotle produced his theory of contradiction and drew the logical conclusions from it; see Aubenque, *Le Problème de l'Etre*, pp. 124ff. See Aristophanes, *Clouds* 112; 882; Plato, *Phaedrus* 267A; etc.

63. See H. Mutschmann, "Die älteste Definition der Rhetorik," *Hermes* 53 (1918), pp. 440ff.

64. Plato, *Sophistes* 234B–C.

65. Hesiod, *Theogony* 27.

66. I here follow Aubenque, *Le Problème de l'Etre*, pp. 98–106.

67. Gorgias, *Helenēs Enkōmion, ap.* Diels, *Fragmenta Veterorum Stoicorum*[7], vol. 2, p. 290.17ff. On Hermes and *logos*, see Wilhelm Heinrich Roscher, *Hermes der Windgott* (Leipzig: Teubner, 1878), p. 28 nn.105, 106. See Vernant, in *M.T.*, p. 135 n.42. At the level of language one can detect a continuity in every way comparable to that noted by Vernant between the *epimēlios, polymēlos* Hermes who makes cattle grow and multiply, and the Hermes who is the god of commerce and the *tokos*, interest that "reproduces" itself. On the relations between βία and πειθώ, see pp. 58–59 above. Aspects of *psychogogia* are successfully studied by Koller, *Mimesis in der Antike*, pp. 88–99, 127, 131, 136, 145, 160ff., 192, 193, 195, 203.

68. Gorgias, *Helenēs Enkōmion* 8, *ap.* Diels, *Fragmenta Veterorum Stoicorum*[7], vol. 2, pp. 290, 18ff. See Charles P. Segal, "Gorgias and the Psychology of the Logos," *Harvard Studies in Classical Philology* 56 (1962), pp. 99–155.

69. A point often noted, e.g., by Dupréel, *Les Sophistes*, p. 72. See Plato, *Thaeatetus* 167B.

70. Clement of Alexandria, *Stromateis* 1.8.39ff. Plato, *Phaedrus* 272D–E: τὸ παράπαν γὰρ οὐδὲν ἐν τοῖς δικαστηρίοις τούτων ἀληθείας μέλειν οὐδενὶ ἀλλὰ τοῦ πιθανοῦ.

71. Hippias was the inventor of a technique of memorization: Xenophon, *Symposium* 4.62; Plato, *Hippias Major* 285E; *Hippias Minor* 368D (see Nestle, *Vom Mythos zum Logos*, pp. 365ff.). The *Dissoi Logoi* sing the praises of memory (*ap.* Diels, *Fragmenta Veterorum Stoicorum*[7], vol. 2, p. 416.13ff.). The dialogue between Socrates and Strepsiades, in Aristophanes' *Clouds*, shows clearly how important memory was for the Sophist (see l.414; l.483; l.484–85; l.629; l.631; l.785). The same point is made by a passage in the *Laws* (908B–C) (trans. A.E. Taylor, in *The Collected Dialogues of Plato*) in which Plato distinguishes between two kinds of people who do not believe in the existence of the gods. The second kind is more dangerous and includes a hodgepodge of "diviners and fanatics for all kinds of imposture, . . . dictators, demagogues, generals, contrivers of private mysteries," not forgetting "the so-called Sophist" (908D). All are "full of plentiful subtlety and guile"; above all they are characterized by the "possession of a vigorous memory" (μνῆμαί τε ἰσχυραί) and "a keen intelligence" (μαθήσεις ὀξεῖαι). It is worth noting that *phronesis* also requires a good memory. Aubenque, *La Prudence chez Aristote*, p. 159, cites the Aristotelian texts and, in particular, a remark of Alexander's in *Met.* 30.10ff. Hayduck: "*Phronesis* is precision and clarity in images and the natural ability in practical conduct that is to be found in beings endowed with memory." See Ernst Wüst, *s.v. Mnemonik, R.-E.* (1930), c. 2264–2265. The secularization of memory was an important part of the advent

of the city, as François Chatelet, *La Naissance de l'histoire* (Paris: Editions de Minuit, 1962), has successfully shown in connection with the Greek historians.

72. It is therefore most remarkable that, while sophistry represented the triumph of ambiguous speech, it was also largely responsible, through its use of opposed speeches and its analysis of the different modes of discourse, for the formulation of the principle of identity and the development of a logic based on the exclusion of contradictory propositions.

73. Among the representatives of this type of thought, we should include magi, inspired poets, and semihistorical, semilegendary "divine men," such as Aristaeus, Abaris, Hermotimes, Epimenides, etc., but also the Orphics, the Pythagoreans, and probably the initiates of the "golden tablets." For a good analysis of ancient traditions on magi and Pythagoreanism, see Walter Burkert, *Weisheit und Wissenschaft: Studien zu Pythagoras, Philolaos und Platon* (Nuremberg: H. Carl, 1962), pp. 98-142. See also F.M. Cornford, *Principium Sapientiae: The Origins of Greek Philosophical Thought* (Cambridge: Cambridge University Press, 1952), pp. 89ff., who successfully shows the affinities between this type of magus and diviners and inspired poets; K. Meuli, "Scythica," *Hermes* 70 (1935); E.R. Dodds, *The Greeks and the Irrational* (Berkeley: University of California Press, 1957), pp. 135ff. Against the "shamanistic" thesis of Meuli and Dodds, it is necessary to point out the importance, within these circles, of a doctrine of the soul that is specifically Greek and is not at all characteristic of shamanism (see Marcel Detienne, *De la Pensée religieuse à la pensée philosophique: La Notion de Daimon dans le pythagorisme ancien* [Paris: Editions les Belles Lettres, 1963], pp. 60ff. See Jacques Brunschwig, "Aristote et les pirates tyrrhéniens," *Revue de philologie* [1963]). Vernant, *Origins of Greek Thought*, provides information on the sociological aspects of these circles, religious or philosophicoreligious sects (particularly pp. 57-60). See also Vernant, in *M.T.*, pp. 75-105; 106-25; 343-75.

74. Vernant, in *M.T.*, p. 119 n.8, puts his finger on an essential difference between the religious thought of the sects and philosophical thought: "The 'wisdom' of the philosopher aims to establish an order within the city, whereas all considerations of political organization remain totally foreign to the spirit of the sects." But in *Origins of Greek Thought*, pp. 76-78, Vernant dwells on the figure of Epimenides, an example of a magus who did work within the city and who played an important role in the history of archaic Athens.

75. Plutarch, *De Defectu oraculorum* 22.422B (= Petron of Himerus, *ap.* Diels, *Fragmenta Veterorum Stoicorum*[7], vol. 1, p. 106.13ff.); on Petron, see Albert Rivaud, *Le Problème du devenir et la notion de matière dans la philosophie grecque* (Paris: F. Alcan, 1905), p. 100 n.216; Robert Eisler, *Weltenmantel und Himmelszelt*, vol. 2 (Munich: Beck, 1910), p. 461 n.6; p. 722 n.6. See also M. Timpanaro-Cardini, *Pitagorici*, vol. 1 (Florence: La Nuova Italia, 1958), pp. 70-72; *contra*,

J. Kerchensteiner, *Kosmos, Quellenkritische Untersuchungen zu den Vorsokratikern* (Munich: Beck, 1962), pp. 209–11.

76. See Marcel Detienne, "La Notion mythique d'ΑΛΗΘΕΙΑ," *Revue des études grecques* 73 (1960).

77. Plato, *Phaedrus* 247B.

78. *Ibid.* 247C, trans. R. Hackforth, in *The Collected Dialogues of Plato.*

79. *Ibid.* 248BC.

80. *Ibid.* 248C.

81. Proclus, *In Platonica ad Rempublicam* 2.346.19 (W. Kroll, ed.).

82. Plato, *Republic* 621A. In the image of the river Amelēs, Vernant (in *M.T.*, pp. 106–25) draws attention to the transposition of an infernal water charged with a power of defilement: among the religious brotherhoods and philosophical sects, the river "without *meletē*" becomes a symbol of death, a term synonymous with *Lēthē.* The opposition memory-oblivion corresponds to the pair *Meletē-Amelēs.* There would appear to be a connection between these religious traditions and the idea of *Metameleia* mentioned by Plutarch, *De Genio Socratis* 592B; and Plato, *Phaedo* 113E. See Robert Joly, "Note sur μετάνοια," *Revue histoire des religions* 160 (1961), and "Le Tableau de Cébès et la philosophie religieuse," *Collection Latomus*, vol. 56 (Brussels: Latomus, 1963). We know that Metameleia, the daughter of Epimetheus, stands in opposition to Promētheia, the daughter of Prometheus, just as Prometheus is opposed to Epimetheus, his double and his contrary (*Scholia in Pindar, Pythian* 5.35A [Drachmann, ed.] vol. 2, 1910, pp. 176, 19ff.). On Meletē, see also Jacques Brunschwig, *Revue Philosophique* (1963), pp. 267–68.

83. See Vernant, in *M.T.*, pp. 75–105.

84. The text of the "tablets of gold" may be found in *Orphicorum fragmenta*, frag. 32, (Otto Kern, ed.) (Berlin: Weidmann, 1963) and in Diels, *Fragmenta Veterorum Stoicorum*[7], vol. 1, pp. 15ff. See the general study by W.K.C. Guthrie, *Orpheus and Greek Religion* (London: Methuen, 1952). For our purposes, it does not really matter whether they were Orphic (Guthrie), Pythagorean (Thomas), Orphico-Pythagorean (Ziegler, Cumont), or Eleusian (Boyancé, Picard): the beliefs expressed there are inseparable from all the speculation on memory, time, and the soul.

85. Plato was heir to an important attempt to transpose religious themes to philosophy. Ernst Heitsch, "Wahrheit als Erinnerung," *Hermes* 91 (1963), underlined the importance in the Platonic theory of knowledge of the link between the representation of truth and the role of memory.

86. See Diels, *Fragmenta Veterorum Stoicorum*[7], vol. 1, p. 360.4ff.; pp. 374ff. For Empedocles, see Jean Bollack, *Empedocle*, vol. 1 (Paris: Editions de Minuit, 1965).

87. On this concept of memory, see Vernant, in *M.T.*, pp. 75–105. Burkert did not know of this important article and consequently seriously underestimated the role played by memory in ancient Pythagoreanism; see Burkert, *Weisheit und Wissenschaft*, pp. 144ff.

88. As Vernant points out in *M.T.*, pp. 106–25, the insistence on total knowledge is in a way reminiscent of the strict obligation not to forget anything at all in religious ritual, which calls to mind the diviner's quality of νημερτής.

89. See Marcel Detienne, *La Notion de daimôn dans le pythagorisme ancien* (Paris: Editions les Belles Lettres, 1963), pp. 60–92.

90. See *ibid.*

91. See Diels, *Fragmenta Veterorum Stoicorum*[7], vol. 1, p. 32.17ff. On Epimenides, see Herbert Demoulin, *Epiménide de Crète* (Brussels: Office de Publicité, 1901); Burkert, *Weisheit und Wissenschaft*, pp. 127–28; R.F. Willetts, *Cretan Cults and Festivals* (London: Routledge & Kegan Paul, 1962), pp. 216, 242, 311; Vernant, *Origins of Greek Thought*, pp. 77ff.; Dodds, *The Greeks and the Irrational*, pp. 141–46.

92. According to Diogenes Laertius, 1.114, Epimenides claimed to be Aeacus, the brother of Minos.

93. See Cicero, *De divinatione* 1.30, Aelien, *Hist. Var.* 3.11 (R. Hercher, ed.). It is tempting to compare these religious traditions on visions of truth, obtained during states of ecstasy, with Plato's myth of the cave, which seems to be a philosophical transposition of them. On two occasions (*Thaeatetus* 152C; 162A), Plato alludes to the mysteries of *Alētheia*, who sometimes speaks from deep within her sanctuary (ἐκ τοῦ ἀδύτου) and sometimes reveals herself in secret (ἐν ἀπορρήτῳ).

94. One of the most remarkable aspects of the continuity from one level to another is the persistence of the "wide" meaning of *Alētheia* as a synthesis of the past, present, and future. First, on the level of inspired poets, the Muses declare *Alētheia*: "what is, and what is to be, and what was before now" (Hesiod, *Theogony* 28; 38; cf. 32, trans. Richmond Lattimore [Ann Arbor: University of Michigan Press, 1959]). Second, at the level of diviners, the nocturnal visions of dreams are *Alēthosunē*; they cover "the past, the present, and all that has to be for many mortals during their dark sleep" (Euripides, *Helen* 13ff.). See Calchas, according to *Iliad* 1.70, "the best of diviners who knows the present, the future, and the past." Third, at the level of the philosophicoreligious circles, as is attested by (1) the connection between the divinatory power of Epimenides ("who made revelations not on future things, but on *things past, things invisible*"; *ap.* Aristotle, *Rhetoric* 3.17.1418A.24) and his vision of *Alētheia* in the cave of Zeus Diktaios (cf. Diels, *Fragmenta Veterorum Stoicorum*[7], vol. 1, p. 32.17ff.) and (2) passages such as Plato, *Republic* 571E; Aelien, *Hist. Var.* 3.11 (R. Hercher,

ed.); Cicero, *De divinatione* 1.30 (see Detienne, *De la Pensée religieuse*, pp. 76–77), in which prophecy and cataleptic experiences are intertwined. (It is worth noting that, in a story concerning a tripod related By Diogenes Laertius, 1.33, the oracle prescribed sending the religious object to the house of a wise man, defined as such by his knowledge "of the past, the present, and the future," which indicates the affinities between the Wise Man [a figure of the same type as the Seven Wise Men] and the inspired poet. Elsewhere, in Aristophanes' *Clouds*, philosophical meditation is permeated by features of incubatory practices [see André Jean Festugière, *Contemplation et vie contemplative selon Platon*, 2nd ed. [Paris: Vrin, 1950], pp. 70ff., who emphasizes the similarity between this type of meditation and the technique described in the *Phaedo*.) In all these religious experiences, it is striking that *Alētheia* is defined, as on other levels of thought, by its synthesis of past, present, and future. That same synthesis was to reappear, this time with a cumulative perspective, in secularized thought: in the famous theory of "prognosis" in rational medicine, it is reflection on *present* cases (τὰ παρεόντα) and comparison with *past* ones that make it possible to *foresee* (προλέγειν τὰ ἐσόμενα) (see the texts cited by Louis Bourgey, *Observation et expérience chez les médecins de la collection hippocratique* [Paris: Vrin, 1953], pp. 220ff.); in sophistry, discourse presupposes memory of things *past*, knowledge of things *present*, and foresight on things *to come* (Gorgias, *ap.* Diels, *Fragmenta Veterorum Stoicorum*[7], vol. 2, p. 291.5–9; see also Plato, *Republic* 515C–D).

95. See Diels, *Fragmenta Veterorum Stoicorum*[7], vol. 1, pp. 15.31; 16.17; 16.22; 17.13. Compare the demonic status in the Pythagorean sect or the divine status of Empedocles.

96. See Diels, *Fragmenta Veterorum Stoicorum*[7], vol. 1, p. 311.6; p. 355.12–356.2. On the *pistis* of Empedocles, see Wilhelm Jacob Verdenius, "Notes on the Presocratics, VIII. The Meaning of πίστις in Empedocles," *Mnemosyne* (1948), pp. 10–12. The association of *Alētheia* and *Pistis* is particularly explicit in Parmenides (see p. 131 above).

97. Plato, *Gorgias* 493Aff.; Vernant, in *M.T.*, pp. 115ff., explains the Empedoclean origin of this myth.

98. See Vernant, in *M.T.*, pp. 117ff., who also (*M.T.*, p. 122 n.53) recalls the texts of Plutarch, *De sera numinis vindicta* 566A and *De oraculis Pythiane* 397B, in which *Hēdonē* is associated with *Lēthē* and *Atē*. On the chasm known as *Lēthē* in Plutarch's *De sera numinis vindicta*, see Yvonne Vernière, "Le 'Lēthē' de Plutarche," *Revue des études anciennes* 66 (1964).

99. For an entire tradition, "to take part in persuasion" is "a remnant of the earthly weakness of an animal that is subject to death" (Ecphantus, *Traité de la royauté*, pp. 278, 2ff. [Hense, ed.] *ap.* Louis Delatte, *Les Traités de la royauté d'Ecphante, Diotogène et Sthénidas* [Liège-Paris: Editions Droz, 1942], p. 51f.).

On the relation between forgetfulness and persuasion, see Plato, *Republic* 412E–413C. On ἀπάτη as a synonym for *Lēthē*, see the remarks of Robert Joly, "Le Tableau de Cébès," pp. 36ff.

100. On these various points, see Marcel Detienne, "Héraclès, héros pythagoricien," *Revue de l'histoire des religions* (1960). In this theme of choice, the notion of *metameleia* may have played a role of self-reassessment, a self-awareness that paved the way for the choice of salvation. In the Judgment of Paris dramatized by Sophocles (in the play entitled κρίσις, see Athen., 15.687C=frag. 334N²), the choice is between Athena-Aretē (or Phronesis) and Aphrodite-Hēdonē. With no proof, M.C. Waites, "The Allegorical Debate in Greek Literature," *Harvard Studies in Classical Philology* 23 (1912), takes this to be an older version than that in the *Cypria* (see Albert Severyns, *Le Cycle épique dans l'école d'Aristarque* [Paris: Editions Champion, 1928], pp. 261ff.).

101. One will doubtlessly object that the image of a choice was already found in Hesiod's *Works and Days* (l.286ff.): a choice between the steep, rugged path of virtue and the level, easy path of wretchedness. But the choice in Hesiod is not the same as that for the philosophicoreligious sects. Vernant, "Hesiod's Myth of the Races: An Essay in Structural Analysis," in *M.T.*, pp. 3–33, shows that, while the myth of the races has a tripartite structure, the logic of the myth is for its part dualist. It is the tension between *Dikē* and *Hybris* that gives, in an appropriate way for each, an element of polarity to each of the three functional levels (p. 23). In religious thought constructed around polar tensions and antithetical relationships, there can be no choice entirely free from ambiguity. The philosophicoreligious sects gave choice the character of an alternative.

102. Plato, *Gorgias* 524A.

103. Diels, *Fragmenta Veterorum Stoicorum*⁷, vol. 1, p. 17.11.

104. *Ibid.*, vol. 1, p. 352.20ff. and p. 365.5ff. While frag. 122 (Diels, *Fragmenta Veterorum Stoicorum*⁷, vol. 1, p. 361.3ff.) refers to the meadow of *Atē* (on the difficulty of this passage, see "La 'Démonologie' d'Empédocle," *Revue des études grecques* 72 [1959]), it also contains a particularly rich description of the ambiguity of the terrestrial world, in which Beauty is matched by Ugliness, Sleep by Wakefulness, Silence by Speech, Truth by Uncertainty.

105. On the process of abstraction in archaic thought, see T.B.L. Webster, "Personification as a Mode of Greek Thought," *Journal of the Warburg and Courtauld Institutes* 17 (1954), and "Language and Thought in Early Greece," *Memories and Proceedings of the Manchester Literary Philosophical Society* 94.3 (1952–53). Philosophical thought was left to complete that process and separate out nature, the gods, and man, concepts that mutually define and counterbalance one another (Vernant, in *M.T.*, pp. 343ff.).

106. In the vast body of literature devoted to Parmenides, I have above all

made use of Mario Untersteiner's excellent aid to research, *Parmenide: Testi-monianze e frammenti. Introduzione, traduzione e commento* (Florence: La Nuova Italia, 1958). (See, however, Jacques Brunschwig's justified reservations on cer-tain points of interpretation, in *Revue Philosophique* [1962], pp. 120–23.) This work does full justice to the literature predating 1958. In the discussion that fol-lows – and I must apologize for its brevity – I consider not so much Parmenides himself but his relationship to certain forms of thought and problems, for which he at times represents the extreme culmination. But I will leave to historians of Parmenides the task of assessing the precise importance of the prehistory *Alētheia* for an understanding of the author of the *Treatise on Nature*. I am simply ven-turing to make a few suggestions.

107. These affinities were noticed long ago and have been meticulously cataloged; see, e.g., Hermann Diels, *Parmenides' Lehrgedicht* (Berlin: G. Reimer, 1897), pp. 10–11; Louis Gernet, "Les Origines de la philosophie," *Bulletin de l'enseignement public du Maroc* 183 (1945), pp. 2ff.; Fränkel, "Parmenides-studien," *Wege und Formen*, pp. 158ff. (who compares the *daimones* guiding the mares to the Muses in Pindar, *Olympian* 4.22–27); Cecil Maurice Bowra, "The Proem of Parmenides," in *Problems in Greek Poetry* (Oxford: Clarendon Press, 1953), pp. 38ff.; Bruno Snell, *Die Entdeckung des Geistes* (Hamburg, 1955), pp. 196–97; Gregory Vlastos, "Parmenides' Theory of Knowledge," *Transactions of the American Philological Association* 77 (1946); Wolfgang Jäger, "Parmenides' Mysterium des Seins," in *Die Theologie der frühen griechischen Denken* (Stuttgart, 1953); Mario Untersteiner, "La ΟΔΟΣ di Parmenide come 'via' all'Eon," in *Parmenide* (Florence: La Nuova Italia, 1958); K. Diechgräber, "Parmenides' Auffahrt zur Göttin des Rechts," *Abhandl. Akad. Wiss. Lit. Mainz, Geistes-und sozialwiss. Klasse* 11 (1958); Hans Schwabl, "Hesiod und Parmenides. Zur Formung des Parmenideischen Prooimions (28 B 1)," *Rheinisches Museum für Philologie* 106 (1963) (who rigorously pursues the parallelism between Hesiod and Parmenides, in line with his important articles in *Serta philologica Aenipontana* [1966], *Hermes* [1962], and *Hermes* [1963]). See also Edwin F. Dolin, "Parmenides and Hesiod," *Harvard Studies in Classical Philology* 66 (1962).

108. See A. Francotte, "Les Disertes juments de Parménide," *Phronesis* 3 (1958).

109. Diels, *Fragmenta Veterorum Stoicorum*[7], vol. 1, p. 233.4ff.

110. *Ibid.*, vol. 1, p. 234.34.

111. On Parmenidean *dikē*, see Fränkel, *Wege und Formen*, pp. 162ff.; André Rivier, "Pensée archaïque et philosophie présocratique," *Revue de théologie et de philosophie* 3 (1953), p. 99.

112. See Diels, *Fragmenta Veterorum Stoicorum*[7], vol. 1, p. 230.12; p. 236.5; p. 237.8; p. 239.6–7; pp. 275ff., in Clemence Ramnoux, *Héraclite ou l'homme*

entre les choses et les mots (Paris: Editions les Belles Lettres, 1959), who also points out the importance of *pistis* in Heraclitus and Empedocles.

113. See Diels, *Fragmenta Veterorum Stoicorum*[7], vol. 1, p. 239.8.

114. In Plato, certain uses of *Alētheia* retain an ontological sense; see Eduard Des Places, "La Langue philosophique de Platon: le vocabulaire de l'Être," *Comptes rendus des séances: Academie des Inscriptions et Belles Lettres* 1961 (1962). It is worth noting that there are certain affinities between the religious world in which a divine decision is effective and action that comes to pass (see *Iliad* 1.41; *Odyssey* 5.170, where the expression νοῆσαί τε κρῆναί τε is used) and the world of Parmenides, in which Being and Thought coincide.

115. It is not Parmenides who poses the problem of Being but Aristotle, who later asks, What is Being? (see Aubenque, *Le Problème de l'Etre*, pp. 13ff.).

116. See Ernst Hoffmann, *Die Sprache und die archaïsche Logik* (Tübingen: J.C.B. Mohn, 1925), pp. 10ff.; Ramnoux, *Héraclite ou l'Homme*, esp. pp. 291ff.

117. See Diels, *Fragmenta Veterorum Stoicorum*[7], vol. 1, p. 238.7; p. 239.8; Untersteiner, *Parmenide*, pp. 158ff.

118. Emile Benveniste, *Problèmes de linguistique générale* (Paris, 1966), pp. 70–71. More generally, see Louis Auguste Paul Rougier, *La Métaphysique et le langage* (Paris: Flammarion, 1960).

119. See Jean Fourquet, "La Notion de verbe," *Journal de psychologie normale et pathologique* (1950), pp. 93ff. On the problems of logic posed by Parmenides, see Guido Calogero, *Studi sull' Eleatismo* (Rome: G. Bardi, 1932).

120. The ontological meanings of Parmenides' *Alētheia* have been emphasized particularly strongly by Wilhelm Luther, "Der frühgriechische Wahrheitsgedanke im Lichte der Sprache," *Gymnasium* 65 (1958), pp. 84ff.

121. See Aubenque, *Le Problème de l'être*, p. 157.

122. As has been pointed out by Vernant, *Origins of Greek Thought*, p. 45 n.10, the problem of the One and the Many expressed in Orphism and "strictly" formulated at the level of philosophical thought refers one to a fundamental contradiction in social practice: the state is single and homogeneous, but humanity is composed of many heterogeneous parts (see Aristotle, *Politics* 2.1261A.18ff.). In the *De Mundo* 396B, the Pseudo-Aristotle refers to the admirable political concord that produces "a disposition that is single out of what is multiple and, out of what is dissimilar, a way of thinking that is similar." Elsewhere, political thought opposes the simple (ἁπλοῦς) character of the law to the diversity of men, actions, and different cases: Plato, *Pol.* 294B; Aristotle, *Nicomachean Ethics* 5.15.1137B.25. See also Vernant, in *M.T.*, pp. 212–34.

123. See Aeschylus, frag. 288 (H.J. Mette, ed.) (ἁπλᾶ γάρ ἐστι τῆς ἀληθείας ἔπη); *Prometheus* 610, 686; Euripides, *Phoenician Women* 469 (ἁπλοῦς ὁ μῦθος τῆς ἀληθείας ἔφυ) (see Nestle, *Vom Mythos zum Logos*, p. 290 n.99); frag. 289, 2 N²;

frag. 206 N[2]; Plato, *Hippias Minor* 364B (the ἀληθής τε καὶ ἁπλοῦς Achilles is opposed to the πολύτροπός τε καὶ ψευδής Odysseus); Plato, *Republic* 382E (god, ἁπλοῦν καὶ ἀληθές) (see *Cratylus* 408C); Aristotle, *Rhetoric* 1416B.25; 1438B.21; *Ethica Eudemia* 1233B.38; etc. In Xenophon, ἁπλοῦς is opposed to ἐπίβουλος (*Memorobilia* 3.1.6) and to ἀπάτη (4.2, 4.16; 4.18).

124. The complementarity of the way of *Alētheia* and the way of the *doxai* has been recognized in a number of studies; see Hans Schwabl, "Parmenides," *Anzeiger für die Altertumswissenschaft* 9 (Innsbruck: Universitat-Verlag Wagner, 1956) (see "Sein und Doxa bei Parmenides," *Wiener Studien* 66 [1953], pp. 50–75); Jean Bollack, "Sur deux fragments de Parménide (4 et 16)," *Revue des études grecques* 70 (1957) (who acknowledges the perspicacity of Jean Beaufret, *Le Poème de Parménide* [Paris: Presses Universitaires de France, 1955], pp. 31ff., 48ff.); Untersteiner, *Parménide*, ch. 4.

In a discussion of the work of Karl Deichgräber in *Gnomon* 38 (1966), pp. 321–29, Bollack stressed the unity of Parmenides' poem and the interaction between the *doxai* and the Eon.

125. In two passages of the *Thaeatetus* (152C and 162A), Plato alludes to a *revealed* truth (ἐν ἀπορρήτῳ and ἐκ τοῦ ἀδύτου), but it is a truth revealed by Protagoras!

126. It is striking that, in the Proem, the daughters of the Sun use persuasion, resorting to *caressing* words and *parphasis* (Diels, *Fragmenta Veterorum Stoicorum*[7], vol. 1, p. 229.15–16: τὴν δὴ παρφάμεναι κοῦραι μαλακοῖσι λόγοισιν πεῖσαν ἐπιφραδέως) in order to get to *Alētheia*. From the very beginning of the poem, *Alētheia* and *Apatē* are related. Schwabl, "Hesiod und Parmenides," has established a comparison with the Hesiodic Muses (*alēthēis* and *pseudēis*).

127. See Diels, *Fragmenta Veterorum Stoicorum*[7], vol. 1, p. 239.10ff. In connection with this, I am following the interpretation defended by Jeanne Croissant, "Le Début de la Doxa de Parménide," in *Mélanges Desrousseaux par ses amis et ses élèves, en honneur de la cinquantième année* (Paris: Hachette, 1937). For other interpretations, see Untersteiner, *Parmenide*, p. 121 n.15.

128. The way of Being is opposed by the second way, that of Non-Being, the way of ἀμηχανία, taken by "men who know nothing," men "with two heads" (δίκρανοι), incapable of choosing and judging (ἄκριτα φῦλα) (Diels, *Fragmenta Veterorum Stoicorum*[7], vol. 1, p. 233.3ff.). These epithets all emphasize that this is a world of pure *confusion*.

129. See Vernant, *Origins of Greek Thought*, p. 58.

130. This type of truth is attested only in Plato, *Gorgias* 487E, but it is quite decisive there (on this subject, see Chaim Perelman, "De la Preuve en philosophie," in Chaim Perelman and Lucie Olbrechts-Tyteca [eds.], *Rhétorique et philosophie* [Paris: Presses Universitaires de France, 1952]). This is certainly a characteristic of the rational truth of Greece and the West as a whole. There

does not seem to have been any such concept in the East. "There, truth is not understood as the horizon of an indefinite series of investigations, nor as an enquiry into being and intellectual possession of it" (Maurice Merleau-Ponty, *Signes* [Paris: Gallimard, 1960], p. 167). Vector-truth is closely allied with dialogue-speech (and hence to sophistry), whose development is in turn linked to the existence of egalitarian social relations. India certainly produced debate and confrontation, but, in the Brahmanic and the Upanishad texts, the discussion does not aim to convince. The debate is a game of riddles, with questions and answers, a duel to the death between two monolithic kinds of knowledge (see W. Ruben, "Über die Debatten in den alten Upanishad's," *Zeitschrift der deutschen morgenlandischen Gesellschaft*, vol. 8 [Wiesbaden: Franz Steiner, 1929]). Thus, discussion in India is no different from certain oracular procedures used in Greece.

CHAPTER SEVEN: AMBIGUITY AND CONTRADICTION

1. See Maurice Merleau-Ponty, *Signes* (Paris: Gallimard, 1960), p. 287, in connection with the "spiritualists" of 1900.

2. The expression is borrowed from Louis Gernet, "Droit et prédroit en Grèce ancienne," *L'Année sociologique*, 3rd series (1948–49) (1951), p. 117.

3. See Jean-Pierre Vernant and Louis Gernet, "Social History and the Evolution of Ideas in China and Greece from the Sixth to the Second Centuries B.C.," in *Myth and Society in Ancient Greece* (New York: Zone Books, 1988). On the permanence of certain religious representations and mythical themes within philosophical thought, see, e.g., Marcel de Corte, "Mythe et philosophie chez Anaximandre," *Laval théologique et philosophique* 14 (1960), and "Anaximène," *Laval théologique et philosophique* 18 (1962).

Complementary Bibliography

For the benefit of readers perusing this book after its original publication in 1965, I would like here to draw attention to a selection of works that have since developed around the questions raised by the genealogical inquiry into truth.

In an inquiry into the meaning of truth in the system of Xenophanes, Ernst Heitsch, "Das Wissen des Xenophanes," *Rheinisches Museum für Philologie* 109 (1966), sketches a history of *Alētheia* from Hesiod to Parmenides. In the spirit of his earlier works, he ascribes much importance to the "Heideggerean" category of "what is not hidden" (*Unverborgenheit*). Tilman Krischer, for his part, in the course of his remarks on the two levels of thought represented by ἔτυμος and ἀληθής, *Philologus* 109 (1965), usefully warns against any assumption of an absolute equivalence between *Alētheia* and *Unverborgenheit*. Finally, Wilhelm Luther, *Wahrheit, Licht und Erkenntnis in der griechischen Philosophie bis Demokrit: Ein Beitrag zur Erforschung des Zusammenhangs von Sprache und philosophischen Denken* (Bonn, 1966), states conclusions drawn from studies he began in 1935. While his analyses of the systems of thought in which *Alētheia* has a place and his inquiries into the organization of the semantic field of *Alētheia* from Homer to Democritus make many positive contributions toward a history of Greek "truth," the entire program seems to me to depend on W. von Humboldt's philosophy of language, which postulates a fundamental relationship between the internal form of a language (*innere Sprachform*), a particular conception of the world (*Weltansicht*), and the spirit of the people in question (*Geistesleben*). This method leads Luther to write a history of *Alētheia* that doggedly supports this philosophy and has little in common with my own, much more limited study.

Two critical analyses also deserve particular mention: Maurice Caveing, "La Laïcisation de la parole et l'exigence rationnelle," *Raison présente* (January 1969); and Jeanne Croissant, "Sur quelques problèmes d'interpretation en l'histoire de la philosophie grecque," *Revue de l'Université de Bruxelles* 3-4 (1973).

On "mythical thought," see Marcel Detienne, *The Creation of Mythology*, trans. Margaret Cook (Chicago: University of Chicago Press, 1986); "Afterword: Revisiting the Gardens of Adonis," *The Gardens of Adonis*, trans. Janet Lloyd (Princeton: Princeton University Press, 1994); and Paul Veyne, *Les Grecs ont-ils cru à leurs mythes? Essai sur l'imagination constituante* (Paris: Seuil, 1983).

Studies of religious thought, rationality, and various branches of knowledge and society include Jean-Pierre Vernant, *Myth and Thought among the Greeks* (London: Routledge, 1983); Geoffrey Lloyd, *Magic, Reason and Experience: Studies in the Origins and Development of Greek Science* (Cambridge: Cambridge University Press, 1979); and *The Revolutions of Wisdom: Studies in the Claims and Practice of Ancient Greek Science* (Berkeley and Los Angeles: University of California Press, 1987). On memory, the muses, and truth, see Michèle Simondon, *La Mémoire et l'oubli dans la pensée grecque jusqu'à la fin du Ve siècle av. J.-C.* (Paris: Editions les Belles Lettres, 1982). On a number of concepts and categories whose institutional meanings are found in my study, see Emile Benveniste, *Le Vocabulaire des institutions indo-européennes* (Paris: Editions de Minuit, 1969). On cunning, trickery, seduction, and persuasion, see Laurence Kahn, *Hermès passe, ou les ambiguités de la communication* (Paris: Maspero, 1978); Pietro Pucci, "Odysseus Polutropos: Intertextual Readings," in *The Odyssey and the Iliad* (Ithaca, NY: Cornell University Press, 1987); Louise H. Pratt, *Lying and Poetry from Homer to Pindar: Falsehood and Deception in Archaic Poetics* (Ann Arbor: University of Michigan Press, 1993); Marcel Detienne and Jean-Pierre Vernant, *Cunning Intelligence in Greek Culture and Society*, trans. Janet Lloyd (Chicago: University of Chicago Press, 1991). On problems of speech, see Marie-Christine Leclerc, *La Parole chez Hesiode* (Paris: Editions les Belles Lettres, 1993); Pietro Pucci, *Hesiod and the Language of Poetry* (Baltimore: Johns Hopkins University Press, 1977); Jesper Svenbro, *La Parola e il marmo: Alle origini della poetica greca* (Torino: Boringhieri, 1984); and, more specifically on the semantic field of *muthos* in Homeric epic, see Richard P. Martin, *The Language of Heroes* (Ithaca and London: Cornell University Press, 1989).

There has been no shortage of interpreters of Parmenides. See Nestor Luis Cordero, *Les Deux chemins de Parménide* (Paris and Brussels: Vrin, 1984); Lambros Couloubaritsis, *Mythe et philosophie chez Parménide* (Brussels: Editions Ousia, 1986); Pierre Aubenque (ed.), *Etudes sur Parménide*, vol. 1-2 (Paris: Vrin, 1987), (vol. 1 and the translation of Parmenides' poem are the work of Denis O'Brien, in collaboration with Jean Frère, as is the critical essay). On the sophistic movement see Barbara Cassin, *L'Effet sophistique* (Paris: Gallimard, 1995).

On *Alētheia*, its original essence, the evolution of the interpretation constructed by Heidegger, and the paradigms of Antiquity that have been used, two different approaches are found. See Marlène Zarader, *Heidegger et les paroles de l'origine* (Paris: Vrin, 1990); Barbara Cassin, "Grecs et Romains: Les Paradigmes de l'Antiquité chez Arendt et Heidegger," in *Ontologie et politique: Hannah Arendt* (Paris: Tierce, 1989). On *Alētheia* and on *alēthes*: the semantic analyses and philological interpretations of Jean-Pierre Levet, *Le Vrai et le faux dans la pensée grecque archaïque: Etude de vocabulaire* (Paris: Editions les Belles Lettres, 1976); Bruno Snell, *Der Weg zum Denken und zur Wahrheit* (*Hypomnemata* 57) (Göttingen: Vandenhoeck und Ruprecht, 1978), pp. 91–104; Thomas Cole, "Archaic Truth," *Quaderni urbinati di cultura classica* (1983), pp. 7–28 (together with the critical remarks of Gregory Nagy in "Autorité et auteur dans la *théogonie* hésiodique" in *Hésiode*, Fabienne Blaise, Pierre Judet de la Combe, Phillipe Rousseau [eds.] [Paris, 1994]), who appears to have read everything except *The Masters of Truth*. On the part played by truth in the inquiries of historians: Catherine Darbo-Peschanski, *Le Discours du particulier: Essai sur l'enquête hérodotéenne* (Paris: Seuil, 1987). On writing, democracy, public space, and new branches of knowledge, see Marcel Detienne (ed.), *Les Savoirs de l'écriture en Grèce ancienne*, 2nd ed. (Lille: Presses Universitaires de Lille, 1992 [1988]).

Index

This edition designed by Bruce Mau
Type composed by Archetype
Printed and bound Smythe-sewn by Maple-Vail
using Sebago acid-free paper